Appalachian White Oak Basketmaking

Appalachian White Oak

BASKETMAKING
Handing Down the Basket

Rachel Nash Law and
Cynthia W. Taylor

Illustrations by Alison Bruce Wieboldt

The University of Tennessee Press

Knoxville

To Basketmakers

Library of Congress Cataloging in Publication Data

Law, Rachel Nash, 1955 —
    Appalachian white oak basketmaking : handing down the basket /
by Rachel Nash Law and Cynthia W. Taylor; illustrations by Alison Bruce
Wieboldt. — 1st ed.
        p.   cm.
    Includes bibliographical references.
    ISBN 0–87049–668–9 (cloth: alk. paper)
    ISBN 0–87049–672–7 (paper: alk. paper)
    1. Basketmaking — Appalachian Region.   2. Basketwork — Appalachian Region.
3. White oak.   I. Taylor, Cynthia W. (Cynthia Wieboldt), 1950–   .   II. Title.
TT879.B3L395   1990
746.41'2'0974 — dc20   90–12043   CIP

Contents

Illustrations

Plates

Color Plates *(following page 200)*

Preface

The idea for this book grew out of a desire to understand more fully the extensive white oak basket traditions of the central Appalachian region and to explore in more depth particular contributions made by traditional white oak basketmakers. For this book, concentrated research on white oak basketmaking has been going on since 1982. During these years we have focused on documenting both white oak baskets and white oak basketmakers.

Originally we looked at baskets as a series of techniques and were mainly object-oriented. After examining baskets in numerous private and public collections, we became aware that different basket styles or techniques dominated in different regions. We came to recognize that these distinctions represented traditional ways of making baskets and in fact constituted regional styles.

Our research took us to people who gave us a larger outlook, and we began to see basketmakers as part of an ongoing tradition. This view then helped us to appreciate the traditional nature of basketmaking and to understand many of the influences that caused makers to change their ways and try new styles, techniques, or materials. Our findings were confirmed by oldtime basketmakers who explained how they had learned to build a basket from a parent, relative, or community member. Some recalled why they had made changes in the traditional way their group or clan had always worked. Furthermore, as they explained or demonstrated distinguishing details of their own basketwork, we realized that within a particular tradition, individual variations exist that allow one to say with some confidence who made a basket.

This book is a survey of white oak basketmaking of the central Appalachian mountain region and neighboring territories. It documents traditions still existing among basketmakers of those areas. The emphasis in this study is on baskets which have been produced within the limits of tradition and region, with special attention given to the diversity of styles and construction techniques exhibited in these traditional baskets.

Books which set a foundation for this survey include the regional studies of Stephenson, Lasansky, and Irwin. The work of Sue H. Stephenson,

Basketry of the Appalachian Mountains, provides a good overview of basket styles and working techniques. Jeannette Lasansky's book *Willow, Oak, and Rye,* is helpful in understanding Pennsylvania basket traditions. John Rice Irwin's *Baskets and Basket Makers in Southern Appalachia* documents many of the styles and stories about baskets of eastern Tennessee. Background studies of European basketry by Wright and Will also are helpful in understanding the European forms which are the antecedents of American forms. Other works of interest are listed in the bibliography.

Perhaps one of the most significant contributions this book makes is in providing a comprehensive understanding of a little-known American basket form: the oak rod basket. In 1977–78, Law studied traditional willow basketry at the Staatliche Fachschule für Korbflechterei (National Tradeschool for Basketmaking) in Lichtenfels, West Germany. During this time she saw museums and basketmakers in other parts of Europe. These contacts and friends became invaluable resources for answering both technical and historical questions relating to oak rod baskets. Lasansky, Stephenson, and Irwin all have noted the existence of the white oak rodwork, which is normally confused with willow or reed wickerwork. In the regions we studied, white oak rodwork is surprisingly widespread and in some locales even appears to have been the dominant basket type. Unfortunately, in the latter half of the twentieth century this basketry tradition has all but disappeared.

The Subject

Having seen many fine examples of traditional white oak baskets made in a variety of ways, we wanted to learn more. What were the different types of white oak baskets? When and where were they made? Who made them? Why were they made? Were there different methods of preparing the basket materials? Do oak baskets differ from region to region? Is there any relationship between basket styles or construction details and the ethnic traditions of the makers? How do current traditional makers talk about their work? The questions keep coming, and the results of this survey raise yet more questions and leave room for much more research. The preliminary research suggested the organization for the book—dividing oak baskets into three major groups: *rib, rod,* and *split,* each group named for its chief structural element. A chapter is devoted to each type. In addition, the first chapter develops an understanding of the traditional craft and some of the influences on this ongoing tradition. The second chapter discusses the processes of finding and preparing oak for basketmaking.

We have defined our area of focus as the "central Appalachian region." This area includes core regions of white oak work in areas of Pennsylvania, Virginia, North Carolina, West Virginia, Kentucky, Tennessee, and Ohio. We hope that our focus on a definable region gives enough depth to provide a sound basis for future studies within this region or at other geographical locations.

We realize that our inclusion of the areas of central Tennessee and southcentral Kentucky in the "Appalachian region" may be controversial. However, we feel strongly that these regions should be included in this study, because these western areas share many cultural similarities with eastern mountain regions (Glassie 1968, pp. 38–39). Moreover, the oak basketmaking tradition in these regions is very strong and well documented. Today, in terms of numbers of baskets produced, these regions have the strongest ribwork tradition. Finally, because of extensive marketing outside the region, baskets made in central Kentucky and Tennessee often are wrongly attributed to other areas.

Why white oak baskets? White oak is the basketmaking material most widely used in the Central Appalachian Mountains. While there are many species of white oak, only two are commonly used for basketmaking (see range map, figure 2.2). The range map shows that white oaks grow throughout the eastern United States. However, the densest oak forests are located in the central and southern states.

Today both traditional basketmakers and revivalists make white oak baskets. While there are contemporary revivalists who make very fine baskets, we have not included them in this book. Our interest is in documenting the lives and work of traditional basketmakers who learned their craft informally from relatives or members of their communities.

Theory

We believe that by recording and analyzing the basket's construction, its structural details, and relationships between these basket styles or details and particular geographical locations, it often becomes possible to link baskets to specific makers, regions, and ethnic traditions. When a particular basket style or technique is repeated, it might signify that it was preferred by a basketmaker or a basket user. In all probability, the style also reflects features of a cultural group to which the basketmaker belonged. One must also consider the inventiveness of the individual basketmaker and the possibility of outside influences, such as the demands of the marketplace. The fact that a particular style is commonly associated with a region may also suggest hidden patterns of cultural migration or diffusion of ideas through common trade routes. We do not attempt to answer such questions, but we do hope to provide a foundation for future studies, which are best achieved at a local level where one can more easily and accurately study the work of a particular region.

Terminology

There was a definite need to develop a vocabulary which allowed for clear descriptions and comparisons of basketwork. Without a detailed vocabulary to describe structure or details, it would be impossible to compare or analyze similarities and differences among forms. Most makers just made baskets and had a minimal technical vocabulary. They knew what they were doing and didn't need lots of words to explain it. In choosing key terms, we tried to pick familiar ones, but on occasion we have chosen a less common term in order to avoid confusion among basket types.

Traditional makers use the term "split baskets" to describe any white oak basket, including not only split baskets but also rib and rod baskets. To add to the confusion, some basketmakers use the term "split" for both "round rods" and "flat splits." In order to distinguish the three basket forms, the authors have chosen to call "split baskets" only those baskets made chiefly of long flat strips of wood.

The term "split" has been selected over "splint," although some basketmakers use the words interchangeably. In New England the term "splint" prevails, and most Cherokees use the word "splint," which also refers to strips of rivercane (M. Ross, 8 May 1985). In the central and southern Appalachian regions, however, the term most frequently used by non-Native American white oak basketmakers is "split."

We have tried to be careful, consistent, and clear. Descriptive names have been given to techniques and details for reference purposes. In chapters 1 through 4, we have relied on the basketmaker's word choice as much as possible. In chapter 5, because of the relationship and similarity of American rodwork to European willowwork, we have relied on the terms used by Dorothy Wright, A.G. Knock, Thomas Okey, Alastair Heseltine, and Christoph Will, writers and scholars of English and German basketry. Due to the paucity of oak rod basketmakers, it was not possible to draw on informants' interviews for vocabulary to describe the range of techniques in rodwork.

Key terms are introduced in boldface, alternative terms are given in quotes, and short definitions of significant terms are offered in the glossary.

Procedure and Recording

Initially we began to record, through photographs and illustrations, the baskets and basketmakers that we found closest to home. Then we expanded our field, relying on knowledgeable collectors or researchers in other geographical areas who kindly shared their findings with us. Whenever a new style or basket detail was seen, it was our practice to document the basket through photographs or illustrations and record any "reported" information, even though some of this information later might turn out to have been inaccurate. A particular basket style may have been recorded three or four times before that basket or style was attributed to a specific region.

A catalogue system was developed to keep accurate records on each basket and the information known about its creation or use. As each basket or maker was recorded, each was compared to those already on file; thus the data continued to accumulate as more and more variations were discovered. Literally thousands of baskets have been observed, and roughly eight hundred were selected to be catalogued and recorded in more detail. Of these, no two are exactly alike. This fact attests to the creativity of individual basketmakers. The baskets selected for this book were chosen to represent the work of particular basketmakers, to point out features characteristic of a particular region, and to show examples of fine craftsmanship or unusual details.

Preliminary sketches were made while viewing the baskets, and, when it was deemed necessary to confirm the accuracy of our descriptions and illustration, copies were made using specific techniques. Our sketches were meticulously rendered into clear line drawings by illustrator Ali Wieboldt. The drawings are designed to present accurate and concise images which clearly show the working methods of particular basketmakers or the construction details of specific baskets.

When possible, baskets or makers were photographed by the authors. Doing our own photography gave us much better control over this crucial element of the book, recording the makers at work, the baskets themselves, and their important details. A rich variety of baskets and details is included here, to convey the diversity of basket styles and regions. In the captions, information is included (if known) about the maker, dates of the photo, where the basket was made, and the basket's dimensions. Dimensions are listed in the following order: base size; top opening; side height (s.h.), from basket base to the top rim; and overall height (o.h.) from the base to the top of the handle.

One of the most crucial questions is: How accurate is our information? Information presented in this book was carefully screened. Utmost care was taken to find reliable sources of information about local baskets or basketmaking. Most oral interviews were taped and then transcribed. There were cases when recording equipment might have intimidated informants, and on such occasions notes were taken. Many basketmakers also are fine storytellers, so please remember that, as with all oral folk tradition, there is natural hyperbole and room for personal interpretation. For this reason, we have often relied on exact quotes.

While we have made an attempt to be comprehensive and accurate, we know there is much yet to be recorded. It is hoped that this survey will be of value by pointing out some of the distinguishing characteristics of white oak basket constructions and by opening avenues for continued research on the subject. We also hope that more studies of individual makers and their traditional settings will be done, so that we can better understand the traditions of white oak basketmaking in the central Appalachian mountain region.

Acknowledgments

A great number of people have contributed in many ways to the research and writing of this book. We would like to thank everyone involved, for each has given his or her own unique type of help.

Several people have supported the project from the beginning and/or offered insights which at some point made major differences in concept, direction, and fieldwork: James M. Gentry, Scott Gilbert, Larry Hackley, Elizabeth Harzoff, Beth Hester, Loyal Jones, Rosemary O. Joyce, the late Catherine Candace Laird, Jeannette Lasansky, H. Wayne Law, Nancy J. Martin-Perdue, J. Roderick Moore, Mary M. and C. David Nash, Sue H. Stephenson, Michael B. Taylor, Alison Bruce Wieboldt, and Thomas F. Wieboldt.

Special thanks also go to historians, researchers, basketmakers, and institutions in Europe who provided background information on European basketmaking and willow culture.

England: Dorothy Wright Dix and Alastair Heseltine. Andrew Jewell and Sadie Ward, Museum of English Rural Life, Reading. K.G. Stott, Long Ashton Research Station, Bristol.

France: École Nationale d'Osiériculture et de Vannerie, Fayl-Billot.

Holland: Mrs. G.M. Pot–van Regteren Altena, the late A. Westendorp, Arie and Epona v'ant Hoog, and Ir. W.D.J. Tuinzing.

Scotland: Hugh Cheape, National Museum of Antiquities of Scotland, Edinburgh. M.J. Wilton, Highlands and Islands Development Board, Inverness. R. Ross Noble, Highland Folk Museum, Kingussie. Mrs. Clare Kyle.

Switzerland: Werner Turtschi.

Wales: Welsh Folk Museum, Cardiff. Dan Theophilus.

West Germany: Carola Kindle, Michael Thierschmann, and Christoph Will. Staatliche Fachschule für Korbflechterei, Lichtenfels, with special appreciation to Alfred Schneider and Wilfried Popp. Deutsches Korbmuseum, Michelau.

To the traditional basketmakers and their families with whom we shared baskets, meals, and stories, we owe more than thanks. They have given us the energy and dedication to pursue this work: Curtis Alvey, Leroy Alvey, Clovis and Roxie Boyd, Tishie Caldwell, Ralph and Trula

Chesney, Lestel and Ollie Childress, Lucy and William Cody Cook, W. Bill Cook, Betty Curry, Bill and Ida Pearl Davis, Oliver Day, Thelma and Billy Hibdon, Martha and Dan Jones, Edna Knott, Elmer E. Knott, Elmer L. Knott, Bill and Glenna Luke, Bob Mansberger, Donna Billetter Moore, Edith Billetter Myers, Irskel and Charlotte Nicholson, Oral W. Nicholson, John Peters, Elmer D. Price, Sr., Jake Ratsford, Ed Rector, Martha Ross, Nora Rutter, Dwight Stump, Homer and Juanita Summers, Earlean and Lawson Thomas, Charlotte Tracey, Pete Ware, Estel Youngblood, Gertie Youngblood, and Paul Younger.

Many other individuals also gave their knowledge, advice, time, hospitality, or baskets: Jack Adamson; Ralph and Sarah Arthur; Chris Benson; Jim Blackaby; Elizabeth Byrd Boggs; Carol and Jim Bohn; John Briley; Mayfield and Teresse Brown (at Grandmother's Antiques, Celina, Tennessee); Robert S. Brunk; Mr. and Mrs. Dennis R. Bruton; Jesse and Roxine Butcher; Emma Bybee; Robert Cogswell; Orlela and Adrian Combs; Alma and Jerry Cowherd; Allison Cusick; Kathleen and Ken Dalton (Coker Creek Crafts, Coker Creek, Tennessee); Jerry Devol; Datha Doolin (Country Village Antiques, Lancaster, Kentucky); Edd and Peggy Elkins; Jane and Ken Farmer; Charles and Teresa Faulkner; Cathy Fernandez; Barbara and Josh Gammon (Tin Rabbit Antiques, Marietta, Ohio); Linda Gardner Gant; David Gardner; the late Terry Gardner; Frank and Jane George; Earl and Mildred Gladden; Bert T. Glaze; Vernon Gunnion; Hazel Hamilton; David Haney (Fort Harmar Antiques, Marietta, Ohio); Roger Hankins; Marion Harless; Alice Hartman; Bruce and Mildred Helsley; Dr. and Mrs. Donald M. Herr; Robert M. Hicklin, Jr.; Maxine Hill; Patricia Hodges; Martha Howard; C.B. and Donna Huddleston; Walter Hyleck; Norman and Dorothy Irvine; John Rice Irwin; Judy Jones (Sign of the Times Antiques); John and Sue Kelleher; Marilyn Kemble (Norwich, Ohio); Ted Kessel; Denis O. Kiely; Marcus Farthing King; John Kraft; Sue Kurginski; Robert and Shirley Kuster; Fred Lamb; Drew Langsner; Shereen LaPlantz; Janice and Ted Law; John Lewis; Tim Lloyd; Benny and Janet Long; Burt Long; Kip Lornell; Susan Lott; Harry Mahoney; Mary Ann, Max, and Therese Malone; Robert Maslowski; Rosemary Maxwell; Connie and Tom McColley; Jorene McCubbins; Paul McGinnis; Dianne and Kelly Mink; Lynwood Montell; Michael Mullen (Marietta [Ohio] Historic Calendars); Michael Mullins; Valeria Smith Murphy; James O'Donnell; Charles L. Perdue. Jr.; Tim Pyles; Bill Richardson; Robert Richardson; Bruce Rigsby; Betty and Dick Robertson; Joe Roby; Smith G. Ross; Catherine Rubin; Barbara and Robert Schafer; Nancy and Peter Schiffer; Jerry

Schureman; Sandy See; Joan and Palmer Sharpless; Annie Handley Shobe; Rocky Simonetti; Willie Fay Spurlock; Karen Stollar; Nathan Taylor; Lois Unger; Bill and Dot Van Corbach (Split Rail Antiques, Elizabethtown, Kentucky), Ray and Sally Waters; Elizabeth C. Watts; Vaughan Webb; Martha Wetherbee; Blair White; E.F. and Mary Ann Wieboldt; Tanya Wilder; Sandy Worley; Aaron Yakim; Bud and Margaret Young; and Namuni Hale Young.

Institutions and foundations which have lent support in various ways include:

Kentucky: Appalachian Studies Foundation, Doris Ulmann Foundation, Hutchins Library, Settlement Institutions of Appalachia, all at Berea College, Berea; Red Bird Mission, Beverly; Folklife Archives and Kentucky Library, Western Kentucky University, Bowling Green; Appalachian Development Center, Morehead; Hindman Settlement School, Hindman; Kentucky Arts Council; and the Hart County Historical Society, Munfordville.

North Carolina: Southern Highland Handicraft Guild and Folk Art Center, Asheville; Museum of the Cherokee Indian, Cherokee; Mars Hill College, Mars Hill.

Ohio: Ohio Arts Council, Ohio Historical Society, and the Center of Science and Industry (COSI), Columbus; Campus Martius Museum, Marietta College, Marietta; and Zoar Village State Memorial, Zoar.

Pennsylvania: Bucks County Historical Society, Mercer Museum, and Spruance Library, Doylestown; Pennsylvania Farm Museum of Landis Valley, Lancaster; and Union County Historical Society, Lewisburg.

Tennessee: Special Collections at the University of Tennessee, Knoxville; Museum of Appalachia, Norris.

Virginia: Virginia Polytechnic Institute and State University, Blacksburg; Folklore Archive, University of Virginia, Charlottesville; and the Blue Ridge Institute at Ferrum College, Ferrum.

West Virginia: West Virginia Arts and Crafts Fair Board, West Virginia Arts and Humanities Council and the West Virginia Governor's Office of Economic and Community Development, Charleston; United States Department of Agriculture, Forest Service, Elkins.

Sincerest thanks to the University of Tennessee Press and its staff, who have made this book a reality.

Appalachian White Oak Basketmaking

Pl. 1.1 "Howdy Folks, you are at Doug's Place. Weaving baskets for the tourist trade is a profitable vocation in some sections of Kentucky. Mrs. Lucinda Allen at Doug's Place on U.S. 25 near Lamero shows her wares to a traveler looking for a souvenir or two." So reads the by-line of a photo in the Louisville, Ky., *Courier Journal* of 4 June 1950. Photograph by James N. Keen, reprinted with permission of the *Courier Journal* and the *Louisville Times*.

Introduction

Before paper bags, tin cans, and plastic containers, our forebears relied on baskets of all shapes and sizes as utensils essential in the daily routines of an agrarian society. A basket's form and construction often reflected its function, so grain riddles and sieves were made with openworked bottoms; winnowing baskets were made shallow to allow the grain to be tossed in the air; "long, open baskets [were designed] for the rolls of the spinners" (Goodrich 1931, p. 18); and the forms of fish and eel traps showed their intended uses. Commonly used for gathering, transporting and storing goods, most baskets served as basic containers and often were named for their contents or use: egg baskets for gathering eggs, coal baskets for hauling coal, berry baskets, pack baskets, clothes baskets, cradles, bobbin and wool baskets, laundry baskets, lidded feather baskets, and sewing baskets. Traditional basketmaker Walter Logsdon recalled, "People just couldn't get along without it [a basket]. Everybody had to have bushel baskets to carry the corn, feed the hogs, and carry around to the barn and feed the different horses" (Montell, 1 Sept. 1977).

As North America was settled by many different ethnic groups, they brought with them the basket traditions of their heritage. In the Central and Southern Appalachian Mountains, immigrants learned to use materials growing locally for their basketmaking. The Appalachian mountain region of the middle eastern United States, with its numerous and varied plant species, offered plentiful raw materials of many different types to satisfy basketmakers' needs and preferences. Suitable were young shoots of native willows and osier dogwoods, a variety of vines, and such tough-fibered plant materials as cattails, corn husks, oat or rye straw, and broomsedge. Rivercane, split into thin strips, was a favorite material of the Cherokee Indians of the region. Woods which were split into thin strips for basketmaking included white and black ash, white and swamp chestnut oak, elm, yellow-poplar, maple, sassafras, buckeye, and hickory. In addition, barks of hickory, white pine, poplar, elm, maple, and willow were stripped from tree trunks and used for weaving (Cl. Pl. 1).

Although many of the plant species mentioned above were used for basketmaking, white oak became the material most commonly used for baskets in the central and southern Appalachian mountain regions. Frances Louisa Goodrich, who came to western North Carolina in

1890, made these observations about white oak basketmaking in the mountain region:

> The craft of basket making would seem to have been brought from the old countries by settlers in the southern mountains. The change to the New World made possible and even necessary changes in materials, and in this respect something may have been learned from the Indians. For large or strong baskets osiers were exchanged for splits of white oak or of hickory wood. Much work and much skill goes into the making of a split basket. First the tree must be chosen not over one foot in diameter at the butt, of straight growth, and of firm fiber. Even best judges are sometimes mistaken in a tree, finding it twisted or of loose growth, and are obliged to abandon it after felling. When the trunk has been sawed or chopped into convenient lengths, these are split into halves and again into quarters and eighths, from which the ribs and hoops and "weavers" can be rived off. In this way every split that is used in the basket is worked out with the grain of the wood, instead of being cut across the fibers as in machine-made baskets, and in this the durability and beauty of the hand-made basket largely consists. (Goodrich 1931, p. 17)

In the central and southern Appalachian regions (Fig. 1.1), one finds three major types of white oak baskets: **rib baskets, rod baskets,** and **split baskets**, named for the chief structural element of each form (Pl. 1.2; Fig. 1.2). Geographically, there are isolated pockets as well as widespread regions where one particular form is the dominant basket tradition, often reflecting the ethnic background of the settlers of that region.

The distinctive feature of rib baskets is the structural framework which includes curved foundation pieces, commonly called **ribs**, which govern the graceful curves and rounded shapes most characteristic of these baskets. This structural framework makes the rib basket deceptively sturdy. Rib baskets were made throughout the Central Appalachians; however, regional pockets where rib basketmaking is dominant occur in those areas heavily settled by Scots-Irish and Germans. Goodrich observes the dominance of rib baskets: "The most common shape is what is known as the melon basket or hip basket. It is interesting to note that this shape is to be seen in pictures in the *National Geographic Magazine*, from Ireland, Roumania [*sic*], and Jamaica, and has been found throughout central and southern Europe. Perhaps the idea is a very ancient one, and therefore is widespread." She then goes on to mention baskets "on another plan, but still of the dependable splits," undoubtedly, split baskets (Goodrich 1931, pp. 17–18).

Baskets constructed chiefly of long flat strips of wood known as **splits** are called "split baskets." The round, square, or rectangular split baskets are the simplest of all the white oak basket constructions. Despite its

Fig. 1.1 Map of the central Appalachian region.

simplicity, splitwork also shows a wide range of craftsmanship, with some baskets exhibiting skillfully carved handles or elaborate top rim treatments. This form is the most widespread of the three basket types, but there are distinctions in construction and detail work which can be associated with particular regions.

Rod baskets are made with long slender **rods** which have been split and shaped from white oak. As a basket form, rodwork is nearing extinction, as few makers continue the tradition. The task of making rods and weaving them into baskets has no known precedent in Europe. Rodwork appears to be a distinctively American adaptation of European willow basketwork. Exactly when and why basketmakers turned to rodwork can only be guessed, but the tradition was quite widespread. From Pennsylvania to

Pl. 1.2 Basket group showing the three major types of white oak baskets: rib, rod, and split.

Fig. 1.2 Key to basket group: (a) oak rod sewing basket with wrapped handles; (b) shallow round split basket; (c) small rib melon basket; (d) rib wall basket; (e) square split basket; (f) lidded twill-woven rectangular split basket; (g) swing-handled round split basket; (h) small urn-shaped split basket; (i) rib basket with decorative braid; and (j) round rod basket with solid handle. Collection of Cynthia W. and Michael B. Taylor: a, b, j. Collection of Linda and Terry Gardner: c, d, h, i. Collection of Ray and Sally Waters: g. Private collection: e, f.

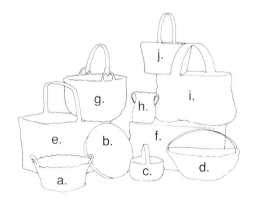

North Carolina and as far west as Indiana, oak rod baskets are found, although often their creation was localized in areas settled by Germans, such as the Shenandoah Valley of Virginia and Landis Valley of Pennsylvania (Pl. 1.3).

There are significant and consistent, although often minor, departures or variations in technique which occur within these basket types. Each basketmaker has a particular way of making a basket. When makers used certain techniques or construction features that were continued by descendents (Pl. 1.4) and other members of the basketmaking community, a regional style developed. Many of these techniques are continued today by basketmakers who often cannot explain why they construct baskets the way they do. Irskel Nicholson, a basketmaker in Shenandoah County, Virginia, patiently explained the way his family had always "built" split

Pl. 1.3   Henry Landis, cofounder of the Pennsylvania Farm Museum, with a group of Pennsylvania baskets. Early in the twentieth century, the Landis brothers began to collect a variety of objects representing rural Pennsylvania life. Their collection became the foundation of the Pennsylvania Farm Museum of Landis Valley. Landis is holding an oak rib basket typical of the region. The large oak rod cradle holds other forms common to the area, including more rib baskets, coiled straw baskets, willow baskets, and a hexagonally woven basket. Photograph courtesy of Pennsylvania Farm Museum of Landis Valley, Pennsylvania Historical and Museum Commission.

baskets and added, "We have a name for everything, it may not be right, but it is a family tradition and we stick with it" (16 Mar. 1985). While it is possible to document specific changes made in basket technique and construction and link these to specific makers, a large number of the variations presented in this book can be attributed only to region.

Basketmaking as a Tradition

While there were isolated individuals who learned to make baskets on their own or from a neighbor, evidence suggests that the majority of basketmaking is perpetuated through a family network. One well-documented study of basketmaking traditions being passed on in families was done by Nancy J. Martin-Perdue. The research reported in her "Case Study: On Eaton's Trail: A Genealogical Study of Virginia Basket Makers" (1983) documents six generations of known basketmakers among the Nicholson, Corbin, and Cook families and traces their shared lineage back to a common Nicholson ancestor who was born in Cumberland County, England, in 1704.

A white oak basketmaker's education has been informal, learning by watching a family member or other basketmakers in the community. "I just wanted to learn to make baskets," said Carol Welch, a Cherokee basketmaker. "I was only twelve when I started weaving. My mama didn't *teach* me exactly; I would just watch her, and finally I started to use the white oak strips the same way that she did. My daughter fools around with some of the pieces that I cut, but it's probably just play. She's only seven" (United States Department of Interior, 1977).

White oak basketmaking is time-consuming and has never paid well in terms of the time invested. However, it is a craft which requires relatively few tools and produces a marketable commodity. Basketmakers not only made baskets for their own use, but also sold or traded their products. In rural areas where individuals may have relied on farming, coal mining, chairmaking, stonemasonry, or bootlegging as their major source of income, basketmaking was a way to bring in extra money or goods.

Many basketmakers peddled their own wares. Some went by foot, a mode of transportation appropriately referred to as the "bone wagon" (Eaton 1937, p. 177). Residents of Pendleton County, West Virginia, can remember when Levi Eye (Pl. 1.5) came to their door peddling his baskets (Elizabeth Boggs, 10 Feb. 1986). Other peddlers who were not makers,

Pl. 1.4 Round split baskets made by three generations of the Billetter family of Belmont County, Ohio. All three baskets are made from a variety of native woods and show a continuity of tradition in style and technique. The basket on the left, made by Sarah Wayt Billetter (1835–92), is the only one made of white oak. She taught her son, Samuel E. Billetter (1870–1957), who, beginning at the age of seven, became a very prolific basketmaker in the Sewellsville, Ohio, area. Billetter used a variety of woods, including oak, elm, and ash, to weave identical forms (center basket). The tradition was passed on to his son, Charles A. Billetter (1902–1982), who made the basket on the right (Gladden, 28 Sept. 1984; Horward, 4 Apr. 1951; Myers, 10 Oct. 1984). Collection of Edith Billetter Myers.

such as William Nicholson, bought baskets from their relatives. In the region around Old Rag, Virginia, Nicholson was known as "Jake the Peddler" and "the Calculator," because of his facility with numbers. He made a large wooden frame which extended several feet over his head, attached many baskets to the frame and traveled the long roads selling his wares (Martin-Perdue 1983, pp. 95–96).

In some areas baskets were nearly legal tender. Baskets were traded to neighbors and local storekeepers for goods and services. The value of the basket as a barter item kept many families actively making baskets.

> My grandmother . . . made, and my mother. . . . We made baskets. We had to make 'em, take 'em to the store for our living. They wouldn't give you no money on 'em. So you had to take 'em to the store and trade 'em for groceries to live on. (Thomas and Thomas, 30 Nov. 1984)

> They all made baskets, bottomed chairs and things like that. . . . They'd just

take a big rope and tie a big bunch of baskets, throw 'em over a mule and go to the grocery. . . . Whatever Mama needed. . . . What she didn't take up in groceries, they'd give her money for it. ["or a due bill" said Lestel] . . . If she wanted anything like the old Victrola that you turn . . . then she'd make baskets for 'em. (Childress and Childress, 23 Mar. 1984)

In southcentral Kentucky, basketmaking and selling grew into a sizeable cottage industry, with the marketplace extending far from the homestead. One well-documented basket "industry" was centered around Cub Run (known as Crossroads before 1874), Hart County, Kentucky (Alvey, 23 Jan. 1986; Brown and Schottenfeld, 14 Sept. 1977; Childress and Childress, 23 Mar. 1984, 20 Feb. 1985; Davis and Wilson, 29 Sept. 1977; Hall and Hall, 30 Sept. 1977; Hall and Moody, 19 Oct. 1977; Harzoff, 14 and 19 Sept. 1977; Jaggers 1971; Kiely, 30 Sept. 1977 and 1983; Korn and Kiely, 16 Sept. 1977; Ludden, 5 Sept. 1977; Marshall and Schottenfeld, 23 Sept. 1977; Montell, 1 Sept. 1977; Montell and Collins, 1 Oct. 1977; North 1975; Ostrofsky and Brown, 28 Sept. 1977; Payton, Fall 1977; Judi Sadewasser, interview with Logsdon, 15 July 1974, and "Folkways," 1974; Judi Sadewasser and Steve Sadewasser, 27 June 1974; Schottenfeld 1977; Sutherland 1971; Waldrop, interviews with Logsdon, 15 and 28 Nov. 1975, and "Basketmaking," 1975; Wilson [1977]).

While it is not known exactly how many people from southcentral Kentucky made or peddled baskets, interviews with individuals from the region indicate the number was quite large. Anderson Childress, basketmaker and local historian, estimated that between Cub Run and Sandhill, five hundred to six hundred families were involved in the basket trade. Those were not small families, as most had six to fifteen children. Childress claimed there were two classes of basketmakers, each with about equal numbers of members: those who made baskets whenever they had the time, and those "basketmakers [who] didn't do much of anything else. They didn't worry about farm work. If they farmed, it was secondary, basketmaking was their primary vocation" (Marshall and Schottenfeld, 23 Sept. 1977). Some names of basketmakers and those involved in the trade were: Jaggers, West, Miles, Dennison, Alvey (Pl. 1.6), Waddle, Childress, Cottrell, Trulock, Kessinger, Taylor, Logsdon, Higdon, and Gunterman. Many of these families are still making and selling baskets in Kentucky today. Walter Logsdon, a basketmaker from Edmonson County, recalled, "Buying and selling baskets was a industry. Even in the newspapers, they published it around the stores at Cub Run, 'Farm Baskets A Speciality' [sic]. They specialized in farm baskets. They [the merchants] wanted all

Pl. 1.5 Levi Eye (1842–1926) of Pendleton County, West Virginia, peddling baskets in 1921 in Franklin, West Virginia. Born to one of the early families (settled 1768) of the county (Morton [1910] 1980, pp. 167, 205–207; Elizabeth Boggs, 10 Feb. 1986), Eye is credited with making seven thousand baskets and was a well-respected master of his trade. Eye also served in the 62nd Regiment, Virginia Infantry, during the Civil War (Elsie Boggs 1960, p. 112). Photograph by Elsie Boggs, courtesy of the Elizabeth Boggs estate.

of 'em they could get. And they'd buy great loads of 'em there and hoard um up, and stack 'em up til the time come to peddle 'em out" (Judi Sadewasser, 15 July 1974).

According to Anderson Childress and Rec Childress, both of whom were involved in the basket trade in this region of Kentucky, long-distance basket peddling began soon after the Civil War, as a few baskets were added to wagons carrying locally quarried grindstones to outside regions (Marshall and Schottenfeld, 23 Sept. 1977; Brown and Schottenfeld, 14 Sept. 1977). Soon long-distance basket peddling developed into a fulltime occupation for many individuals. Many peddling trips lasted weeks and even months, as the basket peddlers traveled great distances with mules or horses pulling their specifically designed wagons, loaded with hundreds of baskets. At first, the "farm baskets" or "bushels" were the chief item of trade, because of the demand for them in many grain-producing areas of the Midwest: Indiana, Illinois, Ohio, Missouri, and particularly Iowa (Montell, 1 Sept. 1977). The bushel baskets were tied by the handles, four to a bundle, and piled high on the wagons which had been custom built to carry the load. Anderson Childress described the basket-peddling wagon in great detail:

> The old farm wagon had high wheels in back and low wheels in front. The frame was made on two poles that were hewed out. . . . They'd let the running gear out to make a long wheelbase and they'd put a long bed on it. There was a round or partly round pole on each side. They bored auger holes in it and they'd sit these poles in these auger holes. They didn't have to be heavy because a basket load was light. Across the top there was a split out piece. It was about six feet from the wagon bed to the top of the pole. They had enough of these upright pieces to keep the baskets from rolling out. . . . They had a little dog house of a thing built on the front of the wagon, waterproof, some covered with tin, some with tarp, I suppose, that they could sleep in it in the rainy weather and they kept their bedrolls, frying pan, coffee pot, whatever in that in the dry. They'd sit on the front of it. (Marshall and Schottenfeld, 23 Sept. 1977)

Merchants and individuals alike purchased baskets from peddlers who had traveled far from their home territory. Consequently, an old bushel basket found in Cleveland, Ohio, or Chicago, Illinois, might have been purchased locally but made in central Kentucky or Tennessee.

Pl. 1.6 Leroy Alvey, Grayson County, Kentucky, ca. 1962. Alvey operated a general store in Wax, Kentucky, and accepted baskets in trade. Like his father, Thomas Alvey, who operated the store before him, Leroy was also the postmaster. At the time of this photo, Leroy was still "dealing and trading groceries and supplies for baskets, from approximately twenty families." He would also pay cash for the baskets purchased, but in earlier years, when money and credit were tight, Thomas Alvey accepted baskets in trade, issuing a "due bill" for the change owed to the basketmaker (Alvey, 27 Jan. 1986). Photograph courtesy of Emma Bybee, Leroy Alvey, Jerry Schureman, and East Kentucky Power.

1. White Oak Basketmaking   13

Influences on the Tradition

White oak basketmaking has always been dependent on the availability of good basket timber, a market for handmade baskets, and the basketmaker's opportunities for better employment. In the last hundred years there have been important economic, ecological, and social changes which have had a significant impact on the lives of the basketmakers as well as on the baskets they built.

As a traditional craft, some elements of white oak basketmaking have remained relatively unchanged from generation to generation, while other aspects of the craft have changed significantly. Many of the tools and techniques used to split the oak log into basketmaking materials have remained constant, but as a consequence of advances in technology and transportation, modern basketmakers may use chain saws or motorized transportation. Basket forms and distinguishing details in style or technique have undergone a continuing evolution, as basketmakers draw from their traditions but also express their own ingenuity, copy models (Pl. 1.7) provided from the outside, or respond to the demands of a changing marketplace.

Toward the end of the nineteenth century, basketmaking in the Southern Appalachians was influenced significantly by the Handicraft Revival. The revival began when outsiders, influenced by the Arts and Crafts movement and the social reform programs of early urban settlement houses, came to the southern mountains. With renewed interest nationwide in oldtime crafts creating a market for handcrafted items, the newcomers offered guidance in the production of handicrafts. The impact of the Handicraft Revival was quite extensive and remains controversial. (Readers may want to investigate Eaton's book, *Handicrafts of the Southern Highlands*, and two more recent books, Whisnant's *All That Is Native and Fine* and Shapiro's *Appalachia on Our Mind*, for three different perspectives.)

Numerous regional groups and organizations became active in the Handicraft Revival and together founded their own "Fireside Industries." One of the first and most successful of the handicraft enterprises was Allanstand Cottage Industries (ACI), organized in 1902. Frances Louisa Goodrich, Allanstand's founder, was born in New York, was raised in Cleveland, Ohio, and attended Yale Art School. In 1890, employed as a social worker in the schools of the Women's Board of Home Missions of the Presbyterian Church, she settled near Asheville, North Carolina, and soon became actively involved in reviving the handicraft work of the local

Pl. 1.7 Imported baskets have long served as models for traditional basketmakers. The imported basket on the left was purchased at a local flea market by traditional Tennessee basketmaker Estel Youngblood, who used it as a model to fashion, from white oak, his own version, which he calls the "Moses basket." While there are many similarities in the two baskets, Youngblood has used native materials and incorporated into the new form techniques traditional in his region, including the bow wrapping, woven handle, and a decorative braid added to the handle hoop (Youngblood, 30 Nov. 1984).

people (Russell 1976, pp. 55–59; Eaton 1937, p. 64; Goodrich 1931, pp. 21–30). According to Goodrich, Allanstand was established with three purposes in mind: "To save the old arts from extinction; to give paying work to women too far from market to find it for themselves; and, more important than all, to bring interest into their lives, the joy of making useful and beautiful things" (1931, p. 25). In 1908 the handicraft sales location was moved from Allanstand to a permanent salesroom and distribution center in Asheville, North Carolina, which continues in operation today, under the auspices of the Southern Highland Handicraft Guild. A price list from the 1930s (see Pl. 1.8 for a 1917 price list) advertises the Allanstand Cottage Industries as the "Pioneer Exchange for Handicrafts of the Southern Mountains."

In *Mountain Homespun*, Goodrich describes her "discovery" of basketmaking in the mountains, the baskets typical of the region, how they were

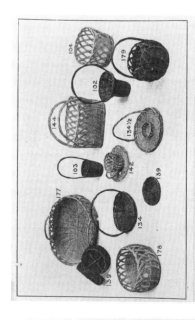

No. 142—Cup and Saucer_____25c
No. 144—Parcel Basket_____50c, 75c, $1.00
No. 177—Baby Basket_____25c
No. 178—Darning Basket _____60c
No. 179—Egg Basket _____75c

MISCELLANEOUS
No. 202—Work Basket of Honeysuckle Vine____50c to $1.50
No. 203—Honeysuckle Covered Bottle_____40c to $1.00
No. 220—Pine Needle Basket_____$1.00
No. 222—Pine Needle Tray_____50c, 75c, $1.00

Many Other Styles Not Listed

CONDENSED PRICE LIST OF WEAVINGS AND OTHER ARTICLES

COVERLET WEAVING, light weight, in many patterns, for bedspreads, couch covers, hangings, table covers and cushion covers, $2.50 per yd.

HEAVY WEIGHT COVERLET, material for floor rugs. Made to order in any length desired.

LINSEY WOOLSEY, for sport suits, $1.75 a yard and up, depending on color and weave.

ALLANSTAND BLANKETS, for hangings and couch covers, $1.75 a yard up.

KNOTTED AND TUFTED COLONIAL BED-SPREADS, with fringe, $16.00 up.

QUILT TOPS, in old designs.

SILK TAPESTRY, woven to order.

HAND-WOVEN CANVAS, embroidered for bedspreads, hangings and table covers, as well as by the yard.

BRAIDED AND CROCHETED COLONIAL RUGS.

RAG RUGS woven to order..

KNOTTED FRINGE—60c a yard up.

SHUCK HATS—$1.50 to $3.00, according to size and fineness of braid.

HEARTH BROOMS, of broom corn, 40c.

Prices vary according to design and color of material

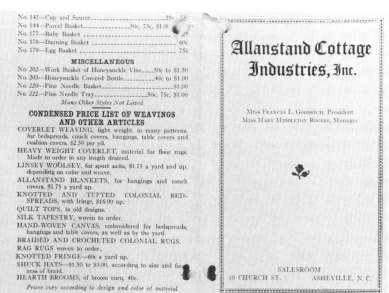

Allanstand Cottage Industries, Inc.

Miss Frances L. Goodrich, President
Miss Mary Middleton Rogers, Manager

SALESROOM
10 CHURCH ST.   ASHEVILLE, N.C.

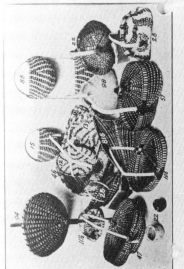

Price List

OAK SPLINT BASKETS

No. 6—Fruit Tray_____60c and 75c
No. 11—Round Bon-Bon Tray_____25c
No. 11½—Oval Bon-Bon Tray_____30c
No. 12—Oval Sandwich Tray_____45c
No. 13½—Square Sandwich Tray_____50c
Nos. 15, 16, 17, 19—Tyrol or Wall Baskets_40, 50, 75, $1.00
No. 22—Melon Favors, 1½ to 2½ inches, each_____15c
No. 22—Melon Baskets_____20c to $5.00
No. 24—Hamper _____$2.50
No. 26—Violet Canoe_____35, 50, 75, $1.00
No. 26½—Rose Basket_____$1.25
No. 28—Low Melon_____60c to $1.00
No. 29—Fruit Basket_____75, $1.00, $1.25
No. 30—Apple Basket_____$1.15, $1.30
No. 34—Canoe _____$1.25
No. 36—Oval Fruit Basket_____$1.00 and $1.25
No. 46—White Rock_____50c to $2.00
No. 47—Fruit Boat (not always available)____50, 75, $1.00
No. 57—Watermelon_____50, 75, $1.00
No. 64—Wood Basket_____$1.00 to $2.50
No. 74—Bird Nest _____45c
No. 76—Knitting Basket_____$1.25
No. 80—Sewing Table_____$3.50
      Curate or Muffin Stand with Three Trays____$4.00
No. 86—Picking Basket_____80c
No. 88—Double Tyrol_____$1.25, $1.65
No. 94—Garden Basket, Round_____$1.30
No. 94—Garden Basket, Canoe Shape_____$2.00, $2.50
No. 98—Old Kentucky or Jug Basket_____75, $1.00, $1.35

WILLOW BASKETS

No. 102—Nasturtium _____60c
No. 103—Hanging Flower_____50c, 75c
No. 104—Jardinere _____75c
No. 131—Work Basket_____75, $1.00, $1.25
No. 134—Sandwich Tray_____35c
No. 134½—Sandwich Tray and Keeper_____50c
No. 139—Round Trays or Bag Bottoms____10c to 30c

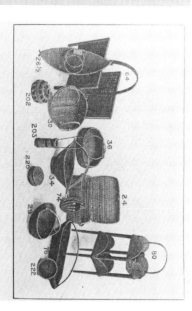

Pl. 1.8   Price List of Allanstand Cottage Industries, Asheville, North Carolina, ca. 1917. Forty-five styles of baskets are listed, all made from native materials: oak, willow, honeysuckle, and pine needles. The catalog shows both traditional basket forms and many new ones developed during the Handicraft Revival. The use of color is evident on many of the baskets pictured. Courtesy of the Southern Highland Handicraft Guild, Folk Art Center, Asheville, North Carolina.

named, and which ones provided models for many of the baskets sold through Allanstand:

> Our venture in basket-making, which has grown to such large proportions, came almost by accident. A man who had become a cripple from rheumatism moved into Brittain's Cove, hoping to find help there in supporting his family. He had taken up the making of baskets and made good, firm, split baskets of the traditional melon shape. These he sold to his neighbors for the small sums they could afford to give him, but it was not an adequate wage for the work and unusual skill and care involved. Telling him that we could market his baskets at a fair price if he would keep up to standard, improving in the smoothing of the splits, we took his whole output, which became considerable. He kept to his part of the bargain, and I look now in vain for baskets to match his, in shape and workmanship. He made a good support for his family as long as he lived. . . . As the years went on other basket-makers came in our way, a few other shapes were discovered and others evolved to make the great variety sold today.
>
> From White Rock, Madison County, came the basket with squared ends which we named the White Rock basket. One man brought us our first boat or canoe basket, copied from the Indians, and someone else seeing it, evolved a "picking basket" by joining two canoes at one end, leaving the other ends wide apart. The basket is held in place against the waist of the picker by a thong around the neck.
>
> In Munich one of us saw a basket which was just half of the melon basket, and this, suggested to the workers, was successfully made of splits and took its place as the Tyrol basket.
>
> Kentucky furnished the pattern for the Jug basket of "Old Kentucky." A large flat oval shape was brought in one day and explained as the quill basket, used by weavers in old times to hold the quills for the shuttles. It is easy to see how the "Watermelon" got its name and the "Muzzle" and "Half-Muzzle." In the "Clover Basket" the ribs are so placed in the weaving that when closely made it will hold a seed as small as clover. There are over twenty shapes now on our list. The melon basket is made in all sizes from the big chip-basket for the hearth to the favors, two inches across. (1931, pp. 27–29)

Fireside Industries not only encouraged the making of regional basket styles, but also introduced new styles and encouraged the creation of new forms. Ironically, many of the "new basket styles" became traditional forms for basketmakers of later generations and today are accepted as traditional forms in the Appalachian mountains. One noteworthy example is the rib wall basket or "wall pocket" or "key basket," as it is commonly named in the mountain region. As noted by Goodrich, this form was based on a basket seen in Germany. The Allanstand sales brochure (ca. 1917) called it the "Tyrol" basket (Pl. 1.8).

Hindman Settlement School, founded in 1902 by May Stone and Katherine Pettit, was active in promoting and encouraging both white oak and willow basketmaking (Nason 1932) (Pls. 1.9 and 1.10). In the same manner that the "Tyrol" basket was introduced by Goodrich and her associates, new shapes also were introduced into the eastern Kentucky mountains through Hindman Settlement School. According to Elizabeth Watts, who came to the school as a teacher in 1908 and later became its director, "In the old days they made melon baskets and then they made the shapes we asked them to make. . . . People would bring in baskets from outside the area—they would pick up a basket which they thought would be nice for them to make. Miss Stone would pick up baskets on her travels too, and others would bring them in" (26 Nov. 1984).

In addition to suggesting new shapes in baskets, the new mountain industries demanded a high level of workmanship and promoted the use of color in baskets. The naturally light-colored white oak splits were easily dyed with native plants and, in later years, commercial dyes. According to Goodrich, the practice of coloring basket splits was introduced into the North Carolina mountains: "Though we had never seen color in a mountain basket we suggested to this man to color some of the splits with a native dye and these, in brown and white, proved to be more marketable than the all-white baskets" (1931, p. 27).

After 1910, many basket forms became more decorative. Changes in agricultural methods, as well as the availability of alternative containers and cheaper baskets made from machine-veneered splits, reduced the demand for handcrafted utility baskets. The new appreciation of handicrafts brought about by the Arts and Crafts movement also influenced the demand for handcrafted white oak baskets. White oak basketmakers made a wide variety of baskets in many shapes, sizes, and colors, in response to the changing demand. Many of these baskets were smaller than the bushel size, more varied in shape, and often decorated with colored splits. "Fancy baskets" and "novelties" were two terms applied to the new products, which included not only baskets, but also flower vases, trays, decorative wall pieces and fans. The brochure issued by the Allanstand Cottage Industries about 1917 boasted twenty-nine different styles of white oak baskets for sale, perhaps reflecting the peak of basket production; by the 1930s, the number of basket styles had dwindled to thirteen (ACI ca. 1930).

Another important force influencing markets for baskets was improvement in transportation systems. Some of the Fireside Industries found that business was great enough to establish sales outlets in urban centers (Eaton 1937, pp. 252 and 295) and publish mail-order catalogs. Parcel post

Pl. 1.9   Bird Owsley, basketmaker from Knott County, Kentucky, ca. 1922, holding two styles of baskets he made and sold through the Hindman Settlement School's Fireside Industries. In his left hand is a traditional melon-shaped rib basket, woven with dyed splits. Hanging from his right arm is a tall rectangular split basket with colored splits, a shape he may have been asked to make by the settlement school. Photograph courtesy of Settlement Institutions of Appalachia Collection, Southern Appalachian Archives, Berea College.

and rail express allowed quick, direct shipments to customers far from the point of origin. Access to easier transportation expanded basket sales, which in turn influenced the number of basketmakers and the volume of their output.

Developments in the road and railway systems also broadened the markets for long-distance basket peddlers in southcentral Kentucky and Tennessee. Peddling vehicles changed. Mule-driven road wagons were replaced by spring wagons and eventually by gasoline-powered trucks. The newer vehicles provided greater comfort and could travel greater distances more quickly, but they held a much smaller load. As a result, peddlers often replenished their basket supply by receiving rail shipments. Stanley Cottrell (Pl. 1.11) described one of his peddling trips using a truck around 1930: "I piled them [baskets] clear up high as we could pile them and

Pl. 1.10 Aunt Cord Ritchie, Knott County, Kentucky, known for her willow basket-making, and a group of other basketmakers, bringing their baskets to the Hindman Settlement School. Photograph courtesy of Settlement Institutions of Appalachia Collection, Southern Appalachian Archives, Berea College.

then I'd pick up baskets about every other day, in different towns. Shipped them to me by Express. Went to the Express office and picked them up. The Express man [said], 'God damn am I ever glad to see you . . . the place is filled up'" (Harzoff, 19 Sept. 1977).

Rec Childress claimed that his father, Elijah Tom, bought a thousand-mile railway ticket for twenty dollars. He boarded the train with three sample baskets, of bushel, half-bushel, and peck sizes. As he traveled, he took orders for the baskets and had the merchants pick up their baskets at the train depot. As many as 1,500 baskets were shipped by rail to different points on his sales trip (Brown and Schottenfeld, 14 Sept. 1977).

In central Tennessee, Earlean and Lawson Thomas, basketmakers from Woodbury, Cannon County, peddled baskets by truck from about 1929 to 1940, when they left Tennessee for better employment in the North. Selling their own baskets as well as those which they had bought from local

Pl. 1.11 Stanley Cottrell, Hart County, Kentucky, at his home relating peddling stories. Cottrell helped his mother make baskets as a youngster, and when older he became a peddler. Several merchants depended on him to sell their baskets. Two tales regularly told to increase sales were "the timber was running out so they better buy now" (in later years, that wasn't too far from the truth) and "buy now because they were so far away from home and might not be back for a long time." Cottrell peddled baskets into Indiana with Elijah Tom Childress, "King of the Basket Peddlers." Cottrell recalled seeing, on one trip to Richmond, Indiana, "the basket sellingest place I ever seen." He and his traveling partner, after selling at every farm in the area, went on to Richmond to spend the night. In the morning his partner asked why he was "taking so much pains a-cleaning up?" He replied, "I'm gonna call on that wholesale hardware." He sold the hardware a gross (144) of bushel baskets. On a return trip a year later, Cottrell went back to the hardware store but was thrown out. The store had not sold the baskets, due to the fact that Cottrell and his partner already had peddled to the surrounding farms (Harzoff, 14 Sept. 1977). Cottrell made his last peddling trip in late 1938 or 1939, just before going into the Army (Harzoff 1977, p. 6). Photograph taken by, and used courtesy of, Elizabeth Harzoff.

Pl. 1.12 Basket stand along old Highway 31W about two miles north of Munfordville, Hart County, Kentucky, ca. 1931. From Louisville, Kentucky, south to Nashville, Tennessee, numerous basket stands and souvenir shops crowded the two main highways, the Dixie Highway (31W) and the Jackson Highway (31E). Basket stands provided excellent marketing opportunities because of the large number of travelers visiting Mammoth Cave or heading south to Florida (Bavill, n.d.). This small log cabin was built adjacent to the home of Virginia Guess Bruton. Bruton's father and mother, Mr. and Mrs. Bill Guess, made most of the baskets and chairs for sale. The child is June Guess (Murphy and McCubbins, 13 Jan. 1986). Photograph courtesy of Hart County Historical Society, Munfordville, Kentucky, and Mr. and Mrs. Dennis R. Bruton.

merchants, Earlean recalled traveling to Dayton, Columbus, and Cleveland, Ohio, as well as regions of Kentucky and Tennessee. Her husband Lawson added, "In the wintertime, we'd go to Florida. Go down there in the wintertime through Virginia and West Virginia. . . . We went as far south as Florida, Georgia, Alabama, North Carolina, South Carolina. I've been to all those places" (30 Nov. 1984).

During the 1920s and 1930s, the U.S. Department of the Interior formed several national parks in the eastern United States. These included Shenandoah National Park in Virginia, Mammoth Cave in Kentucky, and the Great Smoky Mountain National Park in western North Carolina and eastern Tennessee (Ise 1961). The formation of these parks resulted in relocation of long-established inhabitants. Some of those relocated were basketmakers who gave up their work entirely due to the lack of a timber source (Childress and Childress, 23 Mar. 1984). For others, the impact was more beneficial. With the new parks and the expanded road system into the mountain regions, many tourists and travelers came through the territory. Basket stands (Pls. 1.1 and 1.12) and souvenir shops became a common sight along main highways near the national parks and other well-traveled areas. From 1933 to 1947, Elmer Price operated a souvenir stand in northwestern Virginia on U.S. Route 211, the Luray–New Market road, a main highway to the Luray Caverns and Shenandoah National Park. Price not only sold baskets made by his family, but also bought from a middleman named Harry Campbell, a "big basket man" who traveled from Virginia to West Virginia purchasing baskets for resale (Price, 14 Mar. 1985).

By the 1940s, basketmaking was in decline. Economic and social changes during and following World War II changed traditional work values and family structures. Walton Strange, a former basket peddler who in 1940 was operating a basket stand along U.S. Routes 31E and 31W through Hart County, Kentucky, complained that baskets were getting hard to get. He credited the limited number of baskets to the difficulty in finding good timber (particularly since the development of Mammoth Cave National Park) and the decreasing number of large families. Even at that time, many had given up the trade because they could make more money "on relief and W.P.A." Nevertheless, some in the region would work all day on a basket and then sell it for a quarter (Smith, 24 Dec. 1940).

Industrialization of the country had brought work opportunities for many basketmakers. When the cross-tie industry began to develop in south-central Kentucky, Walter Logsdon remembers:

> They made these cross-ties out of white oak timber. And that was a pretty good job. . . . They made about 10 cents a piece for makin' a tie and they could make eight or ten ties a day. And they would make so much more a hackin' ties . . . than they could making baskets that eventually . . . the basket industry just gave way to a cross-tie industry. Then came the saw log days. . . . And then we had a little upheaval in the industrial world at that time, and people began to go away and leave the county and go to the city and get jobs. . . . [Basketmaking] just faded away. (Judi Sadewasser, 15 July 1974)

(Ronald Eller's work, *Miners, Millhands and Mountaineers*, gives an in-depth discussion of lumbering and industrialization in Appalachia.)

White oak basketmaking continued to decline throughout the central and southern Appalachian region. It was primarily members of the older generation who continued to make baskets. The children of the makers

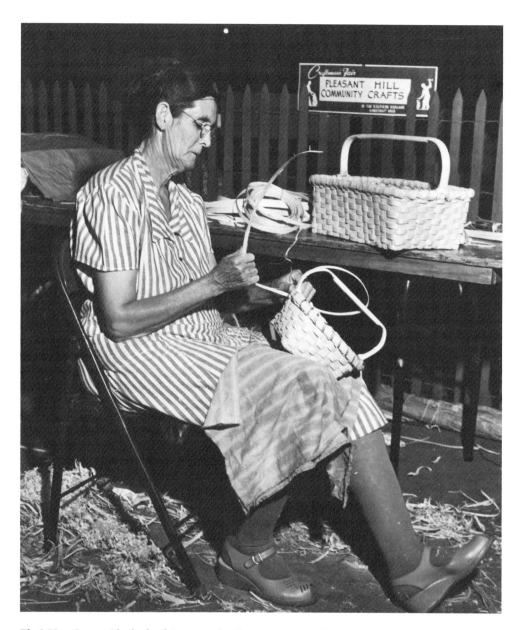

Pl. 1.13　Laura Blaylock of Ravencroft, Tennessee, a small mining community not far from Pleasant Hill, Cumberland County, demonstrating the making of a split basket at the 1952 Southern Highland Handicraft Guild Craftsman's Fair. She learned basketmaking from her parents and continued making baskets as a means of support in raising her eleven children. She marketed her work through the Pleasant Hill Craft Shop (Bullard 1976, pp. 160–62). Photograph by Edward L. Dupuy, courtesy of the Southern Highland Handicraft Guild, Folk Art Center, Asheville, North Carolina.

often eagerly gave up the trade to earn more income through other jobs. Martha Jones, a basketmaker from Warren County, Tennessee, another area with a long history of basketmaking, recalled that her mother, Novella Freed, continued to make baskets, but Martha always "worked at public works, shoe factory, or garment factory" until she started back at the craft about 1980 (Jones and Jones, 7 May 1985). Elizabeth Watts summed up the situation, "When people could make more money doing something else, they stopped making baskets" (26 Nov. 1984).

Continuing Traditions

Because of work by federal, state, and local groups encouraging the practice, teaching, and sales of traditional crafts, there has been a more recent revival of practice and interest in white oak basketmaking. One of the efforts to revive handicrafts came from the Southern Highland Handicraft Guild and Southern Highlanders, who in 1948 organized the first Craftsman's Fair in Gatlinburg, Tennessee (Southern Highland Handicraft Guild 1986). The fair offered not only new sales opportunities, but also education about traditional crafts. Participants were encouraged to demonstrate their skills as well as sell their work. Likewise, numerous other organizations have continued to sponsor yearly fairs, festivals, and markets which have popularized traditional crafts and given some of the traditional makers encouragement to continue their work (Pls. 1.13, 1.14, 1.15).

The American public has become increasingly appreciative of the knowledge and skills of traditional basketmakers. White oak basketmakers who continue to make baskets in the time-consuming old way now are seen in a new light. Martha Jones commented, "People looked down on basketmakers because that was the poorest of the poor who made baskets. Now they look up at you. They are craftspeople" (Jones and Jones, 7 May 1985).

With this improved self-perception, families of basketmakers are developing a new appreciation of their upbringing. As Susan Barret summarized, "Well, its [basketmaking] come down through generations. Just about everybody in our family made baskets, but mostly I would remember my dad and my grandmother as far back as I can remember, we made them in our house. I grew up really just in the shavings, you would say. . . . I really didn't know what an art it was till I got grown to really appreciate what I was coming up with" (Kiely, 30 Sept. 1977).

The renewed interest in basketmaking has resulted not only in a greater

Pl. 1.14   Qualla Cooperative booth at the 1953 Southern Highland Handicraft Guild Craftsman's Fair. This booth exhibit shows the wide variety of white oak, rivercane, and honeysuckle baskets made by the Eastern Band of Cherokee Indians. From left to right are G.B. Chiltoskey, wood carver; Lucy George, known for honeysuckle basketmaking; and Lottie Stamper, an expert in working rivercane (M. Ross, 8 May 1985). Photograph by Edward L. Dupuy, courtesy of the Southern Highland Handicraft Guild, Folk Art Center, Asheville, North Carolina.

appreciation for the talents of the basketmaker, but also in a willingness on the part of the general public to pay higher prices for handmade white oak baskets. The current prices may seem high, but white oak baskets are still relatively inexpensive in terms of the work and time invested to create the object. Current makers are encouraged to demonstrate and sell their work at festivals, markets, and fairs. Guilds, craft shops, galleries, and museums all sell traditional white oak baskets.

As in the years of the Handicraft Revival, the market often dictates the

Pl. 1.15 Claude and Emmer Linville and their daughter Ethel Bias, Lincoln County, West Virginia, ca. 1965. Through the encouragement of Jane Cox of the West Virginia Department of Commerce, for several years (beginning in 1963) the Linville family sent baskets to be sold at the Mountain State Arts and Crafts Fair, Ripley, West Virginia. The Linvilles learned basketmaking from Emmer's grandfather, Manderville Linville (no relation to Claude), who had made baskets as gifts for Emmer when she married. At the time of this photograph, they had made baskets off and on for about fifty years. The family had moved to West Virginia from the small town of Linville, North Carolina. Standing, from left, are Emmer Linville; John Curry, Lincoln County extension agent; Ethel Linville Bias (holding a purse basket of her own design); Jane Cox; and Claude Linville (Cox, 27 Jan. 1968; George and George, 9 Jan. 1985; Higginbotham, 8 June 1965). Photograph courtesy of the Governor's Office of Economic and Community Development, State of West Virginia.

particular baskets which basketmakers produce. (See Alexander 1987 and Cogswell 1986 for background and current concerns regarding marketing baskets in Tennessee and Kentucky.) Many of today's traditional makers, willing to please the customer, weave decorative and novelty baskets, many with colored splits. However, other makers continue to make baskets "in the old way," baskets which may look the same as those made a hundred years ago. Moreover, basketmakers who venture into new shapes tend to keep traditional detail work on their baskets.

1. White Oak Basketmaking   27

The future of traditional white oak basketmaking may be limited, for several reasons. The natural resource becomes more and more difficult to obtain. The good basket timber near where the basketmakers live has been consumed, and the makers have to travel farther and farther afield to find suitable trees. Diseases which have afflicted many of the oaks also have contributed to the decline in available timber (Solomon et al. 1980). Today there are few basketmakers who can live solely on income received from basketmaking. As in the past, today's makers often hold other jobs or take up basketmaking after retirement, when their income needs are less and there is more time to give to a tradition remembered from childhood. The future of the craft really is in the hands of the younger generation, and, unfortunately, at this time, few of the children of these makers choose to continue the tradition. Elmer Price commented about the continuation of the craft:

> The trouble of it is, they just ain't got the patience. I got seven children and it's one of them, no two of them, I'd say that's made maybe two or three baskets in their life. But they wouldn't make them for a hundred dollars a piece. They couldn't set and be that tedious to work all day on something. . . . The trouble is how they gonna learn it, if they don't learn it from some of us old people that's making? What's gonna happen is there ain't gonna be none. There ain't gonna be no baskets. My uncle, Cody Cook, over there, he can't last much longer, and I'm seventy years old. (14 Mar. 1985).

The variety in forms, structures, and finishing details of white oak baskets shows evidence of the large number of people who once knew about white oak basketmaking. As one examines in closer detail the way in which the basket material is prepared and the manner in which a basket is made, the distinctions which often reflect local traditions or some individual interpretations adopted by a particular basketmaker or basketmaking community become more and more evident. However, an accurate understanding of regional distinctions and forms becomes ever more difficult as baskets and people travel, mingling cultures and artifacts.

Timber, Tools, and Traditions

Ain't but one kind that works, that's white oak.
Eddie Nicholson (quoted in Garvey 1975, p. 11)

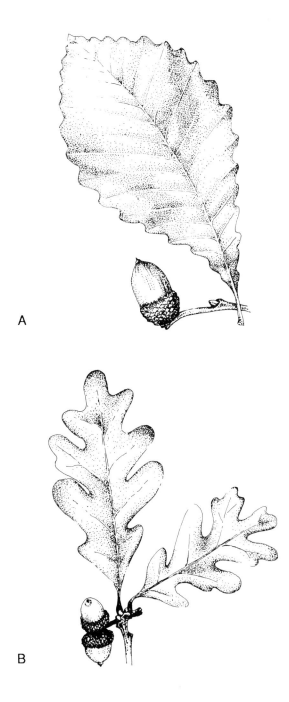

Fig. 2.1 White oak leaves and acorns:
(a) *Q. michauxii* leaf and acorn;
(b) *Q. alba* leaves and acorns.

Introduction

A basketmaker possesses not only the knowledge of how to make baskets, but also a deep familiarity and understanding of white oak as a material. A white oak basketmaker has total control over the entire process, from finding suitable basket timber to splitting and preparing the wood and, finally, making the basket. Many basketmakers consider white oak to be the only material suitable for their work.

Oaks have always been landmark trees in American parks and woodlands. They provide an important food supply and shelter for birds and animals. Oaks furnish more native lumber than any other hardwood species, and at one time the bark was the major source of tannic acid, the curing agent in leather making. Of all the hardwoods in the United States, the oaks, with over sixty species, constitute the most important group of broad-leaved trees.

The oaks are divided into two major categories, the red and the white oaks. In the white oak group, *Quercus alba* and *Quercus michauxii* are considered superior sources of basketmaking materials, because their inherent characteristics make the wood easy to split with consistent results.

Quercus michauxii, the swamp chestnut oak, grows from central New Jersey to northern Florida and west to Texas, with scattered occurrences in central Kentucky and eastern Tennessee. Common regional names for the swamp chestnut oak include "basket oak" and "cow oak." Both swamp chestnut oak and *Q. alba* have light ash-gray bark with flaky scales. Leaves of *Q. michauxii* are five to eight inches long and three to five inches wide (Fig. 2.1-a). The acorns, which are from one to one-and-a-half inches long, with triangular-shaped scales on the caps, are sweet and were often depended on as forage for cows and hogs in the South. Swamp chestnut oaks grow on loamy ridges and bottomlands, in association with white and Delta post oaks and other bottomland hardwoods (Fowells 1965, pp. 622–24; Peattie 1948, pp. 209–11).

The common white oak, *Quercus alba*, is one of the most numerous trees in the eastern woodlands, due to its adaptability and its tolerance for different soils, climates, and elevations. Common names for it, varying regionally, include "stave oak," "fork-leaf white oak," and "basket oak." Its growth range extends from southern Maine to the Gulf states and westward to eastern Kansas, making it one of the most widespread trees of the eastern United States (Fig. 2.2). The leaves are five to nine inches long and two to four inches wide with rounded lobes, while the acorns average about three-quarters of an inch in length and are shiny brown (Fig. 2.1-b). White oak grows best on northern and eastern slopes in deep, well-drained soils and most frequently is found growing in association with hickories and other oaks (Fowells 1965, pp. 631–32; Peattie 1948, pp. 195–201). The two oak species' growth ranges overlap somewhat (Fig. 2.2), but *Q. alba* is the tree most sought and used for basketmaking throughout the southern and central Appalachian region.

When, Where, and What: "Good Basket Timber Is Hard to Find"

"Good basket timber is hard to find." This is a lament common among white oak basketmakers. Despite the abundance of the white oak in the eastern woodlands, those trees having the ideal requirements for basket timber are not easily found. Irskel Nicholson, Shenandoah County, Virginia, commented about the time required and the rate of success involved in the search for good timber: "I'll be honest with you, you can't get in a hurry when you select white oak. . . . my daddy, he'd walk hours and hours up in the mountains. When he'd come back, usually he'd have a piece of white oak that would work. Me, I don't hit it that often. Maybe I hit it fifty percent of the time, but then I get in a hurry sometimes" (Nicholson and Nicholson, 16 Mar. 1985). Finding timber is obviously a most important task for the basketmaker. The time and effort spent in selecting good trees result in increased speed and ease when preparing the wood for basket materials.

Basketmakers in different regions offer conflicting comments on finding and cutting the best timber. Some makers say to cut trees only in the "dark of the moon" and in the months from "October to April" when the "sap is down." Others advise to cut timber only on "the north side of the hill where laurel doesn't grow" (Laird 1967). Each basketmaker learns about the environment and land conditions that produce the best timber. The search for wood depends upon that knowledge.

As a general rule, trees that grow in hollows in rich bottomland soil make good basket timber. Besides the advantage of good soil, trees in hollows are protected from the wind and so grow tall and straight in the process of seeking sufficient light. These trees develop a long, clear trunk, necessary for good basket timber, before forming the first branches. Trees

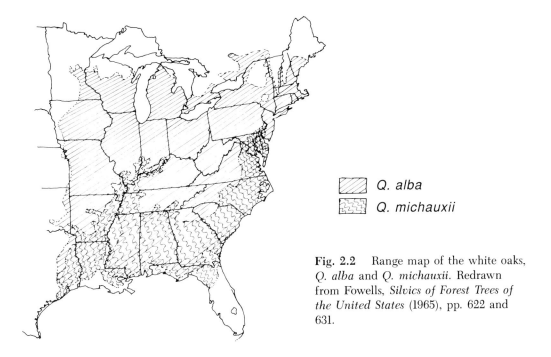

Fig. 2.2 Range map of the white oaks, *Q. alba* and *Q. michauxii*. Redrawn from Fowells, *Silvics of Forest Trees of the United States* (1965), pp. 622 and 631.

Legend:
- *Q. alba*
- *Q. michauxii*

growing near or on top of a ridge are often stunted, low-branched, and twisted from wind action and hence are mostly unusable for basketmaking.

Contrary to popular belief, trees can be cut and worked year round. Timber that is cut in the winter, however, must be allowed to thaw, if necessary, before being worked into basket materials. Frozen wood is practically impossible to split successfully; instead it runs off uncontrollably into short slivers.

The appearance and the size of the white oak for basket timber are the main determining features in selecting trees. In general, trees best suited for basket timber are small, from four to eight inches at the base, approximately twenty to thirty years old, with straight, smooth, light grey bark and with no visible knots or blemishes for four to six feet up the trunk (Pl. 2.1). Such trees are likely to be the straightest and healthiest white oaks in the forest. Growth characteristics which adversely affect basket timber include twisted bark, obvious knots or burrs on the trunk, and low branches. While twisted bark indicates twisted wood grain and a tendency toward uneven splitting, knots, burrs, and low branches signify coarse, knotty wood useless for basketwork. Those trees with unwanted growth characteristics, blemishes, or signs of disease or mortality are left standing.

Pl. 2.1 Lucy Cook, Page County, Virginia, 1985, standing behind her workshop, where she keeps white oak logs to be used for basketmaking. The logs are about eight inches in diameter, with straight, smooth bark. Lucy and her husband, William Cody Cook, learned basketmaking from his mother after they married. For five years, beginning in 1965, the Cooks worked at Colonial Williamsburg, where they made their traditional round and rectangular split baskets, as well as reproductions of eighteenth-century baskets (Casteel 1972, p. 8). The Cooks now make baskets in their home, continuing the distinctive traditional splitwork so characteristic of the Blue Ridge Mountains and the Shenandoah Valley of Virginia (Cook and Cook, 14 Mar. 1985).

White oak is susceptible to many ailments, including diseases, wound damage, insect infestations, and environmental influences. Two common diseases, oak wilt and white patch, are both caused by fungi. Oak wilt attacks the vascular system of the tree, causing the foliage to brown, wilt, and die (Solomon et al. 1980, p. 51). White or smooth patch is a bark infestation. The fungus attacks the bark, exfoliating its outer layers and leaving smooth white areas on the trunk as if bark had been rubbed off (Hepting 1971, p. 425; Lair 1946). Lestel Childress warned against cutting trees which appear as if animals had rubbed against them, as they are usually unsplittable (Childress and Childress, 23 Mar. 1984).

Insects cause much damage to both wood and foliage of growing trees. Woodborers eat through the bark and into the trunk, making holes and staining the underlying wood. Other insects, including the gypsy moth and the forest tent caterpillar, readily devour white oak leaves, defoliating the trees. Although a tree may not sustain much damage from one such defoliation, two or three succeeding years of insect attack will weaken a tree considerably, making it much more susceptible to other diseases and sometimes causing it to die (Solomon et al. 1980; Wargo 1978).

In areas with problems involving air pollution, pesticides, or acid rain, oak trees show the effects of stress and weakening. Sulfur dioxide, ozone, ammonia, and herbicides all cause identifiable foliage blotching, damaging to the leaves. In areas of heavy chemical accumulation, treetops have been noted to be dying due to the foliage damage (Solomon et al. 1980, p. 61). Regardless of the cause of the affliction, and whether it is fatal or not, diseased and infested trees are under stress, which weakens their systems and stunts their growth, often causing the wood to be **brash** — stiff and unsplittable.

Even a tree with all the outward signs of good timber does not necessarily make good splits when it is worked. Some basketmakers test trees to ensure that the wood is suitable for basket materials and worth the haul home. One unusual but deciding test was used by Tom Alvey of Wax, Kentucky, who cut timber for his aunt, Francine Alvey. After the tree was felled, Alvey would bite the end of the tree; from the feel of the bite, he could determine whether or not a tree would make good splits (Jaggers 1971, p. 7). A more common test is to split part of a felled tree on the spot, into the size of materials needed for the basketmaking.

Other basketmakers chip or notch a promising tree before felling to inspect the wood and test its splitting properties. A small chip of wood is cut out near the topmost part of the trunk that would be used for making splits. The notch is cut through the trunk, into the heartwood and about three inches in length. A sample is split out of the chip and bent and twisted to test its pliability. Irskel Nicholson commented on tree testing, offering some safety advice as well:

> Well you can't always go by the looks. You've got to notch it. . . . Notch out a piece as high up here as you can reach. Presume you always have someone with you when you go to get a piece of wood. There is always a possibility that your axe will hit a limb and hit you, cut you. . . . You notch this tree out. . . . You split it down with your pocket knife until you get small billets and then you can split it open, for splits. You can bend it, twist it and see if it stays twisted.

Nicholson went on to say that if the wood did not stay twisted, it was pliable and suitable for basketwork. If the sample remained twisted, the wood was known as being "soapy," tough and unworkable. In case of soapy wood, the tree was left standing, and the search for good timber continued (Nicholson and Nicholson, 16 Mar. 1985).

In communities where basketmaking was a main income source, white oak did become scarce. The search for good basket timber took the makers off their own property and onto neighbors' lands. Those asking permission to cut timber on neighboring property sometimes could get the trees free for the cutting, while other landowners asked for payment. Often the good basket timber simply disappeared. In Hart County, Kentucky, an area where basketmaking was a main economic concern, poaching was a recognized fact:

> Mr. Jaggers said that he could tell a poacher by hearing him chop. When a person needed some timber, he oftentimes would pick up his axe and hunt through the timber of another person until he could find just what he needed for basket-making. He would first make an observation to see if he had been detected in his mission. If all was right he would hit a lick or two, then he would stop and look and listen to see if he had been detected and then he would hit a few more licks, stop to look and listen. When he had finished cutting the sapling he would cut off as much as he thought was suitable for his business. The best wood was almost always of a very small dimension. He would load the pole on his shoulder, gather up his axe and take a course that would be the least detected. (Smith, *Hart County News* [1940])

After a suitable white oak is located, the tree is felled. While axes or handsaws were used in the past, today a chain saw is a more common tool. Notches and cuts are made in a specific manner in order to control the direction of the tree's fall accurately and safely. The direction of the fall is determined by the first notch, which is cut halfway through the trunk about six to eight inches from the ground. The second cut is begun on the opposite side of the trunk, about two inches higher than the first notch. As the second cut is worked through the trunk, the tree leans in the direction of the lower notch, allowing clearance for the saw or axe.

Generally only the **butt log**, the part of the trunk from the base to the first large knot or limb, is considered for basketwork. However, if the tree is exceptionally straight and unblemished, a second length may be cut from just above the first knot or branch. The felled tree, cut to the desired length (averaging three to six feet), is called a "log," "pole," or "stick." It is the butt log which has the clearest and most pliable wood. Farther up the trunk, the wood is often brash, cracking when worked, or impossible to split because of knots from the branches.

Even though one six-foot pole contains enough wood to make approximately eight medium-sized baskets, many basketmakers hunt, cut, and haul several trees at a time, in order to have a supply of timber on hand. Basketmakers often complain of the difficulty of hauling the logs out of the woods. Lilian Meredith of Edmonson County, Kentucky, recalls her efforts to pack timber home:

> Us kids and mother's cut many a stick of timber. Carried it on our shoulders to the house and we didn't [carry] it a short distance either, it was, from my grandaddy's place it was at least two miles from our home down there. We had to come up a hill. . . . She [mother] cut the timber in sticks according to the size of the kids that were going to carry it. She broke them up the sticks she thought they could take to the house. (Ostrofsky and Brown, 28 Sept. 1977)

Today basketmakers may travel hundreds of miles to find good timber and, if they do find it, will cut a truckload (Childress and Childress, 20 Feb. 1985).

White oak must be split for basket materials while it is still "green"— moist from its sap. Anderson Childress agreed, "The timber itself, you have to make it up while it's fresh from the stump, so to speak" (Marshall and Schottenfeld, 23 Sept. 1977). Oscar Peters of Cabell County, West Virginia, advised "not [to] cut more than two or three sticks of timber at once as it don't keep good, seasons out, putting it in damp grass does help" (Oscar Peters, ca. 1966). As soon as a tree is cut, it starts to **season**, to dry out. When the log loses moisture and begins to shrink, radial cracks called **end checks** become visible at each end of the log. Dry wood is stiff, hard, and extremely difficult to work.

Basketmakers have devised various storage methods to keep their logs fresh. Some stack the timber against a shady wall or bury it under leaves, shavings, or sawdust (Chesney and Chesney, 26 Nov. 1984). Stanley Cottrell, Hart County, Kentucky, recalled seeing "people cut timber and bring it in and bury it. Now when they want to use a stick, they pull it out and use that stick up and then uncover another stick. If you've got it covered where the sun can't touch it or the wind can't touch it, it stays in good shape . . . green" (Harzoff, 14 Sept. 77). Other makers use the cellar as a cool storage place or immerse the logs in a stream or pond. Modern technology has created a new storage space—basketmaker W. Bill Cook of Shenandoah County, Virginia, recommends wrapping wood up and putting it in the freezer until needed (6 Dec. 1989).

Timber cut and stored in the fall and winter can remain green, clear, and workable for up to six months. On the other hand, in the warmer seasons, the wood dries out quickly and is susceptible to stain and decay from fungal development. Summer's hot humid weather conditions are optimal for the development of fungi, the most common stain and decay agents (Boyce 1948, pp. 471–74). The fungi, mainly affecting the sapwood, appear as streaky brown or grey discolorations. In the early stages of the fungal development, the sapwood can be split as usual, but in later stages the sapwood becomes brittle and unsplittable. The heartwood is seldom affected by the fungi, probably due to its storage of tannins and other chemical extractives which deter the invasion of the fungi (Boyce 1948, pp. 450–51). In cool, dry weather, stain and decay rarely occur, making the winter months the best time for cutting and storing timber (Boyce 1948, p. 483).

Logs kept under water are not subject to fungal stain or decay, but sapwood staining may occur from the wood reacting with chemicals in the water (Boyce 1948, pp. 452–53; Hepting 1971, p. 451). Chemical staining does not adversely affect the splitting properties, but it makes the wood appear dirty. Some basketmakers who store logs in a stream or pond apparently do not mind the discoloration. Clovis Boyd, Floyd County, Virginia, first splits the wood into billets, then shaves the bark from the sapwood before submerging this wood in water (Pl. 2.2). He sometimes adds Clorox bleach to prevent the wood from becoming slimy and discolored (Boyd and Boyd, 11 Mar. 1985).

Anatomy of the White Oak: Rays, Rings, and Grains

A white oak basketmaker understands the tree structure and uses that knowledge as a guide in splitting and working the wood. Despite the lack of formal training, traditional basketmakers not only learn the outer

Pl. 2.2 Clovis Boyd, Floyd County, Virginia, 1985, splitting a billet. Boyd stores his wood in the long water-filled storage troughs just above his head and directly behind him on the floor. He cuts and splits the wood to fit into the troughs and leaves it soaking in the water until needed for his basketwork. The rib basket on the floor is one that he made, while the darker one at his elbow was made by his father (Boyd and Boyd, 11 Mar. 1985).

characteristics of a good tree, but also develop a good understanding of tree anatomy (Fig. 2.3).

When choosing timber, basketmakers use the **bark** to both identify trees and read the characteristics of the underlying wood. They check the bark for blemishes, signs of disease, color, and "the right feel." Walton Strange of Cub Run, Kentucky, says that "an old hand at gathering the timber can tell the good from the brash in the dark just by feeling of the bark" (Smith, 24 Dec. 1940). Other basketmakers talk about the bark's being straight, smooth, soft, and easily flaked from the tree trunk as indications of good basket timber (Jones and Jones, 7 May 1985; Tracey, 27 Nov. 1984).

Separating the bark from the wood of a tree is the **cambium**, a layer of cells where the new sapwood and bark are formed. In the spring and the summer, the growing season of the tree, the cambium is thick and moist due to the activity of cell division and sap conduction. During this growing time, the bark slips from the wood much more easily than in the winter, when the tree is dormant. Because the cambium is too thin and weak to use in basketwork, it is removed along with the bark in readying the wood for splitting.

The wood of the tree is divided into two sections, the sapwood and the heartwood. The **sapwood**, the active, new part of the tree, is the lighter-colored layer of wood just under the bark and cambium. The main function of the sapwood is conduction of water and sap. Sapwood, therefore, is the moistest and most flexible wood of the tree. As the tree grows older, the sapwood eventually changes into **heartwood**, the brown wood in the center of the tree surrounding the pith. Heartwood is inert but functions as trunk support and as a depository for tannins and other chemical substances. As a result, the heartwood is noticeably darker than the sapwood and sometimes has a distinctly reddish cast.

The use of heartwood and sapwood for basketmaking ultimately depends on the splitting properties of each particular tree. The heart and sapwood in a good piece of timber may split equally well and be used interchangeably for all basket parts. However, as a general rule, the sapwood is used to make thin weaving materials. Heartwood, tougher and drier than the sapwood, is often difficult to work into thin splits and therefore most often is reserved for thick pieces such as handles, hoops, rims, and ribs.

Viewing a white oak in cross-section, one notices the **rays**, the narrow shiny lines radiating from the **pith**, the central core of the tree, to the bark. Oaks are known for their prominent ray formation and sometimes

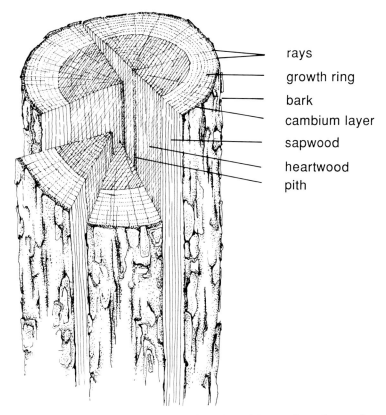

rays
growth ring
bark
cambium layer
sapwood
heartwood
pith

Fig. 2.3 Anatomy of the white oak. Adapted from Alexander, *Make a Chair from a Tree: An Introduction to Working Green Wood* (1978), p. 25.

are specially milled into quarter-sawn lumber to expose the rays. In the preparation of basket material, the log is split along the rays. Splits made in this direction are known as **radial** or **board splits** and narrow the wood to a width workable for hand splitting.

The wood of the tree is made by the formation of **growth rings**, each ring representing the amount of growth of the tree in a single year. The rings appear in cross-section as concentric circles beginning around the pith and continuing out to the bark. Rays intersect the growth rings approximately at right angles.

White oak is categorized as a ring porous wood, a hardwood in which each annual ring is formed from two distinct cell layers of growth. In the spring, the season of a tree's most rapid growth, a narrow layer of large, weak, thin-walled cells called the **earlywood** is formed. Later in the summer, a tree grows more slowly, creating the **latewood**, a broader layer of cells which are more densely packed, smaller, and more thickly walled

(Panshin and Zeeuw 1980, pp. 568–69). In a cross-section of the oak, the cells of both growth layers appear as series of pores. The earlywood layer forms distinctive dark lines, known as **grains** or **grain lines**, which are separated by the lighter latewood. The grains are used as guidelines for splitting wood to a desired thickness. Splits made in this direction are known as **tangential, grain,** or **bastard splits.**

Depending on growing conditions, annual rings are not always evenly spaced. Drought years may be indicated by extremely narrow growth rings, while years with more normal rainfall are indicated by wider rings. Timber found on steep hillsides where one side of the tree receives most of the growing light can show noticeably wider growth rings on that side, sometimes resulting in a tree trunk that is more oval than round. Generally, trees with evenly spaced growth rings of one-sixteenth to one-eighth inch in width make good splitting timber. If the rings are very close together, the wood is difficult to split on the grain lines; on the other hand, if they are too far apart, the wood is likely to be coarse, tough, and difficult to split.

Splitting and Tools

Splitting white oak is a skill which comes only with long familiarity with working the wood. William Cody Cook, a Virginia basketmaker, related his thoughts about working white oak: "Once you see how to weave you can go on with it, but fixing the wood has to be from practice. You can't just see how to do it. If the wood isn't right you won't make a good basket, it doesn't matter how you weave. The feel for the wood comes in your hands, when you've done it a while, but it's like anything else, when you have to do something the knowledge comes with it" (Casteel 1972, p. 10).

The splitting process is a series of halvings to divide the wood. Earlean Thomas of Cannon County, Tennessee, commented, "You start in from that pole of timber and bust it open, then you bust it down, you see that halves it. Then you bust it into a quarter and then on down until we call [it] a slat of timber" (Thomas and Thomas, 30 Nov. 1984). The concept of halving and understanding the wood's dimensions and anatomy are keys to successful material preparation.

In splitting the wood, the basketmaker works with the wood's three dimensions—length, width, and thickness (Fig. 2.4). The initial length is determined when the tree is cut. The basic rules for splitting white oak are: *split radially for width* and *split tangentially for thickness.*

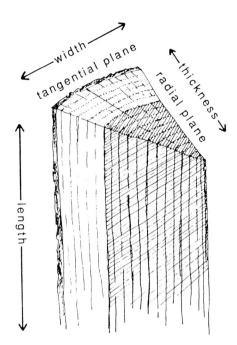

width

tangential plane

thickness

radial plane

length

Fig. 2.4   Wood dimensions and planes.

The tools used for splitting the log and **riving** the splits depend on the basketmaker's practice. Some makers use no more than an axe and a knife, while others depend on a whole workshop, including froes, draw-knives, and shaving horses. Whatever their tool preference, all makers split and finish the materials following a set procedure, with attention to the tree's anatomy.

1. "Busting the Log": Radial Splits

A log is always split starting from the top end. Irskel Nicholson, advised always using the pith as the beginning mark for the first division, whether or not it is exactly centered in the cross-section (Nicholson and Nicholson, 16 Mar. 1985) (Fig. 2.5). The first split, which halves the log, is made by using an axe, sledge hammer, or heavy wooden **maul** and **gluts** or metal **wedges**. The wedges or gluts are driven down the length of the log following the split to force the two halves apart (Fig. 2.6). If stringy fibers remain attached to the halves, these are chopped apart with an axe or hachet.

One half is split into quarters, and then one quarter is divided to make two eighths. Depending on the log's size and the maker's working method, the first two divisions usually are made by driving wedges the length of the pole to force the wood apart.

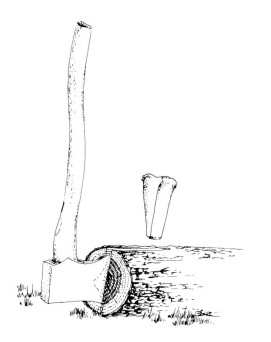

Fig. 2.5 Halving a log.

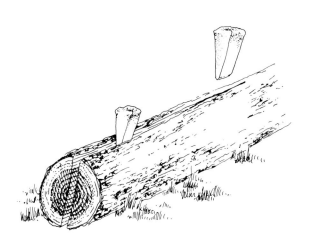

Fig. 2.6 Wedging a log in half.

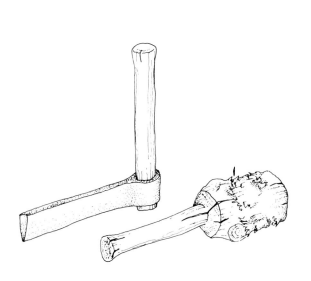

Fig. 2.7 Froe and maul.

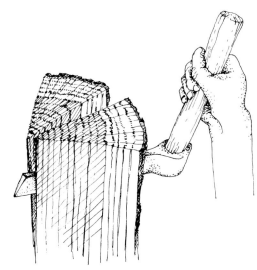

Fig. 2.8 Radial split, using a froe.

The tree is divided further using either wedges or a **froe** and maul (Fig. 2.7). A froe is an L-shaped tool used for riving wood. It is purposely dull-bladed to pry and split wood apart without cutting it. The froe is used with a maul, a heavy wooden mallet made of a tough wood (the root of a dogwood tree is one of the best materials for a maul because of its fine grain and toughness). The froe is struck with the maul to force the blade into the wood. Then it is levered back and forth to force the wood to split (Fig. 2.8). As the froe is worked down the length of the tree, the basketmaker controls the splitting by applying pressure and changing the angle of the blade.

Sometimes a **brake** is used to hold timber which is being split with a froe. A common arrangement for a brake consists of a tree fork with its butt end propped up and two poles crossed through the fork to hold it steady. The end of the basket timber is slipped through the fork of the brake where it is held securely. The brake acts as a fulcrum allowing calculated control of the split as the wood is levered by the froe. When a brake is not used, the end of the timber is simply braced against a support such as a wall or a tree or held between the splitter's knees — any arrangement which secures the end of the wood so that leverage and splitting are controlled.

As the halving progresses, the wood can split unevenly, especially if the initial split was not begun at exactly the half point or if unequal prying force is used on the split. One side may "run off," becoming much narrower than the other. If a runoff begins, the basketmaker applies more leverage against the wider side to force the split to come back toward the center of the wood.

2. "Running on the Grain": Tangential Splits

Once a piece of timber has been reduced to an eighth, the orientation of the splitting changes from radial to tangential, with succeeding splits made perpendicular to the rays in line with the growth rings. Working from top to bottom, the inner half of the heartwood is first split out (Fig. 2.9). This first tangential split is begun in the middle of the heartwood and on a grain line and worked down the length of the eighth. The results of this splitting produce two pieces: a **billet**, also known as a "slat" or "flitch" — a blank of wood to be further rived down into thinner splits or other basket parts — and the dry, knotty, inner heartwood section of the log, which is usually discarded.

Each succeeding split divides the billet in half, beginning as close to the

Pl. 2.3 Stoyd Grant, Edmonson County, Kentucky, ca. 1962 (Bybee 1963; 24 Oct. 1985), using a froe for splitting. Grant is separating the heartwood from the sapwood with his froe, preparing a billet for riving. Photograph by Jerry Schureman, courtesy of the Farmers Rural Electric Cooperative Corporation and East Kentucky Power.

middle of the cross-section as possible and exactly on a grain line. As the wood is split, the basketmaker follows a single grain line (which is also visible on the radial sides). The weak porous earlywood acts as a natural dividing line, easily and evenly separating the denser, more fibrous latewood layers. The second grain split usually, but not always, separates the remaining heartwood cleanly from the sapwood (Fig. 2.10; Pl. 2.3). At this point, if the two resulting billets are wider than desired, they are halved again radially (Fig. 2.11).

When a billet has been split to its final width, it may be **dressed** — cleaning and sizing the wood to the dimensions needed for specific basket parts. A billet is dressed by shaving the radial sides of the wood and thus removing the rough splinters that can cause the wood to veer off grain

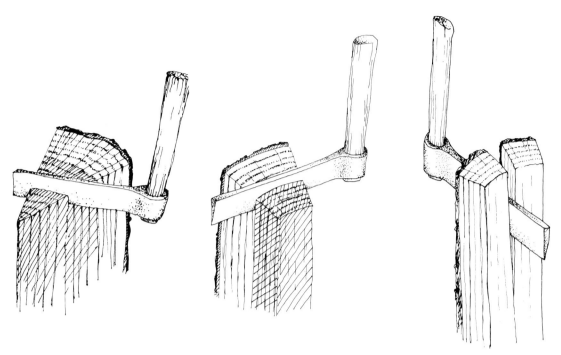

Fig. 2.9 *(Left):* First tangential split, removing the inner portion of the heartwood.

Fig. 2.10 *(Center):* Second tangential split, dividing a billet in half.

Fig. 2.11 *(Right):* Radial split to narrow a billet.

when riving. If a sapwood billet is being dressed, the bark and cambium layer also are shaved off, leaving only the white sapwood. As a result of dressing, the grain lines become quite visible on the radial sides.

Dressing can be accomplished with only a knife and knee pad, to shave the rough sides, but many basketmakers use a **drawknife** (Fig. 2.12) and a **shaving horse** (Fig. 2.13) for smoothing and shaping the billets. A drawknife is a two-handled cutting tool which is pulled toward the user to shave wood. It usually has a beveled edge on only one side of the blade. The frequent companion to a drawknife is the shaving horse, a clamping device typically consisting of a bench with a block or head attached to a post and a foot pedal. A billet is placed under the block and clamped by pressing the foot pedal. The wood is held securely while being worked with a drawknife (Fig. 2.14). Shaving horses vary among makers, from carefully crafted benches to a simple setup in which a board is slipped between two rungs of a ladder and held by pressure from the user's body (Pl. 2.4).

Fig. 2.12   Drawknife.

Fig. 2.13   Shaving horse.

Fig. 2.14   Dressing a billet.

Appalachian White Oak Basketmaking

Pl. 2.4   Ben Tom Alvey, Grayson County, Kentucky, ca. 1965, working down wood for rib basket hoops (Alvey, 27 Jan. 1986). His shaving horse consists of two slats nailed to a forked tree through which a board is inserted. Alvey angles the board, bracing its ends securely between his knees and the slats. The angle of the board against the slats holds a billet in place, while Alvey shaves it with a drawknife. Alvey and his wife both made rib baskets from water maple as well as white oak (Alvey, 23 Jan. 1986). Photograph courtesy of Emma Bybee, Leroy Alvey, Jerry Schureman, and East Kentucky Power.

Structure and Materials:
Splits, Ribs, and Rods

How the basketmaker shapes and uses the wood after it is split into billets depends on the intended basket form and the splitting properties of each particular tree.

All three basket types, rib, rod, and split, are constructed of a **foundation** and **weavers**. The foundation is the skeletal supporting structure for the base and sides of the **basket body.** A basket's foundation materials are usually of a larger dimension, either thicker and/or wider, than the weavers. The weavers secure the foundation and fill in the basket body by interlacing or twisting over and under the foundation at approximate ninety-degree angles.

White oak baskets are constructed from one of two shapes of materials, flat or round. The two basic rules of splitting the wood apply to both flat and round materials: *split radially to achieve width* and *split tangentially for thickness*. Rims, hoops, and handles may be three or four growth-rings thick, while weaving splits are usually rived down to individual or half-growth ring thicknesses. Billets intended for round materials such as ribs and rods are rived into long squared splits approximately the diameter of the finished rod. Specifics concerning materials are discussed in the chapters covering the three basket types. The following sections describe general procedures for making flat and round materials.

1. Flat Materials: Splits

When beginning to rive flat splits, some basketmakers make a slanted cut across the billet's top end, in order to see the grain lines more clearly and as a reminder of which end is the top (Childress and Childress, 23 Mar. 1984). Using a froe or heavy knife, the billet is halved, beginning the division exactly on a grain. When the tool is firmly embedded in the wood, a couple of twists of the handle cause the wood to split further, allowing the basketmaker to get a handhold on each half. The wood is pulled apart along the same grain line down the length of the billet. When the split is on grain, the wood separates easily with a soft popping sound. If the split "runs off" and crosses grain lines, it is harder to pull and has a tearing sound.

The end of the billet is always held firmly, braced either between the knees or under an arm, so that calculated pressure can be applied to the split (Pls. 2.5; 2.6-a, b, c; 2.2). The basketmaker's hands closely follow the

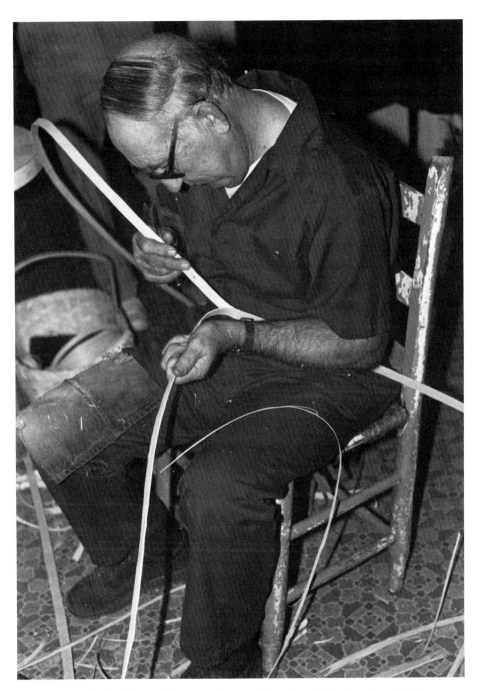

Pl. 2.5 Lestel Childress, Edmonson County, Kentucky, 1984, bracing a billet
under his arm while riving splits. Keeping his hands close to the split juncture as he
pulls the wood apart allows him to feel the thickness of the wood and apply the
force needed to control the splitting (23 Mar. 1984).

Pl. 2.6-a Claude Linville, Lincoln County, West Virginia, ca. 1965, riving weaving splits for a rib basket. He begins the split with his pocket knife. Courtesy of the Governor's Office of Economic and Community Development, State of West Virginia.

Pl. 2.6-b Bracing the wood between his knees, Linville continues the split by hand.

Pl. 2.6-c *(Opposite):* Hand position and close-up view of split.

split as it progresses down the billet. This action allows the basketmaker to feel the thickness of the wood and to control the splitting. Just as with radial halvings, tangential splits may run off grain, with one side becoming thicker than the other. To control the split, more pull is exerted against the thicker side until the split in the wood returns to its original grain line. If the thicker side becomes unmanageable and the split runs completely off, a knife is used to cut into the wood to pick up the original grain. The split is then continued down the length of the billet.

As the halves become thinner from splitting, a knife is used to start the divisions (Fig. 2.15). Centered exactly on a grain line, the knife blade is worked from the corner of the billet, following the grain line across the top end. Once the blade is safely and firmly embedded in the wood, the knife is twisted to force the split, which is continued by hand. According

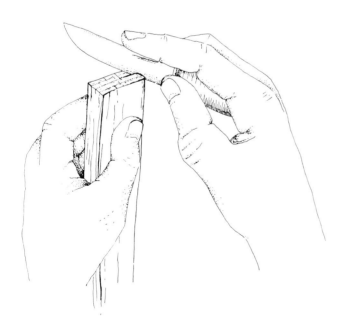

Fig. 2.15   Beginning a tangential split with a knife.

2. Timber, Tools, and Traditions   53

to William and Lucy Cook, if the top end of the billet shows three growth rings and cannot be split exactly in the middle and on a grain line, the split is begun on the grain nearest to the bark side (Laird, "Manufacture of Split Oak Baskets," ca. 1960).

When working wood for thin splits, riving is simply continued until each individual latewood layer is separated. If the latewood layer is thick and a thinner split is required, it is halved again. This final latewood division splits more evenly if it is rived beginning from the butt end (an exception to the top-to-bottom splitting rule). Because the latewood is usually thicker at the butt than at the top (the tree grows with a tapered trunk), the last latewood split often runs off before it reaches the top end. A short split may be run off from the thicker butt end intentionally, in order to make the other longer split a uniform thickness. Since there is no grain line to guide the split, basketmakers rely on their skill and the feel of the wood to run the splits. If the latewood is thick enough, Lestel Childress separates the latewood of an individual ring into three splits (Childress and Childress, 23 Mar. 1984).

Riving by hand is the most common method of making splits, but other procedures also are used. Basketmakers in Arkansas and Missouri shave splits with a drawknife or "split knife," a homemade tool resembling a spoke shave (Betty Curry, 1 Dec. 1989; Curry and Curry 1986; Heidingsfelder 1977, pp. 4–5; Stephens 1975, p. 141). While the split knife's use or prevalence in the Central Appalachians is not clear, old split knives are seen occasionally. Billets are dressed to a certain width, held in a vise, and then the split knife is used to shave off splits (Heidingsfelder 1977, pp. 4–5; Curry and Curry 1986). Splits made by shaving have a different appearance than those which are hand split. Crossed grain lines often are evident and one side of the split is always rougher than the opposite side. Shaved splits are not as strong as hand-rived ones, but shaving is a faster way of preparing materials.

Hand-rived splits usually are scraped with glass, knife, or drawknife, to thin and finish them. Clovis Boyd remembered, "Us kids would take a piece of glass, window glass. My mother would save every piece of glass, a broken table glass or window glass, whatever. She'd save it for us to scrape the splits with, slick them, but I use a knife. I don't use glass" (Boyd and Boyd, 11 Mar. 1985). Basketmaker Mildred Youngblood of Cannon County, Tennessee, recommended scraping splits from the butt end to the top because they scraped better (Benson 1981). The knife or glass is held stationary in an almost vertical position against a pad on the maker's knee. The full length of the rough split is pulled under the stationary blade or edge, which acts as a planer, removing rough spots and smoothing and cleaning the split (Pl. 2.7). The splits are scraped on both sides and sometimes sanded for a finer finish.

Scraping seems to be an arduous chore for many basketmakers. Various tools have been invented to aid with the task of scraping splits. One scraping device, known as a *Schienenmesser*, "split knive," was used by Pennsylvania basketmakers. Two sharpened blades were fastened onto a wooden block at slight angles, making a V-shaped cutting slot. The splits were drawn through the slot, scraping the wood on both sides (Lasansky 1979, p. 30). Another type of scraper was made by Oral ("Nick") Nicholson of Doddridge County, West Virginia (Pl. 2.8). His device consists of a mower's cutter blade fastened to a hinged board. The split is placed under the blade, held down by the board, and pulled through, smoothing one side of the rough split. The split is turned over and pulled through again with the other side scraping against the blade to finish (3 Oct. 1984).

Pl. 2.7   William Cody Cook, Page County, Virginia, 1985, scraping a split to clean and finish it. He holds his knife stationary while pulling the split under the blade. The blade catches on the rough splits, planing and thinning the wood (14 Mar. 1985).

Pl. 2.8   Oral ("Nick") Nicholson, Doddridge County, West Virginia, 1984, cleaning splits with his scraping device. Nicholson made this tool by attaching a tractor mower blade to a hinged board. The split is placed under the blade and then is pulled through, scraping the wood clean (3 Oct. 1984).

After the splits are scraped, they are trimmed, if needed, to even widths with a knife or sharp scissors. The splits may be used immediately or they may be stored until required for basketwork.

2. Round Materials: Ribs and Rods

Billets for rounded materials are split to approximately their finished size and are shaped to their final dimensions with a knife, a shaving horse and drawknife, or a **die**. Rounded ribs used in rib basketmaking and rods used in splitwork typically are shaved with a knife or drawknife. When shaving with a knife, one holds the knife stationary and pulls the wood under the blade, taking off a small curl of wood at a time. The knife blade is held almost horizontally against the wood, to cut rather than scrape. As it is shaved, the wood is rotated to shape and smooth its edges (Fig. 2.16).

Occasionally dies were used for making round ribs and scraping flat splits. One basketmaking family, the Day family of Shenandoah County, Virginia, used such a die (Fig. 2.17). Oliver Lee Day learned basketmaking from his grandfather, Thomas Benton Day (1845–1920), who made his living bottoming chairs and making baskets. Day recalled his grandfather making "oak round for small baskets. He had an iron. He pulled it. Pulled his basket ribs." He also used an "iron" to pull splits "through to dress them down" (13 Mar. 1985) (Pl. 2.9).

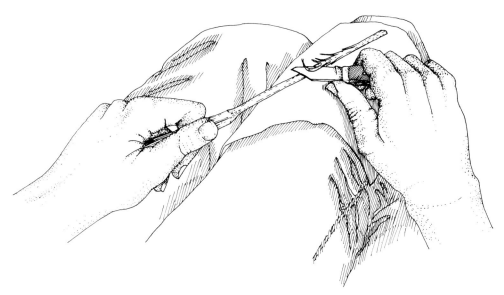

Fig. 2.16   Whittling a round rod or rib. A pad is used above the knee to protect clothing and leg as wood is whittled.

 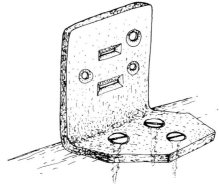

Pl. 2.9 *(Left):* Rib basket made by the Day family, Shenandoah County, Virginia (Helsley and Helsley, 13 Mar. 1985). This melon-shaped rib basket shows different shapes and sizes in the materials used in its construction features. The round ribs on the sides and the flat weaving splits likely were smoothed to their final dimensions by the use of an "iron," while the thick hoops and flat ribs on the base were whittled. Dimensions: 15″ top, 8 1/2″ s.h., 13 1/2″ o.h. Private collection.

Fig. 2.17 *(Right):* Day family "iron." Drawing of the die used by the Day family, Shenandoah County, Virginia, for pulling round rods and scraping flat splits (Helsley and Helsley, 13 Mar. 1985). According to Oliver Day (b. 1906), the tool originated with his grandfather, Thomas Benton Day (1845–1920), who made his living making baskets and bottoming chairs (13 Mar. 1985). The die measures approximately 2 1/2 by 3 inches. The holes progress from 1/32 to 1/4 inch in diameter, and the slits are 1/32 inch wide by 7/16 and 9/16 inch long. The iron is 3/16 inch thick, and both the slots and the holes are relieved to a thickness of approximately 1/8 inch. Private collection.

Rod basketmakers, in particular, used round weaving materials. Some rodwork is made from rods which appear to have little shaping other than being split into long squared splits. The great majority of rod baskets, however, are made from round rods which have been shaped with a die (Pls. 2.10-a, b). The tool typically was made from a metal plate or bar that had holes of graduated sizes punched or drilled through it and sharpened on one side (Fig. 2.18). One end of a rough rod was whittled down to start the rod through the hole closest to its size. The rod was pulled with pliers through succeedingly smaller holes to reach its final diameter.

Pl. 2.10-a *(Left):* Homer Summers, Kanawha County, West Virginia, 1985, pulling a rod through his die. He first splits the wood into small squared strips (as close to the desired diameter as possible), and then he tapers one end to fit through a hole in the die. Pulling the end with pliers, he draws the rod through succeedingly smaller holes to its final size. Summers makes rods from three to five feet long and in three different diameters, for baskets of different sizes. He prepares rods for several baskets at a time and coils them up to dry (Summers and Summers, 13 Jan. 1985).

Pl. 2.10-b *(Right):* Summers' die, made from a hoe head. The die has graduated sizes of holes drilled through it, in approximately 1/64-inch increments ranging from about 1/32 to 3/8 inch. The die is held in a vise which is bolted to a workbench (Summers and Summers, 13 Jan. 1985).

Rodmaker Dwight Stump of Hocking County, Ohio, recommended pulling rods from the butt to the top end to avoid splintering off (Stump and Mansberger, 16 May 1984).

Seasoning and Soaking

Freshly split green wood dries quickly. As wood dries, the loss of moisture causes shrinkage along two wood dimensions: thickness and, more significantly, width. Basketmakers allow for shrinkage by giving basket materials drying time either before or during basket construction. Not allowing the materials to dry will result in a loosely constructed basket.

Thin basket materials, such as weaving rods, splits, and ribs, may be stored indefinitely in a dry place (to prevent mold or mildew). When ready for use, the materials are returned to a pliable state by soaking

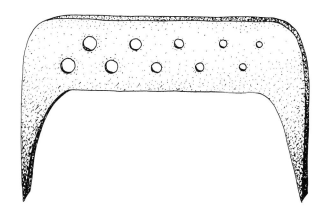

Fig. 2.18   Rodmaker's die. Drawn from a die used in Shenandoah County, Virginia (Helsley and Helsley, 16 Mar. 1989). The plate is 7 inches long, 4 inches high, and 7/32 inch thick. The holes on the top row range from 3/16 to 1/8 inch across, and the holes on the bottom row range in diameter from 1/4 to 1/8 inch. All the holes are relieved by countersinking. The prongs of the plate would have been driven into a bench or board to stabilize the die for drawing rods. Private collection.

them briefly in water. As little water and soaking time is used as possible. The longer white oak is soaked, the more the wood fibers expand, increasing the width dimension, raising the wood grain, and causing the wood to become fuzzy. Earlean Thomas commented on softening splits, "You don't have to soak them [splits] long. Sometime I warm my water and they'll be softer, you know, and then I use rain water. If you use water from the tap it will turn them blue looking sometimes, if you let it stay in there too long. But we use rain water and if we don't have rain water, he [Lawson Thomas] goes to the creek and gets water" (Thomas and Thomas, 30 Nov. 1984).

Depending on the minerals and chemicals contained in the local water supply, the water used to soften the oak can cause chemical staining. Oak has a high tannin content, and the tannin reacts with iron, forming iron tannate, the cause of a light- to dark-grey stain. The stain is fairly permanent, but the effect is a purely aesthetic one, as the strength and pliability of the wood are not affected. This tannate stain is also seen when a basketmaker works the fresh wood with iron tools. A basketmaker often will end the day's work with hands grey from using a knife to split and scrape wood.

Decoration

Decoration of any type of basketry can be accomplished either structurally (during construction), or nonstructurally, by the addition of elements after the basket has been completed (Adovasio 1977, p. 40). Structural ornamentation includes the use of colored elements woven to form designs or patterns, alteration of a weave to form an intentional pattern, manipulations in spacing or sizes of weaving elements, or decorative rim treatments. Nonstructural decorations include applying color after the container is woven and weaving additional elements or attaching elements to the body of the basket (Adovasio 1977, pp. 40, 120).

Many of the baskets in each group of the white oak work show decorative elements. In the structural category, particularly, it is not always obvious if ornamentation was intended or if a decorative detail may be the only technique known by a given basketmaker. This situation leaves the definition of ornamentation open to debate, unless the maker is available to answer this question.

Decoration that is most evident in all basket groups is the use of color. The simplest addition of color in oak basketmaking is the selection of basket materials that alternate naturally-colored dark heartwood and light sapwood. Natural dyes and commercial paints, stains, and dyes also are used for colorwork. In most oak baskets, color is applied to the weaving materials before the basket is constructed.

Today the Eastern Band of Cherokees continues to be well known for its colorful basketwork. The chief sources of natural dyes for the Cherokee remain "puccoon" (bloodroot), butternut, black walnut, and yellowroot (Leftwich 1970, p. 29). In more recent years, however, a wider variety of native dyes and commercial dyes have been used. Martha Ross, a contemporary Cherokee basketmaker who learned white oak basketmaking and the dyeing of basket splints from her mother, Charlotte Welch Lossiah, describes some of the traditional dye plants and procedures:

> It takes about thirty days to scrape up all your splints and get them ready to dye. Use a kettle, put the splints on to dye and sometimes add a little soda to get them all the same color. . . .

You can dye with *butternut* [to get dark brown]. . . . It has the little old round shaped, oblong nut. You can use the bark of the roots. The only time I get the roots is if someone is building a road or something. I have an old rusty tub or black tub to dye it in. It makes even more color. . . . Mama also claimed that you could get a red from the butternut root. She had a cloth bag with ashes in it and she poured water through the ashes and they used this water [lye] for the corn [in preparation of hominy]. She also used the corn water for the dyepot. . . .

This is *staghorn sumac* [pointing to grey colored splits]. You can get a darker grey to nearly a light black if you do it right. . . .

Now *yellowroot*, it's a little old bush and it's yellow top to bottom, even the roots. [It gives the bright yellow]. I take the stems and mash it up with a hammer. I lay it [the yellowroot] in there with a clean pot of water and my splits and let it boil not even thirty minutes and it's through. It just fades out a little bit. . . .

The orange is from *bloodroot*. What you dig is just under the leaves. I learned most every plant by Indian names. That's what my Mother and Dad taught me—how to get the plants for dyes. Boil about two hours. . . .

I'm experimenting with the *angelica plant*. You can get chartreuse and a little bit of green with it. Mama gave me something to put in it, but she never did tell me what it was. (8 May 1985) (emphasis added)

Knowing how to get the right colors is a science. Many dyers had secret ingredients, and sometimes the effects were never fully explained, such as Mrs. Lossiah's recipe for green from the angelica plant.

Many basketmakers during the days of the Handicraft Revival used colored splits to "enhance" their baskets and make them more marketable. Charlotte Tracey of Gaston County, North Carolina, learned dyeing procedures from her parents. The family sold their baskets to the Allanstand Cottage Industries in Asheville, North Carolina. Tracey said that her family made nearly all the baskets out of colored splits when she started making baskets in 1912, at the age of eight. They made their own dyes from native materials but also purchased alum and copperas (ferrous sulfate) from the drugstore to use with their dye-baths. While she also used yellowroot and "puccoon" root, there were other plants which her family commonly used for color:

We'd take the *walnut hulls* and make brown. The green walnut hulls and boil 'em in water and put the splits in it. Could make 'em light brown or anywhere.

Pokeberries made the red. Just take the pokeberries and put 'em in the pot, in your dyepot. We always had old dyepots everywhere. . . . Mama used to make me take 'em to the creek and get sand and scrub them. I hated to do that. You know, maybe get a color in there that wouldn't come out just working at it. But generally, all the time we'd use it, well we'd take and pour the stuff out and wash the pot out. Some of it would come out and some of it wouldn't. . . .

Some people had iron pots and some didn't. Now we'd never have enough iron pots to go around. We had an old iron pot that we boiled ours in. . . . You take that *red oak bark*, skin the bark off. You know, then take the in [*sic*] next to the tree [inner bark] and get that where it's damp. . . . Get that out and just scrape that off the tree and put it in an old pot and boil it. Then you could . . . strain it off of that. . . . You take and put just a speck of copperas in it though and just a little piece of alum. You know, alum comes in little chunks like little rocks. . . . Copperas is kind of green . . . put it on and get it boilin' and when you got it going, just drop your splits in there and it wouldn't be fifteen minutes 'til it'd be colored enough. Green. . . . It made a pretty shade of green. Then after you dyed it and boiled it in that green ooze, and got 'em green, you'd take 'em and lay 'em in lye water and it'd turn 'em a brown. It'd be the prettiest brown, it'd just sparkle like it'd been shined or something.

. . . You take *maple bark*, off a fresh tree. You couldn't use it after it dried out. You take that bark off of that and put copperas with it and it'd make a blue. . . . Just take your knife or ax or something and just take that bark off there and put it in the pot. Boil it in there and then pour that ooze off. . . . over in another pot. . . . Why it'd make the splits speckled . . . wherever that stuff hit 'em it'd leave a dark spot. You almost had to strain the top of your ooze off and then put your alum or copperas or whatever you wanted in it. Where we used the bark that way or *puccoon root* we had to take it and pour it in another pot. Pour the other out, the puccoon root out after it'd boiled, then boil the splits in the water that had come off of it. (27 Nov. 1984) (emphasis added)

When commercial dyes became easily available at competitive prices, many basketmakers relied on them for coloring the oak splits. While the commercial dyes were much easier to use and did not require all the time in collecting plants and preparing the dyepot, the colors were not the same, and some dyers considered them to be inferior products. Charlotte Tracey recalled, "It got to where we used Putnam and Diamond dye to color 'em, but it wasn't as good. It didn't last like the homemade dye did. That homemade dye stayed" (27 Nov. 1984).

Traditions and Signatures

The traditions of past generations are liable to change with present influences and conditions. As some basketmakers find more available materials, they give up the work of finding and splitting the white oak timber. Oliver Day talked about a drought in 1930 which killed a lot of the timber. Around 1948 he could not get white oak, so he purchased round reed for basketmaking (13 Mar. 1985). Day continues to use reed today, to make a variety of baskets quite different from the traditional oak ones he made formerly (Dalke 1979, pp. 4–5). As the materials change, so do the basket forms and many of the techniques used.

Despite the development of technology and the availability of alternative materials, there have always been and still are traditional basketmakers who steadfastly carry on their time-consuming trade, handsplitting and making baskets from the white oak tree, often with only the simplest of tools and facilities. Emma Taylor, Cherokee basketmaker, expressed her feelings about white oak basketmaking and the time involved:

> I think basketweaving is nice work. It's made by hand and just takes one tool, a pocket knife, to fix the splints, and another tool, an ax, to go to the woods and cut the white oak. After you get through cutting your tree down, you bring it home and split it up into quarters. . . . I took all day to go to the woods to only get three trees that were good. One tree makes at least four baskets. It takes one week to prepare the material for eight baskets and another week to weave eight baskets. (United States Department of Interior 1975)

The two work divisions of material preparation and basketmaking require specialized handwork which has never been successfully reproduced by mechanical means. When the whole family was involved in the basketwork, each member contributed her or his special talents. In some families, the men gathered the timber and split the wood, as these chores required much physical strength, while the women, children, and elderly worked the baskets.

Traditions of makers or communities of makers are clearly revealed in their baskets. Each maker, through the details of her or his work, develops a singular basket style. Baskets were seldom if ever signed by the maker, but the style of the maker was always recognizable: "They might as well write their name on them, since anyone in the business will recognize their work," commented Walton Strange, who, at his souvenir stand near Munfordville, Kentucky, sold baskets made by many different makers (Smith, 24 Dec. 1940). An individual basketmaker's signature may be obvious or subtle, but it is nearly always identifiable if one understands the maker's methods of material preparation and basket construction. The knowledge, skills, and traditions which have been passed down through the generations are manifested in the many variations of white oak baskets which have survived years of use, as well as those forms which continue to be made today. The chapters which follow explain in detail characteristics of each of the three basket types—rib baskets, split baskets, and rod baskets.

Rib Baskets

Pl. 3.1 "Cornsheller," ca. 1897, Bucks County, Pennsylvania (Bucks County Historical Society, "Archeology and Colonial History"). The large basket holding corn is a form typical in central and southeastern Pennsylvania, used for many agricultural purposes. Commonly called a "potato" basket, it was made in various sizes. Photograph courtesy of the Spruance Library, Bucks County Historical Society, Doylestown, Pa.

Pl. 3.2 Work basket holding wool to be carded for handspinning, Hindman, Knott County, Kentucky. Baskets of this size were used for many purposes and often were named for the task to which they pertained. Photograph courtesy of Settlement Institutions of Appalachia Collection, Southern Appalachian Archives, Berea College.

Introduction

The rib basket, with its graceful curves, is a deceptively sturdy basket. These baskets are constructed by weaving thin splits through an armature of ribs set into a framework, somewhat like the ribs in a boat. When the framework is filled in with splits, it creates one of the strongest and most durable lightweight baskets in existence.

Ribwork is thought to have originated in Europe (some believe that it may be Celtic), where it has been made and used primarily in rural areas (Wright 1983, pp. 117–20). In Europe these baskets are made chiefly from willow; however, in some areas of the British Isles and on the Continent, large rib baskets were regularly made from other woods, including hazel, ash, and oak (Barratt 1983, p. 4; Will 1985, pp. 82, 141; Wright 1983, pp. 117–27).

In the United States, the rib basket is found throughout the Central and Southern Appalachian Mountains, with concentrations of ribwork in those regions settled by Scots-Irish and Germans. Because of the regional occurrence of the rib basket form, "outsiders" often call these baskets "Appalachian" baskets. Concentrations of rib baskets are evident in central and southeastern Pennsylvania, eastern West Virginia, northwest and southwest Virginia, the western Carolinas, and eastern and central regions of Tennessee and Kentucky. Today the largest ongoing production of rib baskets in the Central and Southern Appalachians is in communities in central Tennessee and southcentral Kentucky.

Rib baskets were made in a variety of shapes and sizes to aid with agricultural (Pl. 3.1) and household chores (Pl. 3.2). Large rib baskets in bushel or two-bushel sizes were used for gathering and storing crops and carrying feed to animals. Smaller rib baskets used in the daily farmwork routine were designated as egg baskets, market baskets, and work baskets. According to Jennie Lester Hill, "No better farm baskets were ever made than are these same melon-shaped mountain baskets, balancing as they do on the hip, or across the neck of a horse in front of the rider. It is the boast of some of the most skilful [sic] old basket-makers that their baskets will hold water, and it is an actual fact that they are sometimes so closely woven that meal can be carried in them" (1903, p. 12). Clovis Boyd recalled his father making oak rib baskets which his family used to scald tomatoes for canning. The basket, full of ripe tomatoes, was lowered into boiling water and left submerged until the skins separated from the fruit. The basket, like a colander, was raised up and the tomatoes allowed to drain before being peeled (Boyd and Boyd, 11 Mar. 1985).

Around the turn of the century, many new styles were developed by rib basketmakers. Color and design were important factors in the new rib baskets, and they were marketed as decorative but functional items. Construction techniques were altered to make a wide variety of forms, some of which were copies or adaptations of foreign models introduced by the workers of the Handicraft Revival. New designs, including trays, flower baskets, picnic baskets, fruit baskets, and wall baskets, were made and popularized as tourist baskets. Other tourist baskets served nontraditional domestic functions as magazine holders, bird houses, fly swatters, fans, and plant stands (Pl. 3.3).

Traditional baskets also were made in various sizes to appeal to buyers. Melon baskets were made in large peck and bushel sizes. Miniature versions called "melon favors," which were only one-and-a-half to two-and-a-half inches in diameter, were listed in the price list of Allanstand Cottage Industries around 1917 (Pl. 1.8). At that time, these favors sold for fifteen cents (ACI ca. 1917), but by 1930, the price had risen to twenty cents (ACI ca. 1930). Basket peddler Elijah Tom Childress, from southcentral Kentucky, often added a little "story" to help the sale of his small baskets. According to local oral tradition, "Ol' Childress, he'd haul baskets up there [Indiana]. He'd get those little bitty baskets an' folks 'd ask who made them an' he'd say that it was little bitty kids, seven or eight years old, and they can't make 'em any bigger or they'd fall over" (Korn and Kiely, 16 Sept. 1977)

Structure and Materials

Rib baskets are made of a framework composed of hoops and ribs. It has been suggested that this style of basket was originally a coracle, a framed boat covered with animalhide (Stephenson, 19–21 May 1986). The most common rib basket form (Fig. 3.1-a) is made with two **hoops** that intersect approximately at right angles. The top half of the vertical hoop arcs across the top of the basket to form the handle, while the bottom half forms the basket **spine**—the central support for the basket body. The hoops are bound at their junction with a split, forming the **wrapping**, the anchoring points for the ribs. The **ribs** complete the framework and finalize the basket shape. The ribbing is filled in with thin **weavers** woven

Pl. 3.3   Arline McCarter, daughter of basketmaker Mac McCarter, Sevier County, Tennessee, holding fans and baskets. The McCarter family made baskets, chairs, and novelties such as fans, which they sold to tourists visiting the Gatlinburg area of the Great Smoky Mountains. Photo by Doris Ulmann, used with special permission from Berea College and the Doris Ulmann Foundation.

from each wrapping to the midpoint on the side of the basket. Feet may be added to protect the base, and occasionally a lid is added to complete a basket. Rib baskets with overhead handles are known throughout Europe and the British Isles. Examples of regional European styles are shown in books by Will; Wright; and Duchesne, Ferrand, and Thomas.

A less common rib basket form consists of a rim hoop to which one or more spines are attached to form the basket frame (Fig. 3.1-b). Baskets similar to this form are known in England as "swills," "slops," or "potato baskets" and are made of various woods, including ash, hazel, or oak for the hoops and ribs, and split oak for the weavers. In the region of Cumbria, England, the baskets were made from oak which had been boiled and then split (Barratt 1983; Hartley 1974, pp. 36–39; Wright 1983, p. 21). These were multiple-use baskets employed for a number of commercial and domestic chores, such as carrying bobbins in cotton mills and disposing of refuse (Barratt 1983, p. 2). A similar form, made in Wales is called a *gwyntell* and is made of hazel or blackthorn hoops, hazel or willow ribs, and willow or hazel weavers (Jenkins 1978, p. 52; Theophilus, 11 Aug. 1978). This basket form is also known in Germany and in France (Will 1985, pp. 82, 17).

While the majority of rib baskets made in the Central Appalachians are constructed entirely of white oak, materials such as shoots, vines, and other woods and barks are used in conjunction with or instead of white oak. Rib baskets framed with oak and woven with honeysuckle vines are made in the eastern Tennessee and western North Carolina mountains. In southcentral Kentucky, where white oak became scarce, sassafras and "water maple" were used for splits (Alvey, 23 Jan. 1986).

In parts of Kentucky and Tennessee, frames and ribs were often made of hickory, known for its dense fiber, toughness, and pliability. Earlean Thomas of Cannon County, Tennessee, commented on the use of hickory: "Now a lot of people thought they were getting hickory baskets. People will ask for them but there's not never been a hickory basket made. They make the hoops out of it and sometimes a little one could make good ribs, but they don't make splits out of them. The splits you get from hickory is the bark and they bottom chairs with it and they have to do that in the spring of the year" (Thomas and Thomas, 30 Nov. 1984). While Thomas was not familiar with splits made from the hickory sapwood, basketmakers from other regions did indeed make splits from hickory. Hickory is more difficult to split than white oak, and the resulting splits are less pliable. Consequently, hickory splits are found in split- and rodwork, but seldom in ribwork.

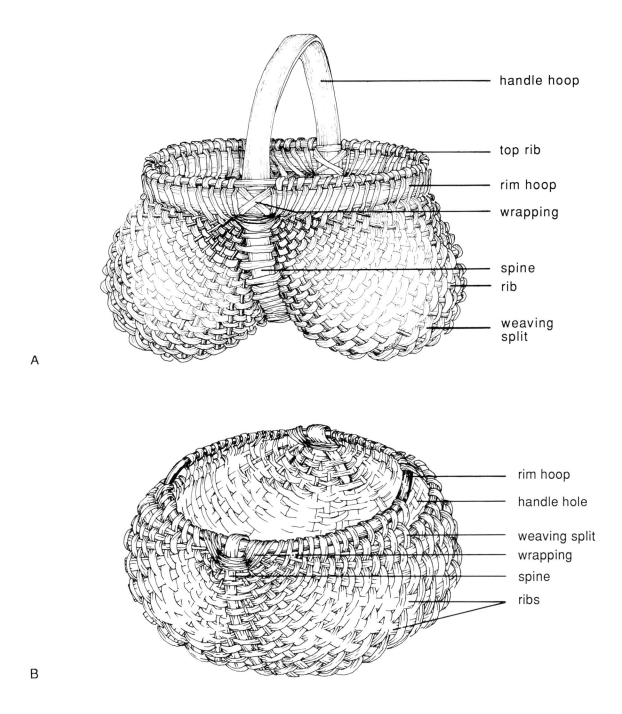

handle hoop

top rib

rim hoop

wrapping

spine

rib

weaving
split

A

rim hoop

handle hole

weaving split

wrapping

spine

ribs

B

Fig. 3.1   Structure of rib baskets: (a) Rib basket with overhead handle, drawn from Pl. 3.14; (b) Rib basket with handle holes, drawn from Pennsylvania basket. Dimensions: 28″ top, 13 1/2″ s.h. Collection of Jeannette Lasansky.

Rib baskets consist of three materials worked and shaped separately—hoops, ribs, and weavers. Usually the sapwood is made into weaving materials, and the heart is used for hoops and ribs. If the tree is particularly fine basket timber, both the heart and the sapwood may be split completely into weaving materials, while a more coarse-grained tree may be worked entirely into hoops and ribs. As baskets increase in size, so do the dimensions of materials: hoop and rib billets are cut longer to increase the basket diameter and thicker to provide support, and the weaving splits are cut wider and thicker.

Basketmakers who make many baskets prepare their materials in quantity, for efficient basket production. Many hoops are made at one time, bent to shape, and left to season until the maker is ready to work on a basket. Ribs are rived and whittled or shaved in numbers. In cross-section, ribs may be round, oval, or flat. The ribs are tapered for a few inches on each end down to a point, to be inserted into the wrapping or hoop frame. Splits for weaving and wrappings are rived and scraped to clean and thin them. The splits are generally very thin—as "thin as paper," according to some basketmakers—to allow for ease of weaving through and around the framework. Splits may be different lengths, some basketmakers preferring short splits while others work better with long ones. The splits are trimmed to width with scissors or a knife.

Rib basketmaking was often a family operation. "Mrs. Cottrell (Mrs. Effie Cottrell, daughter of Nimrod Jaggers) can make them just like shelling corn, and she's got eleven daughters and four boys to help her. She does real well, but it sure takes a big family to do anything with this business" (Smith, 24 Dec. 1940). The labor was often specialized according to the skill of the family member, with each member working tasks best suited for her or his strength and skills (Pl. 3.4). The family formed a production line; the adults, with more experience and strength, would rive out the splits and frame up the baskets, while the children often "filled them in." Walter D. Logsdon of Edmonson County, Kentucky, remembered, "From daylight till dark and even after dark, by candlelight. We'd make [baskets] . . . lived in a large log building and it had a fireplace. We'd load great big loads of wood in there and burn it in the wintertime an' we'd work till bedtime on baskets. I filled a many a basket after supper. My mother would have it framed up" (Judi Sadewasser, 15 July 1974).

Pl. 3.4   Davis and Hibdon family at work, Cannon County, Tennessee, 1985. Billy Hibdon is working on the shaving horse preparing wood for hoops, while Ida Pearl Davis, left, and her daughter Thelma Hibdon, center, are "filling in" baskets. Davis learned basketmaking from her mother, Lydia Murphy Underwood, and has passed the craft on to her daughter Thelma and her granddaughter, Jennifer Dawn Walls. Thelma and Billy split the logs, then Billy splits and roughs out the hoop billets. Ida makes the frameworks creating the shape, and Thelma fills them in. This family continues to make graduated-measure baskets in half-gallon, gallon, gallon-and-a-half, peck, half-bushel, bushel, and bushel-and-a-half dry volume sizes (Davis, Hibdon, and Hibdon, 7 May 1985).

Frameworks: Shaping a Basket

The first influence on the shape of the rib basket begins with the shaping and joining of hoops to make a frame. The size and shape of the hoops determine the overall size and shape of the basket. Hoops may be circular or oval, flattened or squared. The intersection of the rim hoop with the handle hoop or spine determines the depth of the basket, whether its sides

Pl. 3.5 Bird Owsley, Knott County, Kentucky, ca. 1922, working on baskets. His prepared splits and several hoops and frames are hanging within reach. Owsley was one of the most prolific oak basketmakers of Hindman's Fireside Industries. One of Owsley's specialties was the "Kentucky egg" basket (on right), a tall basket which he often wove with brown, walnut-dyed splits. He mainly made rib baskets but also made other baskets as requested, such as the shallow tray basket on the left (Watts, 26 Nov. 1984). Photograph courtesy of Settlement Institutions of Appalachia Collection, Southern Appalachian Archives, Berea College.

will be low or tall, like those of the "Kentucky egg" basket (Cl. Pl. 7; Pl. 3.5).

The rounded basket is the most common shape formed by circular or oval hoops. Round or spherical baskets traditionally are called "melon" baskets (Pl. 3.12), while exaggerated two-lobed baskets (Pl. 3.14) have a variety of names, including "egg," "hip," "buttocks," "fanny," "gizzard,"

Pl. 3.6 Mountain basketmaker. Woman filling in tray basket framework with colored splits. Great numbers of such small baskets, usually with dyed splits, were made and sold through various organizations in the Central and Southern Appalachians. Photo by Doris Ulmann, used with special permission from Berea College and the Doris Ulmann Foundation.

and "butterfly." Both of these forms are begun with circular hoops. Oval hoops create elongated basket shapes (Cl. Pl. 2). An oval handle hoop may span either the length or width dimension across the basket opening, creating two distinctly different basket shapes.

Distinctive shapes are created by sharply flattening one or both of the framework hoops forming D-shaped hoops. A handle hoop with a squared base forms a flat-bottomed basket. Rim hoops placed close to the flattened base result in shallow baskets commonly called "cake" or "pie" baskets or trays (Pl. 3.6). Although the shallow tray baskets occasionally may have been made for home use, the production of large numbers of baskets in this style, many woven with bright colors, came with the development of the large tourist marketplace in the twentieth century. A D-shaped rim hoop, when paired with a handle hoop, produces a "wall pocket" (Harzoff, 19 Sept. 1977) or "side wall" (Davis, Hibdon, and Hibdon, 7 May 1985), a flat-sided basket to hang on the wall. Other common names for

Pl. 3.7 *(Left):* Wall basket, southcentral Kentucky. A flattened rim hoop creates a flat-sided basket. This shape, with the lowered rim hoop and rounded base, the combination of wide flat and narrow round ribs, and an ear wrapping, is typical of many wall baskets made in southcentral Kentucky. Dimensions: 6 1/2″ top, 5 1/2″ s.h., 9 1/4″ o.h. Collection of Bruce Rigsby.

Pl. 3.8 *(Center):* Wall basket with droopy body. Origin unknown. Long ribs and a sagging rim are the main factors in creating the droopy shape. The hoops are nailed together and wrapped with a woven fourfold-bond, a wrapping method often used by makers during the Handicraft Revival. Wall baskets also are known as "wall pockets," "half melons," and "key baskets." Dimensions: 6″ top, 5″ s.h., 8″ o.h. Collection of Datha Doolin.

Pl. 3.9 *(Right):* Scalloped-back wall basket. This basket was bought from the Qualla Reservation, North Carolina (Elkins, 9 May 1985). The techniques of the simple cross wrapping and radiating ribbing are typical of Cherokee ribwork. The extended handle, unusual back treatment, and the yellow, green, and blue weaving make it an extremely decorative wall basket. Dimensions: 10 1/2″ x 5 1/2″ top, 6″ s.h., 17 1/2″ o.h. Collection of Edd and Peggy Elkins.

this form are "key basket" and "half melon" (Pls. 3.7, 3.8, 3.9). This basket was listed in the 1917 Allanstand brochure as "Tyrol or wall basket," named for the central European region from which the model came (Goodrich 1931, p. 27).

Hoops also are bent into rectangular shapes, creating "oblong baskets" or "box baskets," two names used by Tennessee makers (Davis, Hibdon, and Hibdon, 7 May 1985) (Pls. 3.10 and 3.19). Less common than round baskets, rectangular-shaped rib baskets were made throughout the central and southern Appalachian mountain region. Earlean Thomas of Cannon County, Tennessee, calls "the large ones market baskets and the small ones

Pl. 3.10 Mac McCarter, Sevier County, Tennessee, holding a sharply squared rectangular basket. A well-known basketmaker of the Great Smoky Mountains, McCarter, assisted by his wife and several children, made baskets and chairs and sold them from a shop near Gatlinburg along the Sevierville road. The McCarter family made a variety of basket styles: rib baskets, novelties (see Pl. 3.3), and split baskets—baskets with plank bottoms and thick vertical stakes (Maxwell and Exline 1938). McCarter owned a small piece of property which was acquired as part of the Great Smoky Mountain National Park. He was about seventy-seven years old when he died in 1935 (Irwin 1982, pp. 46–49). Photo by Doris Ulmann, used with special permission from Berea College and the Doris Ulmann Foundation.

egg baskets" (Thomas and Thomas, 30 Nov. 1984). The flat bottom of the squared basket was preferred by some Tennessee basketmakers for certain chores, because the basket did not roll (Davis, Hibdon, and Hibdon, 7 May 1985).

The second influence determining the shape and size of rib baskets is the length and curvature of the ribs. Ribs which follow hoop contours may form evenly round or flat-sided baskets. Longer ribs create bulgy-sided, pouchy baskets. Each basketmaker has a formula for measuring ribs to make each style of basket. Ida Pearl Davis uses the bottom of the handle hoop and the middle finger of her right hand to gauge the length of the ribs. She inserts one end of the rib into the wrapping and bends it to form a smooth curve, following the spine. Davis adjusts the rib to an arc somewhat higher than the curve of the spine and measures the resulting space using a certain knuckle or finger length. She uses a specific finger length to measure the arc of the ribs for each size of her baskets. The longest ribs are the ones inserted first into the wrapping; these angle diagonally from the corner of the hoop intersection. Other ribs are added to either side of the first ribs, working the ribbing up to the rim and across to the spine (Davis, Hibdon, and Hibdon, 7 May 1985).

Building Rib Baskets

Rib baskets often are made to a certain dry-volume measure, the most common being peck, half-bushel, and bushel. Each basketmaker has her or his own measurements to create each basket size, beginning with the hoops (Pls. 3.11-a, b, c, d). The length of the hoop billet determines the size of the basket. In measuring the hoop pieces for length, the basketmaker allows several inches for overlapping the ends. After these billets are cut to length, they are split as closely as possible to the desired width and thickness. The width and thickness of the hoop must be substantial enough to support the size of the basket. If the hoops are not thick enough or wide enough, they cannot support the weight of the basket and will bend and sag. Jessie Jones of Scott County, Virginia, suggests that the wood for hoops should measure about one-fourth inch thick by one-and-one-half inches wide (Irwin 1982, p. 115) (Pl. 3.12). The hoop billets are finished by whittling or shaving to shape, smooth, and remove all sharp edges (Pl. 3.11-a). The hoops may be scraped with glass or sanded for a fine finish.

After the hoop pieces are smoothed, the hoop is bent a little at a time

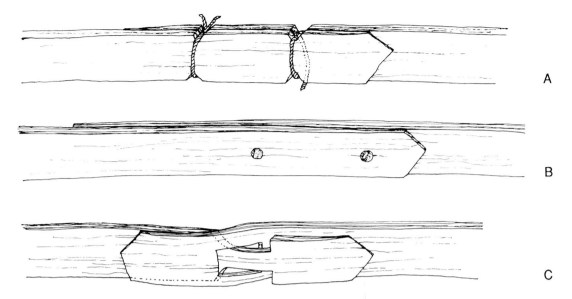

A

B

C

Fig. 3.2   Hoop joins: (a) notched and tied join; (b) pegged join; (c) lock join.

along its entire length, to limber the wood and shape the hoop to the desired form (Pl. 3.11-b). Jones also offered advice concerning the shaping of hoops, saying that the hoops can be bent around a knee, always bending the wood toward the bark side (Irwin 1982, p. 116). The hoops are bent toward the bark side to minimize lengthwise splitting, which can occur as the wood is shaped.

The bent hoops are usually **scarfed** — shaping each end so that the two correspond to each other and can be secured together to form one continuous piece of even thickness. The scarfs are cut, one on the inside and one on the outside of the hoop, beginning a few inches from each end and sloping gradually to a thin end. The scarfed ends are then overlapped and securely joined. There are several methods of joining. The ends can be notched and tied with a cord or thin split (Fig. 3.2-a); they can be nailed or drilled and pegged (Fig. 3.2-b); or the ends can be whittled to make a "lock handle" (Fig. 3.2-c), a join commonly used by Cherokee basketmakers (M. Ross, 8 May 1985).

Some basketmakers are quite particular about the method and fasteners used to join their hoops. Clovis Boyd now uses a copper roofing nail to fasten hoops together, to avoid the stain and rust caused by iron-based nails; however, his wife Roxie commented that, when nails were hard to come by, they used any nail that was available; whether it was an old or a new one, they were just happy to have any (11 Mar. 1985). Ida Pearl

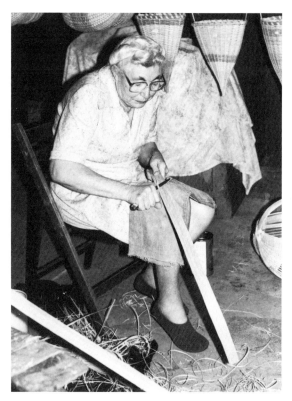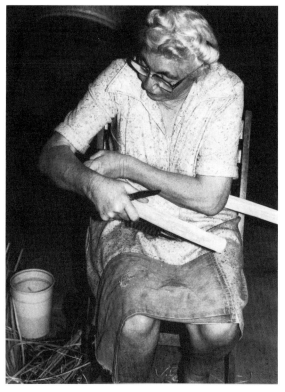

Pl. 3.11-a Making hoops. After Billy Hibdon splits and roughs out a billet on a shaving horse (Pl. 3.4), Ida Pearl Davis "rounds" the hoop edges by whittling and then scarfs the ends for the overlap (7 May 1985).

Pl. 3.11-b Bending the hoop. Davis "circles" the handle hoop against her body, bending it a little at a time until the wood is flexible and forms an even round shape (7 May 1985).

Davis pounds a small brad through the overlapped ends (Pl. 3.11-d) and carefully bends the end over to clinch it and hammer it into the wood (Davis, Hibdon, and Hibdon, 7 May 1985).

Two finished hoops are joined to form a frame or a "set of hoops." The rim hoop is almost always placed inside the handle hoop, although the reverse placement is common among the basketmakers of the Eye and Propst families in eastern West Virginia (Pl. 3.14). The overlap of the handle hoop is placed to the bottom of the basket and the overlap of the rim is usually laid against the handle hoop. Where the two hoops intersect, they are pegged or nailed. Gertrude Lucky of Wirt County, West Virginia, fastened hoops together by heating a nail to red hot and forcing it through both pieces, burning a hole and thus preventing the wood from splitting (Laird ca. 1960).

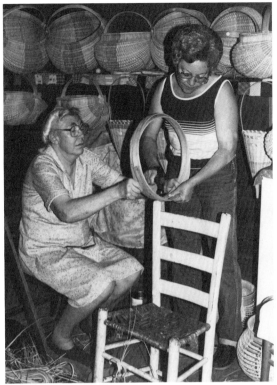

Pl. 3.11-c Measuring the hoop. Davis uses her right arm and hand as a measuring stick to determine the size of the hoop. With her arm bent, she adjusts the diameter of a handle hoop to fit from her elbow to the first joint of her little finger. This is her standard measurement for a half-bushel basket. She overlaps the hoop ends and fastens the hoop with small nails (7 May 1985).

Pl. 3.11-d Nailing hoops. After making the handle hoop, Davis circles a rim hoop to fit exactly inside the handle. Her daughter, Thelma Hibdon, nails both hoops together, using the "ear" of a split-bottom chair as a support. The chair ear is soft enough to prevent the ends of the small nails from bending as they are pounded through the hoops. The nail ends then are bent over and hammered into the hoop to clinch and finish it (7 May 1985).

After hoops have been made and joined together, the basketmaker begins building the framework. The hoops are bound at their intersection with a wrapping to form an anchoring place for the ribs. Wrappings are made with a long thin split and vary from simple crosses to intricately worked weavings. After the wrapping configuration is worked, the ribs are either laid into the pockets created by the wrapping or inserted directly into the wrapping (Pl. 3.13-a) with the aid of a finely sharpened knife or an **awl**, a tool often made by a basketmaker from a nail pounded into a wooden handle and sharpened to a long narrow point.

A top rib is sometimes added above the rim hoop. The top rib may

Pl 3.12 Melon basket made by Jessie Jones, Scott County, Virginia. Jones is a third- or fourth-generation basketmaker who has made baskets since childhood. He uses a combination of flat and round ribs to make this rounded basket. His history and his basketmaking are detailed in *Baskets and Basket Makers in Southern Appalachia* (Irwin 1982, pp. 114–127). Dimensions: 12″ top, 7″ s.h., 11 1/2″ o.h. Private collection.

consist of one continuous rib which has been scarfed to join (Pl. 3.14), or it may be two ribs with their ends anchored in the wrapping or laid behind the handle (Pl. 3.13-b). Russ Rose of Clinton, in Anderson County, Tennessee, said that the top rib added to the life of the basket. He remembered that, while his grandfather had not used a top rib, his father had, and Rose felt that baskets without top ribs, when used heavily, wear out more quickly from broken splits at the rim (Irwin 1982, p. 98). Top ribs are used throughout the regions of rib basketmaking, where the hoops are flat and thin. The top rib appears as a line of beading worked around the top of the basket (Pl. 3.14). In Pennsylvania and other areas, where the hoops are rounder and thicker, top ribs generally are not a part of the basket structure.

After the hoops are wrapped, ribs are inserted into the wrapping to complete the framework. Just as in bending hoops, the ribs are always bent along their whole length from end to end to limber and curve before inserting into the basket. Most basketmakers start with a specific number of ribs on each basket side. A basket may begin with as few as one rib per side, adding in more as needed, or with the total number of ribs inserted all at once. The number of ribs per side may be odd or even at the start but should remain an odd or even number throughout to keep the weaving in pattern. As the ribbing is worked into the basket, an equal number of ribs is used on each side of the spine to keep the basket shape even and balanced, except in asymmetrical shapes such as wall baskets. If the ribs are not inserted all at once, succeeding ribs are added in even numbers on each side, to keep the weaving on its established course. Pairs of ribs are

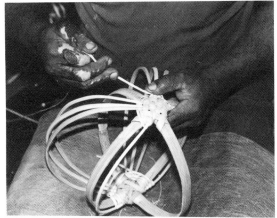

Pl. 3.13-b Weaving and adding ribs. After the first ribs have been added into the sides and the top ribs placed above the rim hoop, Younger begins the weaving with thin splits. As soon as three or four rows have been woven on each end, he adds more ribs to fill in the sides of the basket (15 Mar. 1985).

Pl. 3.13-a Paul Younger, Campbell County, Virginia, 1985, making rib baskets similar to those made by his mother. He begins the ribbing by first inserting the longest ribs into the wrapping to create the framework for the pouchy sides. Younger remembered, as a child, watching his mother work on baskets. He also recalled reluctantly going on trips to help find basket timber; threats of a switching usually overcame his resistance. Younger mainly relies on an axe and knives for his basketwork. He has three large knives, all sharpened somewhat differently, to facilitate the tasks of splitting, whittling, and scraping (15 Mar. 1985).

usually added in close proximity on each basket side to avoid disrupting the weaving pattern.

After the first ribs are added, the weaving begins from the wrapping at either end of the basket. The weaving split is begun from the same point on either end to keep the weaving in pattern. The weaving is worked in **plain weave**, over-one/under-one, and reverses itself as it turns around the rim or top rib and returns to the other side. If no top rib is used, the weaving split may wrap around the rim hoop an extra time, covering the rim completely, a technique common to Pennsylvania ribwork (Pl. 3.17; Fig. 3.17).

The weaving is worked from both ends of the basket, filling in a few

Pl. 3.14 Lobed rib basket. From eastern West Virginia, this basket is characteristic of those made by the Eye and the Propst families of Pendleton County. Made entirely with round ribs, this basket shows an exaggerated pouch, created by adding ribs which are longer than the hoop frame. The basket is made with two round hoops intersecting about midway, with the rim placed on the outside of the handle. A top rib is added above the rim and appears as a beaded edge. Dimensions: 13" top, 10 3/4" s.h., 18" o.h. Collection of Cynthia W. and Michael B. Taylor.

rows on one end and then switching to the other end of the basket to work the same amount, allowing the weaving to progress evenly from each end toward a midpoint on the side of the basket. Weaving the basket from each end insures that the shape of the basket remains even and that the weaving will meet in the middle to complete the basket. As the weaving continues, space between ribs opens; and ribs are added to fill in the sides of the basket (Pl. 3.15).

When a weaving split has been completely woven into the framework and runs out, the weaver is **spliced** by overlapping the finished end with a new split, hiding both ends under ribs. In order to make a smooth splice, the ends of both the ending split and the new split may be shaved thin where they overlap. The weaving is continued with the new split. Splicing is usually avoided across the rim or the spine as it is difficult to make a tight, hidden splice at the hoops.

The shape of the framework influences how the basket is filled in. In many baskets, because of the ribbing, the area to be woven in the belly of the basket is greater than that at the hoops. As side weaving progresses, diamond-shaped spaces become apparent in a basket's sides and these spaces can be filled in by shaping the weavers, narrowing them as they are woven to the top of the basket from the base, a method used by Ida Pearl Davis and Thelma Hibdon (Pl. 3.4).

A more common method of filling in the framework incorporates a series of **turnbacks** (Figs. 3.3 and 3.4). Turnbacks are made by turning the weaver around a rib instead of over the rim hoop, forming short rows across the basket body (Fig. 3.3). Turnbacks generally are not made until

Appalachian White Oak Basketmaking

Pl. 3.15   Francine Alvey, Grayson County, Kentucky, ca. 1971, wife of Ben Tom Alvey, learned to make baskets by watching her father when she was six years old. She could make baskets from miniature to bushel sizes but preferred working on half-bushels and pecks (Sutherland 1971, p. 2; Sutherland 1972). She is filling in a frame, working the weaving toward the center of the basket. Photograph by David Sutherland, reprinted by permission of the Louisville, Ky., *Courier-Journal* and the *Louisville Times*.

3. Rib Baskets   85

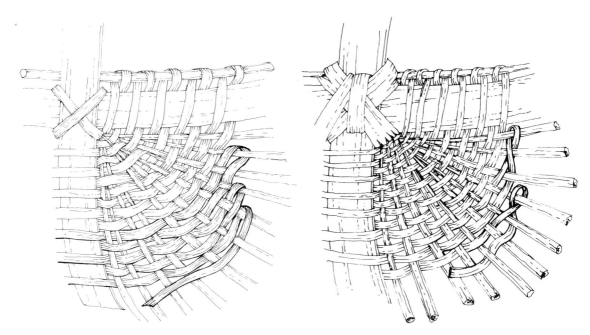

Fig. 3.3   Turnback.

Fig. 3.4   Crossed turnback.

all the ribs have been inserted. The weaver often is tapered for several inches, narrowing to the point of turnback, in order to avoid leaving a small space. Most basketmakers make their turnbacks in a particular section of the weaving on the sides or in the middle of the basket. Claude Linville of Lincoln County, West Virginia, wove until the splits met in the middle of the rim and the spine. He then put the basket aside to allow weavers to dry and shrink, and after a few days, filled in the remaining diamond shaped spaces on each side by turning back from both the rim and the spine (Pl. 3.16) (Laird ca. 1960). Linville did not taper his weaving splits on the turnbacks, but filled in the resulting small spaces with one last row of weaving.

A "crossed" turnback which is common in southcentral Kentucky and central Tennessee is almost invisible (Fig. 3.4). Mildred Youngblood of Woodbury, Tennessee, recommended that this turnback be made at an "under" weave and that the weaver should be trimmed along its bottom edge (next to the weaving) to about half its original width for a distance which would allow the weaver to move over and under about eight ribs (four ribs to the turn and four ribs back). The weaver is then drawn up from the inside of the basket in between the weaving and the turn, so that it crosses over itself and then continues back across the basket. Youngblood made turnbacks randomly throughout the weaving, until the spac-

Pl. 3.16   Claude Linville, Lincoln County, West Virginia, ca. 1965, completing a rib basket by a series of turnbacks (see Pl. 1.15). Courtesy of the Governor's Office of Economic and Community Development, State of West Virginia.

ing was evened and the basket could be woven from rim to rim, completing the basket (Benson 1981).

Another use of turnbacks is to make handle holes in the sides of a basket. On baskets having no overhead handle, handle holes are woven close to the middle of the basket side, just under the rim. The weaving is simply turned around a rib to make an open space for a hand grip around the rim. Sometimes part of the rib is cut out to allow more room for the space (Pl. 3.17).

Decoration and Signatures

The use of color is the most common decorative feature in ribwork. When colored weavers are worked into a basket's sides, the natural curves of the basket accent the resulting stripes (Cl. Pls. 3 and 6). Earlean Thomas, of Cannon County, Tennessee, commented on her favorite colorwork: "I'll tell you the prettiest dyes is, I think, your real heart splits. Now these heart splits won't be the same color every time. The hearts will be different colors. They'll be a brown, but they'll be a different one. I've seen them a reddish brown, some of them are real dark, some of them are lighter" (Thomas and Thomas, 30 Nov. 1984). Whether from the natural wood color (Pl. 3.19) or dyed with natural or commercial dyes, a rib basket with color often was more marketable. Lestel and Ollie Childress of Edmonson County, Kentucky, often use bands of orange and brown in their rib baskets, and sometimes other colors (20 Feb. 1985) (Pl. 3.22). Martha Jones of Warren County, Tennessee, uses bright colors in both her "fan" and her "dolly" baskets. The "fans" have stripings of colors (Cl. Pl. 8), and the "dollies" (Cl. Pl. 9) use the stripes to accentuate the shape of the basket sides (Jones and Jones, 7 May 1985).

Other decorative features of ribwork include structural ones such as wrappings and top borders, and nonstructural treatments such as braids and woven handles. Each of these techniques is discussed more fully in the sections which follow.

Details that establish a basket's identity include the shape of a basket, how the hoops are joined, the wrapping style, how the ribbing is set into a basket's sides, turnbacks, color, and the presence of features such as feet, lids, braids, and borders. Workmanship is also an important clue to identification: whether or not a basket is tightly woven, how the hoops and ribs appear in cross-section, and the width and thickness of the weaving splits.

Details

1. Wrappings

Wrappings used by basketmakers may serve as markers identifying both regions and individuals. Even when the same wrapping is used by different basketmakers within a community, each maker often has a personal mark, such as the width or thickness of the split or a slight variation in working the wrapping. Some of the wrappings on Appalachian rib baskets are: the cross, the ear, fourfold-bond, and ring wrappings. Basketmakers often do not have names for the way they wrap the basket hoops, and sometimes different makers have different names for the same configuration or vice versa.

Usually basketmakers employ the techniques that they see and learn from other basketmakers in their family or community. Sometimes a par-

Pl. 3.17 Large agricultural basket made and used by Peter Weirbach, Bucks County, Pennsylvania, purchased in 1919 by Henry Mercer for five dollars (Mercer 1926, pp. 194–96; Mercer Accession Ledger). This basket has a very substantial framework with thick rim hoop and ribs. The woven wrapping secures the spines to the rim. The edge of the top rib is cut out where the handle holes are woven, to make the space larger. Dimensions: 24″ x 26″ top, 10 1/2″ s.h. Courtesy of the Mercer Museum, Bucks County Historical Society.

ticular type of wrapping is the only one they know. Recently a woman from Florida, wishing to have an old bushel basket repaired, gave it to a southcentral Kentucky basketmaker to restore. The maker studied the basket and was quite able to repair the broken weaving splits, but was puzzled by the damaged wrapping configuration, a "fourfold-bond." The only wrapping method that he knew was the "ear," a wrapping worked regularly in his region. He set out to repair the basket to its original condition, and he tried to find someone in the area who knew how to make a fourfold-bond. When his search failed, he discussed the problem with his client. The woman was pleased to have the basket repaired as he knew how and instructed him to go ahead (Alvey, 23 Jan. 1986). The restored basket, with a fourfold-bond on one end and the ear on the other, may be a curiosity for future generations.

A *cross wrapping* may be worked by itself or as the beginning step of other wrapping configurations. Claude Linville called his wrapping a "basket cross" and made it doubled by wrapping the lashing split twice on the first diagonal and again twice on the returning diagonal across the rim and handle hoop. His wrapping also caught the first ribs, securing them to the hoop frame (Laird ca. 1960) (Pl. 3.18; Fig. 3.5). Similar wrappings are seen on many baskets throughout the central Appalachian region (Pls. 3.10, 3.14, 3.33, 3.38, 3.40-a, 3.41-a, 3.43, 3.46, 3.47, 3.50). A cross wrapping is used by the Eastern Cherokees (Pls. 3.9 and 3.34; Cl. Pl. 3).

A variation on the cross wrapping is the "bow," also occasionally called the "bow tie," made by many basketmakers in central Tennessee (Pls. 3.19 and 3.4; Cl. Pls. 8 and 9). A doubled cross is worked with the wrapping split returning to the center of the cross and looping twice under the cross intersection to form the bow (Fig. 3.6).

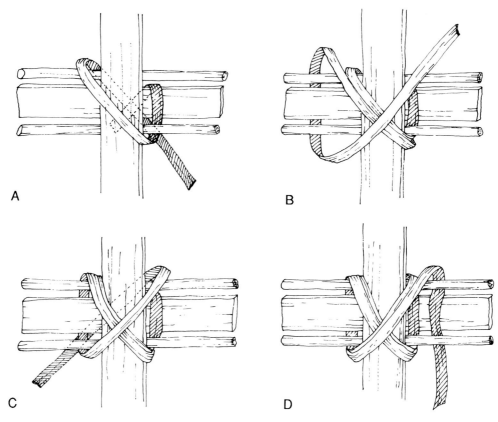

Fig. 3.5 Linville cross wrapping.

Some cross wrappings are made in a figure-eight configuration around the rim hoop, with the wrapping split crossing in the middle of the handle hoop (Fig. 3.7). A figure-eight cross also can be worked with each wrap piling upon itself or worked down the handle hoop, creating a distinctive V-shaped wrapping (Pl. 3.20). Crosses are sometimes interwoven over-one/under-one, as the split crosses diagonally over the intersection of the handle and rim hoops (Pl. 3.21).

The *"ear" wrapping*, as it is called in the southcentral Kentucky region of Hart and Edmonson counties, is also known in that area as a "burr," "tie," or "cross" (Alvey, 23 Jan. 1986). It is the dominant wrapping configuration used in southcentral Kentucky (Pls. 3.22 and 3.7) but also is found throughout the Central Appalachian range (Pls. 3.23, 3.31, 3.49, 3.55). The ear typically begins with a cross worked around the handle and rim junction. The wrapping split is worked over-one/under-one around the rim and spine. The weaving reverses on the rim and is given a half

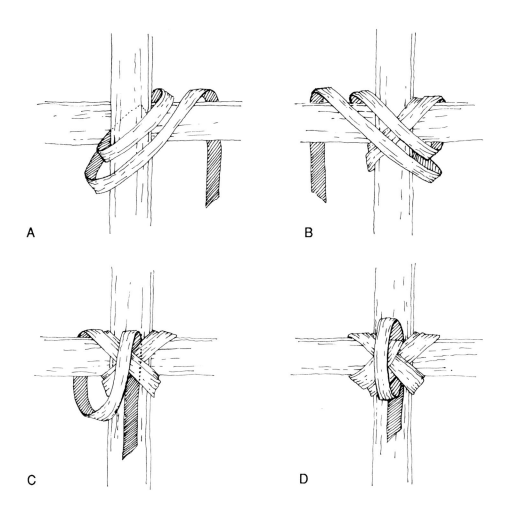

A

B

C

D

Fig. 3.6 Bow wrapping.

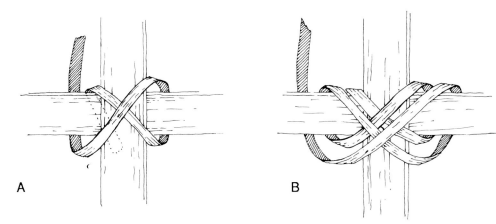

A

B

Fig. 3.7 Figure-eight wrapping.

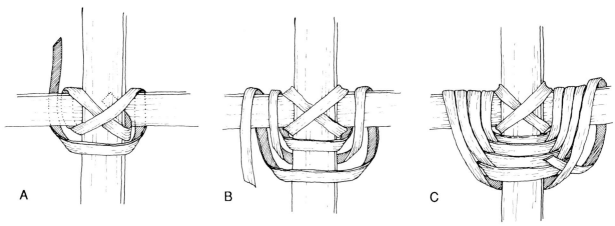

Fig. 3.8   Ear wrapping.

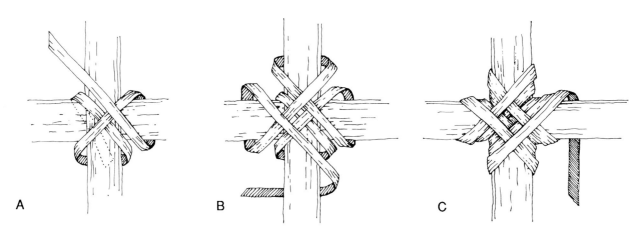

Fig. 3.9   Fourfold-bond wrapping.

twist each time it is woven over or under, allowing the split to lay flat and snug against the previously woven row (Fig. 3.8). The completed wrapping forms a half-moon shape that somewhat resembles a human ear or a "dog ear," another of its Kentucky names (Alvey, 23 Jan. 1986). The wide formation provides ample space for the addition of ribs, which are inserted into the wrapping. Some baskets in the Central Appalachians have an inverted ear wrapping, which is worked up the handle instead of down the spine. Inverted ear wrappings are not common.

The *fourfold-bond* and its variations are common throughout the Central and Southern Appalachians (Pls. 3.24, 3.32, 3.42; Cl. Pls. 1 and 7). The fourfold-bond is worked in a circular fashion, wrapping around the

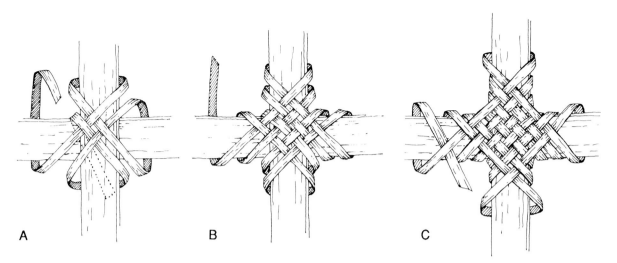

Fig. 3.10   Woven fourfold-bond wrapping.

handle and rim hoops, using all four points (Fig. 3.9). As the fourfold-bond is worked into the diamond shape, the long floats form pockets into which ribs are laid.

A fourfold-bond also may be interwoven as the wrapping is worked around the hoops (Fig. 3.10). The woven fourfold-bond wrapping was commonly used on many later baskets that were made in the North Carolina and eastern Kentucky mountains and marketed through the different handicraft centers (Pls. 3.25, 3.51, 3.56-a, b). Charlotte Tracey of Gaston County, North Carolina, learned this wrapping technique from her father (Pl. 3.26). She calls it a "bow" and continues its use on all the different shapes of baskets which she makes and sells through the Southern Highland Handicraft Guild (27 Nov. 1984). The woven fourfold-bond wrapping makes a decorative center point as well as a strong trap for the ribs (Pls. 3.27-a, b; 3.8; 3.13-b; Cl. Pl. 4).

A triangular wrapping similar to the fourfold-bond is worked on some Pennsylvania rib baskets without overhead handles (Pl. 3.28). It is worked around three points on the rim and the spine into a triangular configuration (Fig. 3.11). This wrapping also forms pockets into which the ribs are inserted.

The origins of the ear and the fourfold-bond wrappings are not known, although both techniques are found throughout Europe. The name "ear" is used in Belgium by the Walloon basketmakers for the fourfold-bond configuration. According to Sue Stephenson, the fourfold-bond configuration is also known as *Ojo de Dios*, "Eye of God," and is a magical symbol

Pl. 3.18   Group of baskets made by Claude Linville, Lincoln County, West Virginia, ca. 1965 (George and George, 9 Jan. 1985). Linville began his baskets with two hoops about an inch wide and a quarter-inch thick. Initial ribs were added both above and below the rim hoop. The cross was worked over the initial ribs to secure them in place. Two long ribs then were added under the cross, and the weaving commenced. The round basket on the right was the typical size and shape that he wove. Dimensions, from left: 12 3/4″ x 16″ top, 6″ s.h., 10 1/2″ o.h.; 6″ top, 4″ s.h., 6″ o.h.; 11 3/4″ top, 8″ s.h., 12″ o.h. Collection of Jane George.

used by some Mexican Indians; it is well known throughout South America and the southwestern United States. Wright adds that this diamond configuration also appears in English corn dollies (Wright 1983, p. 122). In Stephenson's book, *Basketry of the Appalachian Mountains*, a Scottish rib willow basket with a fourfold-bond wrapping is shown (1977, p. 16). Similarly, rib baskets from Germany, made from both hazel and spruce root, use both ear and fourfold-bond wrappings (Will 1985, p. 141). Techniques for weaving both wrappings are illustrated with instructions in Swiss and French basketry training texts (Schweizerischen Vereins 1979, p. 142; Duchesne, Ferrand, and Thomas 1963, p. 158). The use of these two wrappings is widespread.

Ring wrappings are found on baskets scattered in areas of eastern Tennessee, western North Carolina, eastern Kentucky, and Virginia. Most ring wrappings are made with a single split (Pls. 3.29 and 3.30); the wrapping split may either be wound around in a flat ring or be worked by twisting

Pl. 3.19 Set of rectangular rib baskets made by Gertie Youngblood, Cannon County, Tennessee, 1984. Youngblood makes both rectangular and round rib baskets. This fine set is typical of her work and shows many features of central Tennessee basketmaking, including bow wrapping, narrow splits, flattened ribs, and overall basket shape. Youngblood uses great care in her finely prepared materials and basket shaping. The darker stripes are woven with heartwood, a decoration often used to add color. Gertie was asked to make such basket sets by her basket broker, Estel Youngblood. She has made five or six complete sets to date (Youngblood, 30 Nov. 1984). The smallest of the set measures 3″ x 4 1/2″ top, 2 1/4″ s.h., 3 1/2″ o.h., while others graduate up to the largest, 8″ x 12″ top, 6″ s.h., 11″ o.h. Courtesy of Estel Youngblood.

Pl. 3.20 Pennsylvania rib basket similar to those made by the Strauss family, Berks County, Pennsylvania (Lasansky 1979, pp. 49, 54). The wrapping is made in a figure-eight configuration which is worked down the handle hoop. The ribs are inserted into the resulting pockets. The basket has no top rib, and the weaving split is double-wrapped around the rim on each row, completely covering the thick rim hoop. Dimensions: 11″ top, 6″ s.h., 11″ o.h. Courtesy of Pennsylvania Farm Museum of Landis Valley, Pennsylvania Historical and Museum Commission.

Pl. 3.21 Oval rib basket with woven cross wrapping attributed to Fleming County, Kentucky (Hackley, 17 Feb. 1985). The woven cross wrapping is worked in a figure-eight which has been interwoven as it crosses the handle. The oval shape and ribbing make the basket quite distinctive. The ends of the first ribs are overlapped behind the spine to secure them and then are woven. Two of the next ribs are inserted into the wrapping, causing the long unwoven rib float. Dimensions: 9″ x 15″ top, 5 3/4″ x 10″ base, 7 1/2″ s.h., 11″ o.h. Collection of Larry Hackley.

the split a half-turn at each corner of the hoops' intersection. Rings typically begin with a center cross which, as on the basket in plate 3.29, is the only part of the wrapping which binds the two hoops together. Occasionally a ring is worked with a doubled split (or two splits) (Fig. 5.10; Cl. Pl. 6). One ring wrapping on a basket from western North Carolina is ended by making a knot in its center (Fig. 3.12; Pl. 3.30).

Pl. 3.22   Lestel and Ollie Childress, Edmonson County, Kentucky, 1985, are fifth-generation basketmakers who make a variety of rib and split baskets. The Childresses both learned basketmaking from their families as they grew up. Lestel recalled some of the hard work growing up in a basketmaking family: "This guy came. He run a grocery store. He had an old model-A Ford and he drove down to the house one Sunday evening and told Dad, 'I've got an order for 100 bushel baskets, but I have to have them in a week.' There was eight of us in the family. . . . We made a hundred of them in a week and that's the way we paid for our first farm. He got 50 cents apiece for 'em back in 1930s, back during the Depression" (23 Mar. 1984). The large round basket and the rectangular magazine basket that Lestel is holding are two of his specialties. The flower basket on the floor is a design that his mother, Ella Frances Thompson Childress, made, one that he has continued. The Childresses are fulltime basketmakers, carrying on traditional work as well as making original baskets (20 Feb. 1985). The ear wrapping that the Childresses use is common in the southcentral Kentucky region, although the exact working method varies from maker to maker. The ear forms a large knot into which the ribs are inserted.

Pl. 3.23   This melon basket with ear wrapping from northeastern Kentucky (Hackley, 17 Feb. 1985) has details very similar to those seen on baskets of Pennsylvania regions. The basket framework is extremely stout (both hoops and ribs), and the weaving splits are also thicker than those usually found on most Kentucky rib baskets. There is no top rib. The oval shape is accentuated by the ribbing, which creates a wide-bodied basket. Dimensions: 12 3/4" x 13 1/4" top, 8 1/2" s.h., 12 1/4" o.h. Collection of Larry Hackley.

3. Rib Baskets   97

Pl. 3.24 Pennsylvania melon baskets made by Peter Weirbach, Bucks County, ca. 1919 (Mercer Accession Ledger; Mercer 1926, pp. 194–96). Thick hoops, wide flat ribs, double-wrapped rims, four-fold-bond wrappings, and spherical melon shapes are seen in basketwork throughout southeastern and central Pennsylvania. Dimensions, from left: 16 1/2″ x 18 1/2″ top, 8 1/2″ s.h., 16″ o.h.; 13 1/2″ x 15 1/2″ top, 6 1/2″ s.h., 12 1/2″ o.h. Courtesy of the Mercer Museum, Bucks County Historical Society.

Pl. 3.25 "Small rib buttocks basket" made by Mrs. Whyle Hunter, Madison County, North Carolina, in 1917. Purchased at that time for fifty cents (Mercer Accession Ledger). The woven fourfold-bond wrapping allows most of the ribs to be added before the weaving begins. Dimensions: 6″ top, 4″ s.h., 7″ o.h. Courtesy of the Mercer Museum, Bucks County Historical Society.

Pl. 3.26   Charlotte Tracey, Gaston County, North Carolina, 1984, wrapping a hoop frame. On all of her rib baskets, Tracey uses a distinctive woven fourfold-bond wrapping which she calls a "bow." She grew up near Asheville, North Carolina, learning basketmaking from her father, Alec Ballard. Tracey recalls making baskets for Allanstand Cottage Industries: "I went to work for Allanstand when I was eight years old, making my own baskets. . . . I just worked at home and took my baskets in. . . . Most of the time they'd have orders from shops and they'd want certain kinds and certain colors. . . . Most of the time you had to work to get the order out" (27 Nov. 1984). Today Tracey sells many of her baskets through the Southern Highland Handicraft Guild. Different styles of baskets that she makes are: market, wall, egg, melon, tray, and favor baskets. Tracey related a story about making her small favor baskets, one that suggests her familiarity with her work. In preparing for her basketwork, she would whittle out a number of tiny ribs, keeping them in a box. As she worked on the favors, she reached down into the box and, without looking, pulled out the exact number for the small baskets. "It takes ten of these for a basket . . . and I wouldn't miss picking up ten, not one time out of a dozen. Might near every time, I'd get ten, just the feel of them" (27 Nov. 1984).

Pl. 3.27-a   *(Left):* Cone-shaped wall basket. Purchased in Asheville, North Carolina, origin uncertain (Brunk, 27 Nov. 1984). This variation on the woven fourfold-bond wrapping continues its woven pattern as the framework is filled in with ribs and splits. The horizontal ribbing is worked into the wrapping on the basket spine as the basket is woven. This basket is unusual in both its weaving and ribbing methods. Dimensions: 4″ top, 5 3/4″ s.h., 9″ o.h. Collection of Robert S. Brunk.

Pl. 3.27-b   *(Right):* Detail of wrapping and weaving of basket depicted in Pl. 3.27-a plainly shows the insertion of the ribs into the weaving.

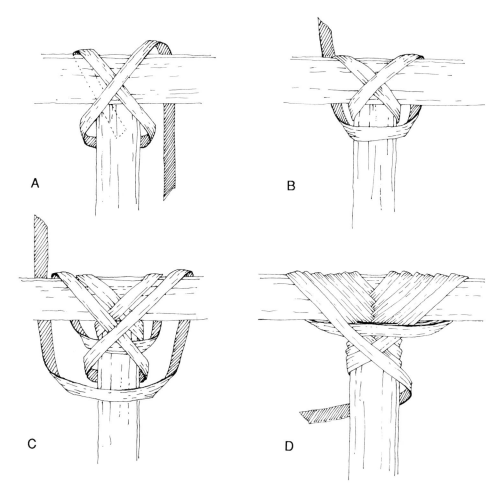

Fig. 3.11   Triangular wrapping.

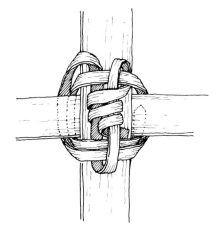

Fig. 3.12   Ring and knot wrapping.

Pl. 3.28 Handleless basket with triangular wrapping, from Snyder County, Pennsylvania (Kuster, 16 Oct. 1984). This rounded basket, made with a framework of a rim hoop and a spine, uses a triangular wrapping worked similarly to the fourfold-bond, but with three points instead of four. This wrapping also forms pockets into which the ribs are inserted. The basket shows the wide flat ribs and characteristic spherical shape of many Pennsylvania baskets. Dimensions: 11 1/2″ x 13″ top, 6 1/4″ s.h. Collection of Robert and Shirley Kuster.

Pl. 3.29 Oval rib basket made by George Bowman (b. 1845), Loudon County, Tennessee (Faulkner and Faulkner, 28 Nov. 1984). Baskets with a cross and folded ring wrapping are found in eastern Tennessee, eastern Kentucky, western North Carolina, and Virginia. The wrapping forms a knot to hold ends of the ribs. Square-cut nails fasten the hoops on this basket, whose high placement of the rim hoop creates a very deep basket. Dimensions: 10 1/2″ x 14″ top, 7 3/4″ side height, 10″ o.h. Private collection.

Pl. 3.30 Basket with ring and knot wrapping from western North Carolina (Elkins, 9 May 1985). The two middle ribs are slipped up under the wrapping to secure the ends. The narrow top and broad belly of the basket create an unusually deep and wide shape. This type of wrapping is not common. Dimensions: 10″ x 13″ top, 9″ s.h., 12″ o.h. Collection of Edd and Peggy Elkins.

2. Ribbings

Ribbing is how the ribs are set into the sides of a basket. Wrappings and ribbings go hand in hand. The wrapping helps determine the type of ribbing used and the shape of the basket. Wide, thick wrappings such as the ear and fourfold-bond configurations allow most or all of the ribs to be inserted all at once. Baskets with wide wrappings are generally quite rounded, with little or no pouching. Narrow wrappings such as the cross and ring cannot hold all of the ribs at one time, so that most of the ribs are anchored into the weaving of the basket sides as the basket is filled in. Baskets with narrow wrappings seem to have more diversity in their shapes than those with wide wrappings.

Baskets with *simultaneous ribbing* have broad and/or thick wrappings into which all the ribs are inserted. This ribbing is common to baskets with fourfold-bond or ear wrappings (Pls. 3.31, 3.32, 3.24, 3.48). In this ribbing method, all the ribs are whittled and cut to length, and the ends are tapered to exact sizes and inserted into the wrapping before the side weaving commences. The sizes and shapes of these baskets are established from the outset, and there is little room to alter the basket shape after the ribs are inserted.

Radiating ribbing (Fig. 3.13) is begun with the initial ribs worked into the wrapping at approximately forty-five-degree angles between the spine and the rim. The first ribs — the center ribs — are the longest and establish the basket's width. The next ribs are inserted on either side of the center ribs, working toward the rim and the spine. Succeeding pairs of ribs are always added next to and on either side of the previously inserted ribs, eventually filling in the sides and the bottom of the basket. This ribbing is readily apparent, as the ribs appear to end directly at the hoops. Baskets with radiating ribbing are common in eastern West Virginia and were made by the Eye and Propst families in Pendleton County (Pl. 3.14) and by other makers in northwest Virginia (Pl. 3.33). Radiating ribbing is also used by Cherokee basketmakers of the Qualla Reservation in North Carolina (Pls. 3.34 and 3.9; Cl. Pl. 3) and is the ribbing method most often worked in rod/rib baskets (Pls. 5.50-a and 5.51).

Baskets with *converging ribbing* (Fig. 3.14) show obvious diagonal lines which begin at the wrapping and continue down the sides. The first ribs are inserted into the wrapping under the rim hoop and alongside the spine, leaving the sides of the basket open. The next ribs are added alongside the initial ribs, working down from the rim and over from the spine to fill in the space. As the basket is woven and more ribs are added, the ends of all the ribs converge along the same diagonal line, giving the

Pl. 3.31 Pennsylvania basket with a wide, thick ear wrapping into which all the ribs are added simultaneously. The ends of the wide ribs are tapered to small points to fit into the wrapping. This basket was intentionally constructed without a handle; the ends of the spine are folded over the rim to the inside and held by the wrapping. Another distinctive feature often found on Pennsylvania baskets is the way the rim is double-wrapped with the weavers, completely covering the top edge. Dimensions: 10″ top, 5 3/4″ s.h. Courtesy of the Pennsylvania Farm Museum of Landis Valley, Pennsylvania Historical and Museum Commission.

Pl. 3.32 Square-rimmed Pennsylvania basket with simultaneous ribbing. All the ribs are laid into the pockets formed by the wide fourfold-bond wrapping. Although the squared shape is somewhat unusual, it is reminiscent of many rib baskets from the British Isles. Dimensions: 13″ top, 5 1/2″ s.h., 10 1/2″ o.h. Courtesy of the Pennsylvania Farm Museum of Landis Valley, Pennsylvania Historical and Museum Commission.

basket its distinctive appearance (Pls. 3.35; 3.44-a, b). Occasionally baskets are made with two lines of convergence, creating more of a pouch on the basket side (Pl. 3.36). Not much is known about this type of ribbing, except that it is found in scattered instances in eastern Tennessee and southwestern Virginia but may not be confined to that region. It is a beautiful ribbing which, through its technique, adds a strong design line to the finished basket.

In *vertical ribbing* (Fig. 3.15), the spine of the basket is used as the guide for inserting all the ribs. The first ribs are added on either side of the spine and conform to the spine shape. Working from the spine up to the rim hoop, succeeding ribs are inserted to align with the previous ribs, gradually filling in the sides of the basket.

A number of baskets with vertical ribbing are attributed to eastern Tennessee and southeastern Ohio, although this ribbing is probably not confined to these areas. One rectangular basket found in southeastern

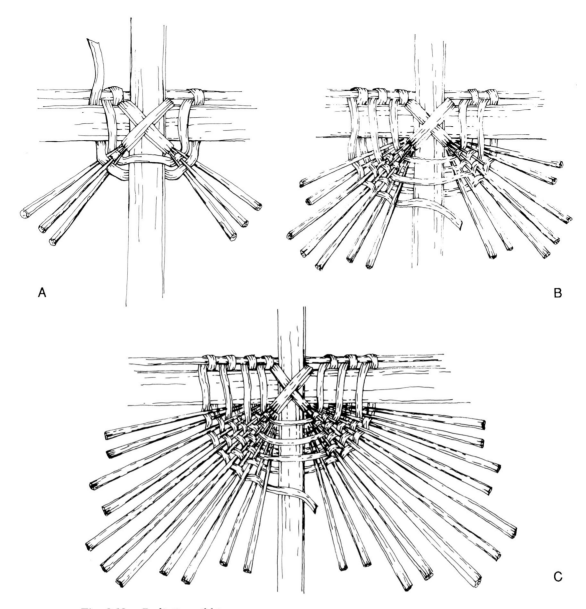

Fig. 3.13 Radiating ribbing.

Ohio (Pl. 3.37) sandwiches the ends of the ribs in place between two rim hoops. The doubled rim not only conceals the ends, but also holds most of the ribs securely in a vertical position. Another basket with vertical ribbing (Cl. Pl. 5), similar to one credited to an eastern Tennessee basketmaker named Waldrip, from Greene County, (Irwin 1982, p. 57), has long tapered ribs which are tucked in alongside the handle hoop. The addition of one shaped rib on top of another creates a graceful S-curve, noticeable

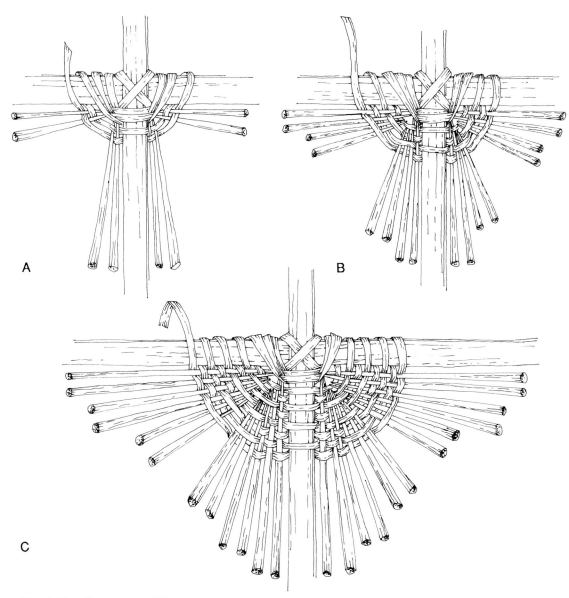

Fig. 3.14 Converging ribbing.

in the side view of the baskets. The combination of flat and round ribs inserted vertically creates a flat base and straight sides in some baskets (Pl. 3.38).

Horizontal ribbing (Fig. 3.16) is built like a rib cage. While vertical ribbing is worked beginning from the spine, horizontal ribbing is worked starting at the rim. The ribs are usually oval or somewhat flattened. Golden Howard of Harlan County, Kentucky, makes horizontally-ribbed

Pl. 3.33 Basket with radiating ribbing, from Shenandoah County, Virginia (Helsley and Helsley, 13 Mar. 1985). This tightly ribbed and woven basket clearly shows the ribs being added from both under the rim and along the spine of the basket. The rim hoop is doubled, and the ends of the handle hoop overlap from rim to rim. The doubled rim hoop allows the ends of the ribs to be concealed between the hoops. Besides the ribbing, details include: the top rib, which hangs over the rim, forming a narrow ledge; the cross wrapping; the shape; and the fine finish of the materials. Several examples of this style of basket have been noted in northwestern Virginia, probably coming from the same maker or family. Dimensions: 12 1/2″ top, 6 1/2″ s.h., 11 1/2″ o.h. Private collection.

Pl. 3.34 Cherokee oval basket with two handles formed by extending the spine above the rim. This basket, with red and blue dyed stripes, begins with radiating ribbing which is commonly used by Cherokee basketmakers. After the ribs have been filled in to the spine, the long sides of the basket are filled in by additional ribs along the rim. Dimensions: 13″ x 18″ base, 9″ x 19 1/2″ top, 8 1/2″ s.h., 10″ o.h. Courtesy of the Museum of the Cherokee Indian, Cherokee, North Carolina.

round, wall, and rectangular baskets. He first makes a cross wrapping with a long split and then wraps the split around and down the spine for several inches to form an anchoring point for the horizontal rib placement. All the ribs are inserted into the wrapping before the weaving is begun (Pl. 3.39).

In other horizontally-ribbed baskets, the ribs are made long enough to circle all the way around the basket, with the overlapping ends lying against the spine. Baskets with encircling ribs often have straight sides. A wrapping split binds the ribs and then continues as a weaver, securing the ribs as the sides are woven. The ribs remain parallel to the rim and are

Pl. 3.35 Basket with converging ribbing. Origin unknown. Converging ribbing has a distinctive diagonal line that is created by the method of adding the ribs. The first ribs are added just below the rim hoop and alongside the spine. Additional ribs are added next to the first ribs, filling in the sides as the weaving progresses. The ends of the ribs are all added in the center of the sides, creating the strong diagonal line. This basket, painted a light yellow-green, has thick hoops, slightly flattened ribs on the base, and round ribs on the sides. Dimensions: 11 1/2″ top, 8 1/2″ s.h., 12 1/2″ o.h. Collection of Bill and Dot Van Corbach.

Pl. 3.36 Flat-bottomed, straight-sided basket constructed with converging ribbing, from Hawkins or Sullivan County, Tennessee (King, 10 May 1985). The ribbing is set into this basket so that two lines of convergence are made on each side of the basket. The wrapping is a cross and circle, with the braid covering the wrapping. This tightly-woven basket has no turnbacks. Dimensions: 9 1/2″ top, 6″ s.h., 9 1/2″ o.h. Collection of Marcus Farthing King.

added one at a time, down to the base of the basket. After the ribs are added to the bottom of the spine, the base is woven in one of two ways. Horizontally-ribbed baskets in the central Kentucky region of Madison and Garrard counties have bottom ribs inserted alongside the handle hoop and under the weaving splits (Pls. 3.40-a, b). The base ribs create a gentle curve at the bottom of the basket, where the base meets the sides. In the

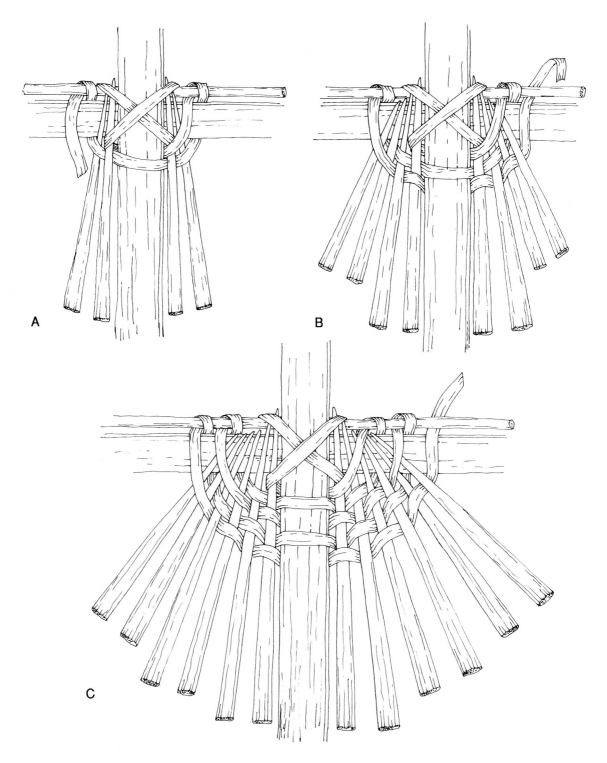

Fig. 3.15   Vertical ribbing.

Pl. 3.37 Vertically-ribbed basket with rectangular rim hoop. Found in Noble County, Ohio (Lott, 30 May 1985; Kemble, 23 Aug. 1985). Vertical ribbing aligns itself to the basket spine and usually follows the contour of the spine to shape the basket. The basket is constructed of flat ribs on the long sides and round ribs on the ends. The basket has a doubled rim, so that the ribs can be slipped in between the rims to secure the rib ends. The rim is double-wrapped with the weaver, and all turnbacks are made in the center. Dimensions: 11″ x 13″ top, 7″ s.h., 11 1/2″ o.h. Collection of Susan D. Lott.

Pl. 3.38 Flat-bottomed basket with vertical ribbing. Purchased in central Kentucky, origin uncertain (Van Corbach, 20 Feb. 1985). The wide flat ribs and the flattened handle hoop combine to create a flat base. The flat ribs are carefully shaped to form the base, and the round ribs on the sides complete the shape. The first rib on either side of the handle is slipped up under the bottom of the wrapping, while the second rib is fitted under the top of the cross. Dimensions: 11 1/2″ top, 7″ s.h., 11″ o.h. Private collection.

Pl. 3.39 Horizontally-ribbed basket made by Golden Howard, Harlan County, Kentucky (Young, 25 May 1983). He makes a cross wrapping which continues around and down the spine to make an anchor for the ribs. All the ribs are added before the weaving begins. Howard sells many of his baskets through Red Bird Mission, Beverly, Kentucky. Dimensions: 11″ top, 6 1/2″ s.h., 11″ o.h. Private collection.

3. Rib Baskets   109

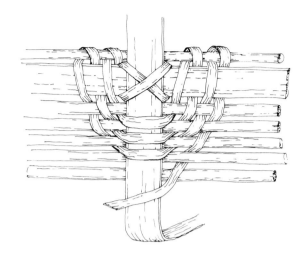

Fig. 3.16   Horizontal ribbing.

Pl. 3.40-a   Small basket with horizontal ribbing, central Kentucky. The horizontal ribbing is added underneath the rim and continues down the spine to the basket base. Begun alongside the spine, the bottom ribbing forms a gently curved base and is worked up to meet the side ribs. Dimensions: 6 1/2″ top, 4 3/4″ s.h., 6 1/2″ o.h. Collection of Datha Doolin.

Pl. 3.40-b   Bottom view of basket shown in Pl. 3.40-a, showing base ribbing added alongside the spine.

Pl. 3.41-b Bottom view of basket in Pl. 3.41-a, showing concentric ribs in the base of the basket.

Pl. 3.41-a Straight-sided basket with horizontal ribbing. Origin unknown. This basket is similar in construction to the one in Pl. 3.40. The base ribbing on this basket, however, is worked with ribs which form concentric circles from the center to the edge of the base. The basket has straight sides, due to the height of the handle hoop and its sharply squared base. Dimensions: 10 1/4″ base, 6″ s.h., 12 1/2″ o.h. Collection of Larry Hackley.

Pl. 3.42 Basket with vertical and horizontal ribbing. Origin unknown. The vertical ribbing begins next to the spine and works out along the rim for a short distance. The ribbing technique then changes to horizontal, which fills in the basket sides. Dimensions: 11 3/4″ top, 6 3/4″ s.h., 11″ o.h. Courtesy of Campus Martius Museum, Marietta, Ohio, Ohio Historical Society.

Pl. 3.43 Rib basket with horizontal and converging ribbing. Purchased in central Kentucky, origin uncertain (Doolin, 19 Feb. 1985). The ends of the hoops are overlapped, grooved, and tied with a rag. The basket is begun with three ribs laid in horizontally and then is completed with converging ribbing, combining round and flat ribs. All turnbacks are made in the center of the basket sides. Dimensions: 10 1/2″ top, 7 1/2″ s.h., 12″ o.h. Collection of Datha Doolin.

second example, the base is filled in by circular rods added in concentric circles as the base is woven. This base allows for a perfectly flat bottom which angles sharply where the sides meet the bottom (Pls. 3.41-a, b).

The explanations given in the preceding descriptions of ribbings deal with "pure" ribbing techniques. Most basketmakers use variations or combinations of these constructions to create distinctive and sturdy baskets. The ribbing style of southcentral Kentucky baskets is particularly identifiable. In these baskets, a large number of primary ribs are inserted into the wrapping. Secondary ribs are then added as the weaving progresses. Most makers from that region use flat ribs for the initial bottom ribs, which fan out from the handle hoop to make the basket body slightly wider than the rim. The remaining space on the side of the basket to the rim is filled in with more rounded ribs which gradually curve up to the rim, creating a rounded basket (Pls. 3.22 and 1.11).

The basket in plate 3.42 is begun with vertical ribbing and then changes to horizontal ribbing on the sides, where the ribs are added below the rim hoop. With its rounded shape, thick rounded hoops, and fourfold-bond wrapping, this basket is similar to ones made in Pennsylvania; however, this ribbing is not typical of Pennsylvania or any known Appalachian region. A German rib basket, made from hazel and spruce roots, uses identical wrapping and ribbing techniques (Will 1985, p. 141). Another rib basket purchased in Paris, Kentucky, has both flat and round ribs and combines horizontal and coverging ribbing techniques (Pl. 3.43).

3. Handles

Rib baskets are made with overhead handles, two handles, or occasionally without handles (Pls. 3.28 and 3.31). The most common overhead handle is formed by the handle hoop. However, occasionally overhead handles are made from separate pieces secured to the rim hoop or the basket body after the sides are woven. A number of oval rib trays with attached overhead handles are attributed to Wythe County, Virginia (Pls. 3.44-a, b) (Moore, 20 June 1984).

Occasionally ribs are added on each side of the handle hoop and woven in place with a split, making a **woven handle** or "muffled" handle, as it is called in southcentral Kentucky (Alvey, 23 Jan. 1986). The "pie" or "magazine" basket (Pl. 3.55) has a woven handle, which is commonly worked on baskets from southcentral Kentucky and central Tennessee. Baskets with a woven handle are not comfortable to carry, and this probably is the reason that this decorative treatment generally is found on small fancy baskets which usually sit in one place.

Two-handled rib baskets are constructed in several ways. In some cases the spine of the basket is made long enough to extend above the rim hoop and serve as handle grips (Pl. 3.34; Cl. Pl. 4). A more common two-handled treatment is the formation of handle holes. Some handle holes are woven in the side of the basket to create an opening below the rim hoop (Fig. 3.1-b; Pls. 3.45, 3.46, 3.17). Other handle holes are created structurally, as part of the basket framework (Fig. 3.17; Pl. 3.48). Two spines, attached to the rim hoop, determine the width of the handle space. The handle hole is completed by attaching a cross-piece to connect the two spines and adding a shorter rib which folds back at the cross-piece. After the rim and spines have been wrapped, the basket is woven from each end, leaving the handle space open. This handle construction is illustrated in a French basketmaking textbook, *La Vannerie* (Duchesne, Ferrand, and Thomas 1963, p. 159), and is also known in West Germany (Thierschmann, Sept. 1987), but its origin is unknown. White oak baskets with the structural handle holes are found in Pennsylvania, in northwestern Virginia, and occasionally farther south.

4. Braids and Borders

When baskets became decorative as well as functional, **borders** and **braids** were often added to make the products more marketable. One decorative treatment is the addition of a braid, i.e., extra weaving that can cover rims, spines, and handles. The large rib basket in plate 1.2 has braids

Pl. 3.44-a Oval tray basket made in Wythe County, Virginia (Moore, 20 June 1984). The framework is constructed with a rim hoop and ribs but no overhead handle hoop or spine for base support. The ribbing converges in the middle of the base, making a distinct line. The sharply squared split-end handle is tacked to the rim, a handle attachment not suitable for everyday carrying. Such baskets probably served as table or work baskets. Dimensions: 10″ x 14″ top, 2 1/2″ s.h., 9 1/4″ o.h. Private collection.

Pl. 3.44-b Detail of basket in Pl. 3.44-a, showing handle nailed to the rim and ribbing converging in the middle of the basket body. The handle appears to have been nailed to the rim before the basket was woven.

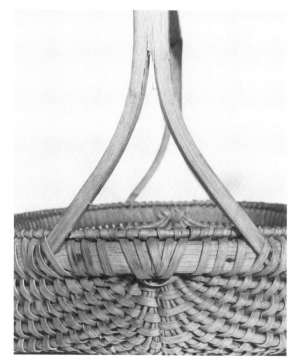

Pl. 3.45 Large basket used for holding wool in wool mills of Rockingham County, Virginia (Helsley and Helsley, 13 Mar. 1985). The basket is woven with a top rib which also extends across the top of the handle hole. The spine is folded over the top rim to the inside of the basket. Dimensions: 18″ x 24″ top, 15″ s.h. Private collection.

Pl. 3.46 Large utility basket constructed with horizontal ribbing and handle holes, Madison County, Kentucky (Hackley, 17 Feb. 1985). Its ribbing technique is the same as that in Pl. 3.40-a. This basket is heavy, due to the thickness of the ribs and the close ribbing. Its large size and the ribbing technique make it unusual. Dimensions: 23 1/2″ top, 24″ base, 19″ o.h. Collection of Larry Hackley.

woven both inside and outside the rim hoop. According to Earlean Thomas (Pl. 3.47), "Everybody calls it a braided hoop. . . . It's newer here lately. People didn't used to do it like that. When I'd work and make 'em for a living, I never braided 'em. None of 'em. You couldn't afford to because you had to make it for a living. You had to make that basket. It's taken me a long time to braid that" (Thomas and Thomas, 30 Nov. 1984).

When ribs are added above or alongside the rim hoop, the top border can be modified with scallops or lips (Pl. 3.49). An oval fruit tray made for Allanstand in the 1920s shows large scallops on either side, which,

Pl. 3.47   Earlean Thomas, Cannon County, Tennessee, 1984. Thomas is a traditional rib basketmaker who learned from her mother. She grew up in Cannon County and remembers making baskets as a child and trading them at Bino's (now Jimbo's) store. She said that she has always made a good basket and prefers working with fine splits. When asked about the time required for making a finely woven basket like those she is holding, she replied by describing how the materials were prepared: "It takes a long time to make that. You don't make that in a day or two. . . . You got to go to the woods to get your timber, get it home, bust it, then make your splits. You got to make your hoops, you got to make your ribs, and how are you going to tell somebody how long you made it. . . . I couldn't tell you how many hours I got in any of them" (Thomas and Thomas, 30 Nov. 1984).

Pl. 3.48 "Coal" basket made by the Day family, Shenandoah County, Virginia (Helsley and Helsley, 13 Mar. 1985). Oliver Day recalled that his father and grandfather made many big coal baskets like this one: "They even made them to order and shipped them on the train to Paw Paw, West Virginia." There they were used at a tannery. "They used bark to make the leather. They peeled it in the spring of the year and carried it to the mill in those baskets." He also remembered that they carried charcoal and corn in such baskets, but they always called them "coal baskets" (13 Mar. 1985). The handle holes are constructed as part of the framework. Baskets with this type of construction are usually quite large and stout, indicating use for big, heavy loads. These baskets were made in central and eastern Pennsylvania, northwestern Virginia, and occasionally farther south. Dimensions: 22″ x 26″ top, 9″ s.h. Private collection.

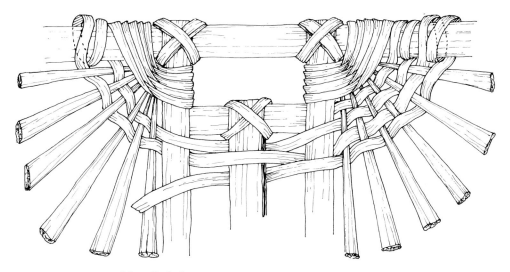

Fig. 3.17   Structural handle holes.

Pl. 3.49 Ruffled pie basket made by Karrie Ayers, Patrick County, Virginia (Lasansky, 15 Oct. 1984). The scalloped top border is made by adding shaped ribs above the rim hoop. The wide ear wrapping is decorative as well as functional. The basket size is appropriate for a single pie. Dimensions: 13″ top, 5″ s.h., 10 1/2″ o.h. Collection of Jeannette Lasansky.

Pl. 3.50 Basket with inner lip from Wythe County, Virginia (Farmer and Farmer, 11 Mar. 1985). Four ribs are added to the inside of the rim hoop and woven as part of the basket body to make an unusual inner lip. Dimensions: 11″ top, 7″ s.h., 11″ o.h. Collection of Ken and Jane Farmer.

Pl. 3.51 Lidded and footed basket. Purchased in Asheville, North Carolina, origin uncertain (Brunk, 27 Nov. 1984). Probably made for the tourist trade, this basket has many decorative features. The flat lid fits inside the rim hoop and has an attached raised handle. The pedestal foot is approximately one-and-a-half inches tall. Everything is covered with braid—rim, handle, foot, and lid pull. The wrapping is a woven fourfold-bond on both the hoops and the lid. Dimensions: 5 1/2″ x 7″ base, 10 1/2″ top, 6 1/4″ s.h., 12″ o.h. Collection of Robert S. Brunk.

Pl. 3.52 Applied skids. Skids on the base of this Pennsylvania melon basket are made like heavy ribs and inserted into the weaving. The skids are tacked to the basket base through the ribs. Protecting and elevating the basket, skids extend the life of the basket. A basket virtually identical to this one is in the Mercer Museum and is credited as having been made by Abram Bergstrasser, 1896, Iron Hill, Pennsylvania (Mercer Accession Ledger). Dimensions: 13 1/2″ top, 7 1/2″ s.h., 13 1/2″ o.h. Courtesy of the Pennsylvania Farm Museum of Landis Valley, Pennsylvania Historical and Museum Commission.

besides being decorative, add higher sides to the tray (ACI ca. 1920s). Similarly, ribs were added above the rim hoops of wall baskets to make an arched back (Pl. 3.9). While both of these construction details are variations which decorate the basket, occasionally border treatments are a regional or maker style. One such is the basket with several ribs woven inside the rim, forming a wide inside lip (Pl. 3.50).

5. Lids and Feet

Lids are not common on rib baskets, but when found, they also are made with rib constructions. Building a lid which fits down into the basket's top opening is a job for a skilled basketmaker (Pl. 3.51). Another type of lid is a swinging lid, attached to the basket frame with hinges. A fine example of a rib basket with a hinged lid is in the collection of the Museum of the Cherokee Indian, Cherokee, North Carolina (Cl. Pl. 3). Holes are bored in the handle hoop to receive the framework of the lid and permit the lids to pivot.

Rib baskets occasionally have **feet** which serve to protect the base, elevate the basket, and allow the rounded forms to rest flat. The feet are of two varieties, skids and pedestals. Skids are found on some Pennsylvania rib baskets (Pl. 3.52) but rarely in other regions. Skids are made like

Pl. 3.53 Ovoid gathering basket, Pennsylvania. In the Scottish Highlands, baskets of this construction, made of willow and other materials, were known as a *mudag* (Grant 1961, p. 233) or *crealagh* (Wright 1983, p. 123). The basket was used to gather bits of wool pulled from hedgerows or sheep. It was also used to hold teased wool by the fire, in order to bring out the natural oils before spinning (Noble, 22 Aug. 1978). In the Hessen district of West Germany, such baskets were called *Nußkörbe* or *Hutzelkörbe* (nut baskets or drying baskets) and apparently were used for gathering and drying nuts (Helm 1961, pp. 48, 50). Dimensions: 22″ long x 14″ in diameter. Courtesy of the Pennsylvania Farm Museum of Landis Valley, Pennsylvania Historical and Museum Commission.

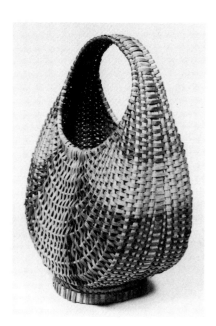

Pl. 3.54 Cherokee "hen" basket woven with grey, orange, and yellow dyed splits. Hen baskets are thought to have originated in Scotland, where it was said they were made to carry a broody hen (Wright 1983, pp. 118–19; Kyle, 31 Aug. 1978). While ribwork is not a traditional basketry type of the Cherokees (Leftwich 1970, p. 45), members of the Taylor family of the Qualla Reservation make this form (calling it a "knitting" or "bird's nest" basket) and other finely detailed rib baskets with an added pedestal foot (M. Ross, 8 May 1985). Dimensions: 5″ x 5 1/2″ pedestal foot, 9 3/4″ wide, 8 1/2″ s.h., 14 1/2″ o.h. Courtesy of the Museum of the Cherokee Indian, Cherokee, North Carolina.

Pl. 3.55 *(Opposite):* "Pie" basket, probably from southcentral Kentucky. Other names for this basket include "magazine" or "wood" basket. A variation of the rim construction creates triangular sides. The rim consists of two pieces both angled down from the handle to form the sloping sides. Baskets of this same basic shape also are made in splitwork (see Pl. 4.22, upper right corner). Dimensions: 10 1/2″ x 20 1/2″ base, 8″ s.h., 12″ o.h. Collection of Willie Fay Spurlock.

thick ribs and are bent to the shape of the basket. They are slipped under the weaving alongside a basket rib and sometimes are nailed to hold them in place. The pedestal foot may consist of a single hoop lashed to the base of the basket or several hoops woven together. A pedestal foot is often applied by Cherokee makers (Pl. 3.54).

Variations in Shape and Construction

Differences in framework construction produce some unusually shaped rib baskets. Two forms, the ovoid gathering basket (Pl. 3.53) and the "hen" basket (Pl. 3.54), are traditional but were modified to suit the tourist trade. In Europe, this form of ovoid basket was used for gathering wool or nuts (Grant 1961, p. 233; Wright 1983, p. 123; Noble, 22 Aug. 1978; Helm 1961, pp. 48 and 50). The basket is made with two oval hoops which intersect at right angles, creating its characteristic football shape. The basket probably is woven from each end, completely filling in the framework except for an opening in the center. Baskets of this same construction were marketed as bird houses and sold by Allanstand Cottage Industries (Pl. 1.8).

Similarly, the "hen" basket (Pl. 3.54), an old form from the British Isles, was made as a popular basket in the Southern Highlands in this country. The basic framework consists of a wide handle hoop sandwiched between two round rings which form the basket opening. Ribs are added between

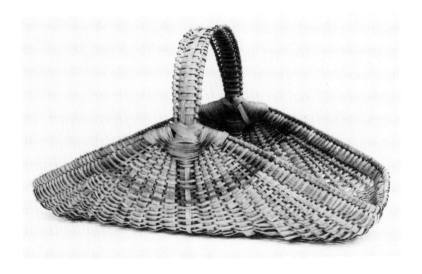

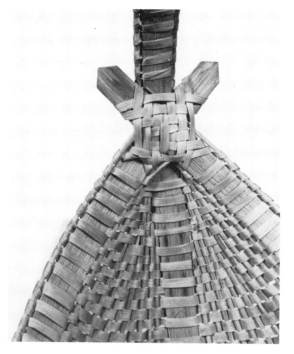

Pl. 3.56-a "Canoe" basket purchased in Asheville, North Carolina; origin uncertain (Brunk, 27 Nov. 1984). The rim hoops on this canoe-shaped basket form its distinctive shape. Two rim pieces cross at the handle and are wrapped with a woven fourfold-bond. Baskets such as these were made for the tourist trade in the Great Smoky Mountains early in the 1900s. Dimensions: 5″ x 9″ base, 9″ x 13″ top, 3″ to 8″ s.h., 13 1/4″ o.h. Collection of Robert S. Brunk.

Pl. 3.56-b Detail of frame construction of basket in Pl. 3.56-a, showing the angle of the rims and the woven fourfold-bond wrapping.

the rings and the hoop to give the basket its shape. Its rounded base was sometimes given a foot, to enable it to sit level.

Another modification of a framework used by basketmakers today — a change influenced by the Handicraft Revival — is made by using two rim sections and altering their angles. The "pie" basket, also known as a "magazine" or "wood" basket (Pl. 3.55), and the "canoe" (Pls. 3.56-a, b) are two styles with some of the other variations depicted in the Allanstand brochure (Pl. 1.8).

Split Baskets

Pl. 4.1   Two-handled clothes basket made by S.E. Billetter, Belmont County, Ohio, ca. 1940. At that time, traditional baskets were still used in many rural regions for a variety of farm and household chores; this split basket also supports Billetter's young granddaughter, Donna Billetter Moore (Myers, 10 Oct. 1984). Photograph courtesy of Donna Billetter Moore and Edith Billetter Myers.

Introduction

Of the three white oak basket types, rib, rod, and split, splitwork has the simplest basket constructions and is also the type most widespread throughout the Central and Southern Appalachian Mountains. The weaves used in oak splitwork are universal and have been employed for basketwork since prehistoric times (Adovasio 1977).

The use of splits from woods, barks, and shoots for basketry is extensive in both Native American and European cultures. Swanton and Sattler cite the southeastern Indians' early use of split cane for mats and baskets (Swanton 1946, pp. 602–608; Sattler 1984, pp. 25–26). In Germany, some of the split-providing woods include hazel, sweet chestnut, pine, spruce, fir, larch, oak, poplar, and aspen (Will 1985, pp. 21–23). These woods or others, depending on what is indigenous to an area, are commonly used throughout Europe and Britain. Shoots of willow also are split into strips called "skeins" for fine basketmaking. Containers made from sheets and strips of birch bark are traditional in Scandinavian countries (Nylén 1977, pp. 383–89). Appalachian split baskets are made mainly from white oak, but also from ash, maple, hickory, elm, and other woods.

Appalachian oak split baskets exhibit a wide variety of forms. In the past, most of these baskets were utilitarian, with a single form having multiple uses. Bushel sizes used for agricultural chores may have been called "feed" or "corn" baskets, while the same basket used in the home was a "clothes" or "linen" basket (Pl. 4.1). Goodrich observed split baskets being used as "hampers for the storing and carrying of grain, and there were long, open baskets for the rolls of the spinners" (1931, p. 18). Other split baskets were made for specific uses, such as cradles (Pl. 4.2), and feed baskets which held grain for mules or horses (Pls. 4.3 and 4.4). As oak is strong and can withstand stress and moisture, oak splits were used for fish-related baskets (Pls. 4.45 and 4.50). Along rivers, streams, and bays, specially designed oak split traps were used by fishermen to catch fish or eels (Pl. 4.5).

By the turn of the century, a new type of split basket had become available at competitive prices. These baskets were handwoven from machined strips of wood, and handles and rims were attached with tacks or staples (Pl. 4.6). Veneer machines had been developed to peel woods such as oak, ash, and pine into thin strips, which were used to make a variety

of baskets for home, agricultural, and commercial use. Veneer baskets were marketed through mail-order catalogues such as Sears, Roebuck.

While veneer baskets were widely available and extensively used, the hand-split oak basket was a stronger product. Machined splits do not have the flexibility and strength of hand-split oak strips and can be woven only into the simplest splitwork forms. The veneering process cuts rather than splits the wood to make thin strips, and the resulting wood strips are susceptible to breakage, particularly where they are bent sharply. Veneer baskets did not completely replace the hand-split baskets. In rural areas, oak split baskets continued to be made for domestic and agricultural use. While veneer baskets (and later cardboard) became the standard containers for packing and shipping produce (Pl. 4.7), some groups continued to use hand-split baskets. In the 1930s, Allen Eaton recounted the use of well-made hand-split oak baskets to carry and ship farm products. He also noted that the Farmers Federation used locally-made split oak baskets in peck and half-bushel sizes to ship a high-grade sweet potato which was grown in the North Carolina mountains (1937, pp. 177–78).

As with rib baskets, the Arts and Crafts movement and the subsequent Handicraft Revival popularized certain forms of split baskets and encouraged the use of color. Some new split forms were introduced, and tradi-

Pl. 4.2 *(Opposite):* Oak cradle purchased by Henry Mercer from a Philadelphia, Pennsylvania, antique shop in 1916 (Mercer Accession Ledger). The simple plaited base has an oval board added to the inside, to strengthen the bottom and provide an attachment for the beautifully shaped rockers. The stakes are split in half, doubling the total number of ends for weaving the sides. The greater number of ends allows an increase in the size of the basket. A thick split bands the bottom of the cradle, covering the edge of the board and finishing the sides. Dimensions: 9″ x 25″ base, 23″ x 30″ top, 11″ s.h., 15″ o.h. with rockers. Courtesy of the Mercer Museum, Bucks County Historical Society.

Pl. 4.3 *(Above):* "Lunch Baskets, Mules Eating Out of Baskets; Delaware Division Canal at New Hope [Pennsylvania], 1899" (Bucks County Historical Society, "Recent History, Natural History and Science"). Dr. B.F. Fackenthal, Jr., reported to the society that while he "was a small boy attending public school (1857–1866) . . . [he] daily passed by the basket making shop of Jacob Gray at Monroe. . . . He made baskets of many kinds and sizes, but his principal trade was making feed baskets for the boatmen on the Delaware Division canal, which flowed close by his shop. These feed baskets were strapped around the heads of the mules, who were required to eat their oats from them while towing the boats. It was said that he made the very best quality of baskets put upon the market, and the boatment [sic] often had to wait their turns to have their orders filled" (1926, p. 196). Courtesy of the Spruance Library, Bucks County Historical Society.

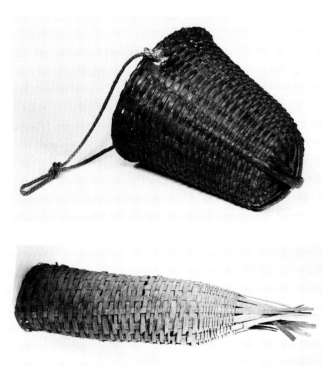

Pl. 4.4 Feed basket used to hold grain for livestock, origin uncertain. The heavy skids which protect the base partially account for the good condition of this basket. Feed baskets have a means of attaching a rope or strap, such as the small holes below the rim of this basket or two small ear handles. Dimensions: 6″ base, 16″ s.h., 14 1/2″ top. Courtesy of Durell Street of Yesteryear, Center of Science and Industry (COSI), Columbus, Ohio.

Pl. 4.5 Fish trap attributed to Haywood County, North Carolina (Elkins, 9 May 1985). Virtually out of existence today, fish baskets were commonly used in many southern rivers. This one is five feet long. The open end of the trap, on the left, is thirteen inches in diameter and then narrows to less than six inches. The funnel mouth allowed fish to enter but not to exit. Smaller baskets of similar design were used to trap eels. Collection of Edd and Peggy Elkins.

tional baskets were modified or given new uses and names. Published price lists of Allanstand Cottage Industries, Asheville, North Carolina, advertise only a few oak split baskets—a "wood basket" with legs, a rectangular "hamper" with side handles and a lid (Pl. 1.8) (ca. 1917), a deep rectangular "thermos lunch basket," a long and shallow rectangular "fern basket (with container)" (ca. 1920s), "garden basket (available in three sizes)," round-based oak "scrap," and a square-based "scrap" basket in "gay colors" (ca. 1930). The Cherokees modified some of their traditional large burden baskets and deep storage baskets to create smaller and more salable wastebaskets (M. Ross, 8 May 1985; Sattler 1984, p. 31) (Pl. 1.14). They also adopted such popular basket styles as flower carriers, handbags, and market baskets (Sattler 1984, p. 31). In southcentral Kentucky, Lestel Childress remembers his mother, Ella Frances Thompson Childress, designing flower-vase baskets which were sold to local florist shops (Pl. 4.8) (Childress and Childress, 20 Feb. 1985). While a few new forms were created or copied from outside sources, the traditional round and rectangular split baskets continued to be made and marketed. In southcentral Kentucky, at tourist stands in the 1930s (Pl. 1.12), 1940s (Pl. 4.22), and

Pl. 4.6   Veneer baskets. Many styles of commercially made veneer baskets were available by the mid-1800s for domestic and commercial uses. The basket on the left, lined with tin, was probably a lunch basket, as was the diagonally plaited one on the right. Courtesy of the Pennsylvania Farm Museum of Landis Valley, Pennsylvania Historical and Museum Commission.

1950s (Pl. 1.1), split baskets were offered along with the more numerous rib forms.

Split baskets continue to be made throughout the central and southern Appalachian region, in traditional sizes and styles. The number of basket-makers who specialize in split forms is small except in the Blue Ridge Mountains of Virginia, where a long ongoing splitwork tradition still continues among members of the Nicholson-Cook clan. William and Lucy Cook and their relatives continue to make sturdy basic splitwork forms and have trouble keeping up with the demand for their work (Cook and Cook, 14 Mar. 1985). William and Lucy Cook's nephew, Elmer Price, of Shenandoah County, Virginia (Pl. 4.32) chooses to makes a variety of functional split baskets and is constantly thinking up ways to improve on old forms. He spoke in particular of a drop-handled picnic basket, with a high domed lid, that he had designed (14 Mar. 1985). Irskel Nicholson, who started making baskets about 1930, states, "I don't take an order or

contract for baskets. What I want to build, I build and what I don't, I don't build. . . . I don't take no orders from nobody, if I want to build something, think of it—when I come up with it, that's what I build" (Nicholson and Nicholson, 16 Mar. 1985).

Structure and Materials

Made in simple geometric shapes (rectangular, square, oval, and round), split baskets show a wide variety of styles and construction details. While rectangular (Fig. 4.1-a) and round (Fig. 4.1-b) split baskets differ in base construction, the weaving techniques and most finishing details can apply to all shapes.

A split basket is made up of foundation elements termed **stakes**, also known as "ribs," "standards," "staves," or "splits," interlaced with **weavers**. Stakes form the structural framework for the basket bottom and sides. A split basket typically is begun by weaving a base. In rectangular- and square-based baskets, stakes are laid out and interwoven with each other to construct a bottom, while in round- and oval-based baskets, stakes are laid out and then interwoven with a separate weaving split. After a base is complete, the stakes are bent up to form the uprights of the basket body, and the sides are woven to the top edge, which is finished with **rims**. Rims encircle the top edge, adding strength and finalizing the basket shape. **Handles** may be added at this point, and, to finish, a **lashing** is worked around the top edge to bind the rims and the handle to the basket body. Occasionally **feet** are added to the bottom, to elevate, strengthen, and protect the base.

As a basketmaker prepares materials for a split basket, the first consideration is the basket's size. Small baskets are often made with fewer

Pl. 4.7 *(Opposite):* Teamsters transporting produce to the B & O Railroad Depot, Marietta, Ohio, 1912 (Devol, 20 Aug. 1989). The area of southeastern Ohio was active in truck farming, and much of the produce was packed and shipped in veneer baskets made by the Marietta Fruit Package and Lumber Company, Marietta, Ohio. According to a 1919 letterhead, the company manufactured "baskets, boxes, crates & fruit packages of all descriptions" from wood processed in its veneer plant in Boyd, Alabama. Photograph by H.P. Fischer, from the collection of J.B. Devol. Photo reproduction courtesy of Michael Mullen.

Pl. 4.8 *(Right):* Flower vase basket designed and made by Ella Frances Thompson Childress. Ella made dozens of these baskets and sold them to be used for floral arrangements. Her son, Lestel Childress, of Edmonson County, Kentucky, continues to make the same form (Pl. 3.22). This basket has an unusual construction: it is begun by weaving splits around a jar, forming a hollow tube. The basket is flared at each end to make top brim and base stand. The woven handle is added, and splits are woven across the base to form a shelf for a container (Childress and Childress, 20 Feb. 1985). Dimensions: 10″ base, 14″ top, 17 1/2″ s.h., 29″ o.h. Collection of Lestel and Ollie Childress.

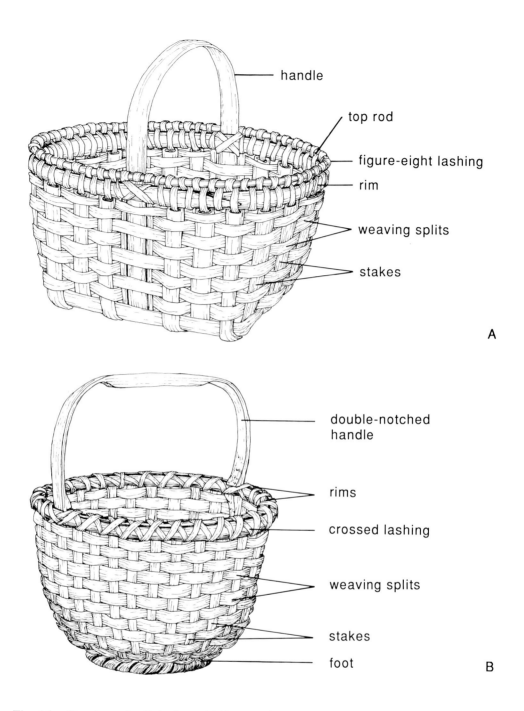

handle

top rod

figure-eight lashing

rim

weaving splits

stakes

A

double-notched handle

rims

crossed lashing

weaving splits

stakes

foot

B

Fig. 4.1 Structure of split baskets: (a) Rectangular split basket, drawn from Monroe County, West Virginia, basket. Dimensions: 6″ x 9″ base, 6 1/4″ s.h., 10 3/4″ o.h. Collection of Jane George. (b) Round split basket, drawn from basket of unknown origin. Dimensions: 6″ base, 7 3/4″ s.h., 13 1/2″ o.h. Collection of Bruce Rigsby.

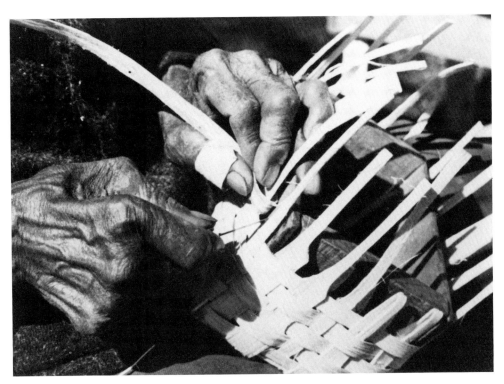

Pl. 4.9 Henry Beverley weaving a rectangular-based split basket on a mold, 1976. At the age of ninety-five, Beverley still enjoyed making baskets. He said, "Live long as you can . . . Don't hurry through life" (Sisto, 17 Apr. 1976). He had molds in several sizes, which he used to make rectangular split baskets. Beverley learned his techniques from watching his mother, who had learned to make baskets from her father David Sanders, who, as a slave in Virginia, had bottomed chairs and made baskets. Beverley worked for many years building railroads, and in 1921 or 1922 he began making baskets for a living. His baskets, woven in plain and twill weaves, had an extra "rib" (rod) above the rim, lashed with a figure-eight lashing. He tapered the stakes at the top to allow room for the lashing (Sisto 1976). The use of molds is rare among white oak basketmakers of the central and southern Appalachian region. Photo by Antonia L. Sisto, used courtesy of the Folklore Archive, University of Virginia, Charlottesville.

stakes, while larger baskets have not only more, but also longer and thicker, stakes. As a general rule, weavers are somewhat thinner than stakes. If the weavers are too thin, then they cannot support the stakes; on the other hand, weavers that are too thick may cause the stakes to bend out of alignment.

Most oak split baskets are made free-form, with a maker's hands and eyes controlling the complete process. However, there are documented basketmakers of the Central Appalachians who used molds for their work. The Calvin Henry family of Centre County, Pennsylvania (Lasansky 1979, pp. 40–41), Henry Beverley of Nelson County, Virginia (Pl. 4.9) (Sisto 1976, p. 3); Elmer Propst of Pendleton County, West Virginia (Laird 1969–72); and David Neff of Rockingham County, Virginia (Garvey 1975, pp. 13–14), are all recorded as using molds. While the practice of using molds was common in production splitwork in New England (Romaine 1939, pp. 57–58; Wetherbee and Taylor 1988; Lester 1987, pp. 42–53), it is not known whether the use of molds for making Appalachian oak baskets was more widespread in the past.

Split baskets show many variations in shape that are directly linked to construction details. Factors influencing the shape of the basket include the structure of the base, the shaping of the stakes, the tension of the weaving, and the shape of the top rim. The base structure determines a basket's initial shape: rectangular, square, oval, or round. Adjustments in weaving tension on the sides can create a certain amount of narrowing and widening in the basket body. A large, lidded storage basket (Pl. 4.10) has an extremely small square base which flares out to rather bulging sides, while an urn-shaped basket (Pl. 4.66) narrows at the top. The shaping on both of these baskets has been controlled by regulating the weaving tension. A straight-sided basket is achieved by maintaining an even tension and equal distances between the stakes after the sides are turned up (Pl. 4.11). Another way to control the side shape is through the shaping of the stakes. Stakes may be shaped to taper or widen at certain points along their length. Tapering the stakes causes a basket to draw in, while widening them causes flaring. The top rim finalizes the shape of the basket body but does not always repeat the base shape.

Weaves

Weaves which form the basis for splitwork are **plain weave** (also known as "checkerwork" and "simple **plaiting**"), **twill weave**, and **hexagonal weave**. In each weave, the elements interlace in a particular series of over/under **movements** (here designated numerically in parentheses after the name of the weave). In *plain weave* (Fig. 4.2), the weaving elements pass over-one/under-one (1/1) approximately at right angles (Adovasio 1977, p. 99). Plain weave is by far the most common weave for split baskets and is used for both base and side weaving (Pl. 4.12).

In *twill weave* (Fig. 4.3), the weaving elements pass over two or more elements before passing under one or more elements approximately at right angles (Adovasio 1977, p. 99; Scholtz 1975, pp. 64–66). The most

Pl. 4.10   Lidded square-based storage basket, purchased in southeastern Ohio; origin uncertain. The small square base appears hardly large enough to support the bulging sides of this basket. The stakes are close together at the base, and then they spread farther apart to create the flared sides. The construction of the lid is different from that of the basket, because of the differences in shape. The lid is begun as for a round base, and then several bye-stakes are added in order to make it large enough to cover the top of the basket. The domed lid fits the rim of the basket and adds additional storage room. The lack of handles on this basket indicates that it was not intended to be moved. Dimensions: Basket: 12″ square base, 20 1/2″ top, 31″ s.h. Lid: 22″ diameter, 10 1/2″ high. Collection of Cynthia W. and Michael B. Taylor.

Pl. 4.11   Straight-sided round basket attributed to Shenandoah Valley, Virginia. From the small round base, the stakes are turned up with a gradual curve to form the straight sides. The broad alternating bands on the side are created by heartwood and sapwood weaving splits. This basket has no handles, and the wear suggests that it often was picked up by the top rims or held under an arm. The basket came from around Winchester, Virginia, and was said to have been used for apple picking, although it is more likely that it was used in its current function, as a wastebasket. Dimensions: 9″ base, 13″ top, 14 1/2″ s.h. Private collection.

Fig. 4.2   Plain weave (1/1) and splice.

Pl. 4.12   Plain woven rectangular-based basket, attributed to southeastern Ohio. Both the base and the sides are woven of plain weave (1/1). This base view shows the contrast between the plain weave of the open base and the closely worked sides. The spaces between the stakes of rectangular bases often are left open intentionally, to allow air to circulate or dirt and debris to drop through the bottom. In this basket, the corner stakes have been divided, allowing the corners to be woven tightly and rounded more. The squared rims have been relieved at the corners to aid their right-angled bends. Dimensions: 8 1/2″ x 10 1/2″ base, 11 1/2″ x 13 1/2″ top, 6 1/4″ s.h., 11″ o.h. Collection of Cynthia W. and Michael B. Taylor.

common twill patterns in oak split work are over-two/under-two (2/2) and over-three/under-three (3/3). In a regular twill pattern, each row of weaving is offset by one stake, creating a distinctive stairstep diagonal pattern. Many variations of twill are possible, some of which produce elaborate patterns. Baskets may have a twilled base but change to plain weaving on the sides, or they may be constructed completely of twill weave (Pl. 4.13; Cl. Pl. 12). A twill-woven base, because of its close structure, requires more stake material than a plain woven base. Twill is used for square- and rectangular-based baskets but only rarely for round ones.

While twillwork is a specialty of the southeastern Indians, it is also used by non-native basketmakers. It appears that the Handicraft Revival encouraged some twillwork designs. In the North Carolina mountains, twill-woven "scrap baskets," garden baskets, and wood baskets were made and marketed through the Allanstand Cottage Industries (ACI ca. 1917,

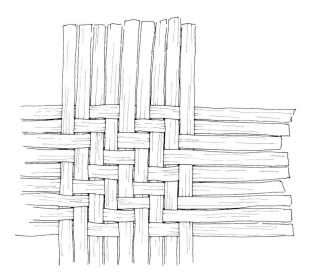

Fig. 4.3 Twill weave (2/2).

Pl. 4.13 Twill basket with dyed weavers. Found in eastern Tennessee (Dalton, 1 Dec. 1984); origin uncertain. Both the base and sides of this basket are woven in twill (2/2), and brown-dyed weavers accent the diagonal pattern created by the twill weave. This twill is spiraled by skipping under one stake instead of two at the beginning of each row. The under-one skip can be seen beginning at the far right of the basket, from which point it moves regularly up the side to the left. Dimensions: 6 1/2″ square base, 6 1/2″ s.h., 11″ o.h. Collection of Kathleen and Ken Dalton.

ca. 1920, ca. 1930). Many of these baskets had tacked rims and handles (see lidded twill basket in Pl. 1.2).

In *hexagonal weave* (Fig. 4.4) the elements are interlaced over-one/ under-one as in plain weave, but in hexagonal weave, no elements interlace at right angles. Instead, the elements interlace at oblique angles, creating hexagonal spaces (Scholtz 1975, p. 107). Baskets made with this weave are not common in the Central and Southern Appalachian Moun-

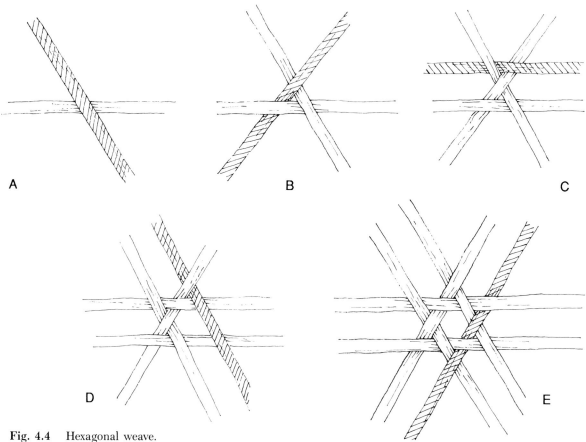

A   B   C

D   E

Fig. 4.4   Hexagonal weave.

Pl. 4.14   Hexagonally plaited oak split basket, attributed to the Rutter family, Athens County, Ohio. Jane Rutter and her daughter Nora Rutter made hexagonally woven "work baskets" in a range of sizes. Family members, both male and female, also made round- and rectangular-based split baskets (Pls. 4.16-a, b), but only the women made ones with hexagonal weave (Joyce, 15 May 1984 and 8 Apr. 1986; Rutter, 19 Aug. 1989; Elmer Knott, 19 Aug. 1989; Knott and Knott, 20 Aug. 1989). The basket was used by the women "for sewing, crocheting, knitting, the like—to hold the yarn and scraps of material for your work" (Edna Knott, 19 Aug. 1989). Dimensions: 8″ base, 11 1/2″ top, 6″ s.h. Collection of Marilyn Kemble.

tains. In the northeastern United States, the Delaware Indians (who were later displaced to Oklahoma) made hexagonally-woven work baskets, which were used by women (Turnbaugh and Turnbaugh 1986, p. 19). In the same region, other large, shallow, hexagonally-woven baskets were used in the making of cheese, while smaller baskets were used as clam baskets and egg baskets. Hexagonally-woven oak split baskets (Pl. 4.14) were made by Jane Rutter and her daughter Nora Rutter, both of Athens County, Ohio, who called them "work" baskets (Joyce, 15 May 1984; Rutter, 19 Aug. 1989; Knott and Knott, 20 Aug. 1989).

Methods used to implement the preceding weaves include **row-by-row** and **spiraling**. On round-bottomed baskets, these methods are begun at the onset of weaving the base; while on rectangular-bottomed baskets, the weaving is started after the base has been completed and the stakes turned up for the sides.

The row-by-row method is worked with an even number of **working ends** (a term used to denote the number of ends of the stakes, rather than

Pl. 4.15   Cherokee double-wall basket from western North Carolina. This basket, worked row by row in plain weave, shows many decorative features used in Cherokee splitwork. Some of the weavers are dyed brown to make small patterns, and a curlicue overlay is added to the baskets' surfaces after the containers are woven. At the top of the back support, edge stakes are turned down every few rows of weaving. This stepped edge creates a decorative back to the baskets. Wall baskets are not common in oak splitwork. Dimensions: 4" x 6" base, 3 3/4" height of each basket, 19 1/2" o.h. Collection of Roddy and Sally Moore.

the number of stakes). This weaving method builds the sides up one row at a time, each row stacking on top of the previous one. A single row is woven and the ends of the weaving split overlapped (Fig. 4.2); the next row is worked beginning on a different side and alternating stakes to continue the plain weave. Row-by-row weaving is most often used for the sides of rectangular baskets woven with plain and twill weaves, and for baskets of hexagonal weave. Rarely is it used for round oak split baskets. This technique is often used with split baskets which are accented by colored bands, such as many of the baskets made by the Cherokees (Cl. Pl. 11; Pls. 4.15, 4.36, 4.48).

Spiraling a weave to build a basket body is common to all shapes of splitwork woven with plain and regular twill weaves. Spiraling is accomplished by using one weaver and an odd number of working ends, or by using two weavers with an even number of working ends. The objective of spiraling is to continue the weaving in pattern as each round of weaving builds upon itself.

Splitting a stake and using a single weaver (Fig. 4.5-a, b) is the most common spiral technique found on plain woven white oak split baskets. Splitting one stake gives an odd number of working ends. The odd number allows the plain weave to spiral continuously, alternating over and under stakes, as the base and/or sides of a basket are woven. While some basketmakers start with one wider stake in anticipation of spiraling with a split stake, most use a stake of the same width and divide it in half, creating two narrower spokes.

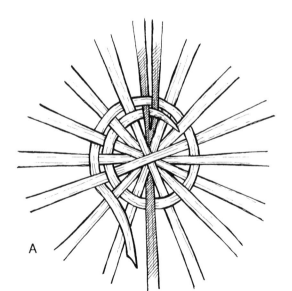

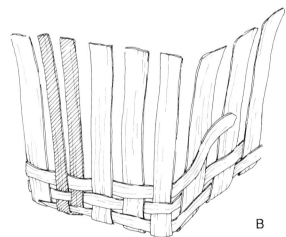

Fig. 4.5   Spiraling with a split stake:
(a) spiraling a round base;
(b) spiraling the sides of a rectangular-based basket.

Fig. 4.6 Spiraling with a skipped stake.

Other less common spiral techniques woven with a single weaver include: the addition of an odd number of **bye-stakes**—short stakes, tapered at one end, that are inserted into the base structure; and spiraling by skipping a stake. The skipped-stake spiral skips over or under stakes (effectively creating an odd number of ends without splitting or adding a stake) at the beginning of each round, in order to keep in alternating pattern (Fig. 4.6). The addition of bye-stakes is most frequent in round- or oval-based baskets, while skipped-stake spirals are used in regularly patterned twillwork and plain-woven baskets. Skipped-stake spiraling often is used only on round bases, but if it continues up the basket sides, a distinct diagonal line is formed where the weaver has skipped stakes from row to row.

A spiral technique termed **chasing** uses an even number of working ends and two weavers (Fig. 4.7-a, b). The weavers are used simultaneously, with one following the other as each moves over and under alternate stakes. This plain-weave technique is particularly well suited for baskets, round or rectangular, that are woven with color. When the stakes and the weavers are dyed, a number of designs are possible. The baskets from Botetourt County (Cl. Pl. 10) and Pulaski County, Virginia (Cl. Pl. 16) are fine examples of chasing with colored weavers.

Splices are made when a weaver is used up and a new piece must be

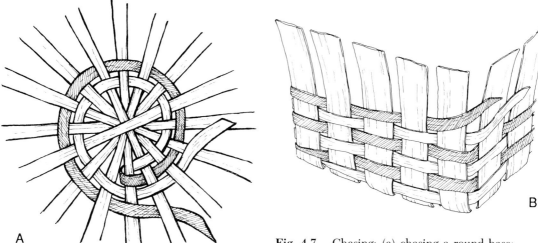

Fig. 4.7 Chasing: (a) chasing a round base; (b) chasing the sides of a rectangular-based basket.

added to continue the weaving. Splices for all three weaves are made by overlapping the ends of the exhausted and new weavers (Fig. 4.2). The overlap is usually long enough to weave through the stakes for at least one movement.

Decoration and Signatures

Ornamentation of split baskets is well known in Cherokee splitwork. The use of color is traditional, with many of the plain-woven baskets showing variations in the widths of the weavers and stakes to emphasize vertical or horizontal designs. When the weaving splits are dyed in twillwork, as is often done in Cherokee basketwork, the diagonal pattern designs are highlighted (Pl. 4.36). In plain-woven baskets, the Cherokees sometimes use a **curlicue overlay**, a technique in which an extra split is threaded through the weaving after the basket body is woven, to form curls on the outer surface of the basket (Pls. 4.15 and 4.47). This type of curl work appeared first in the Northeast ca. 1850, after which it apparently spread to other areas (Turnbaugh and Turnbaugh 1986, p. 115).

Ornamentation is found on non-native baskets as well, but it cannot be identified as belonging to any particular ethnic group. Colored bands are worked with dyed weavers (Cl. Pl. 14), and in some instances color is applied only to specific sections of the stakes or weavers. Decorative weaves are not a regular feature of non-native baskets, but the rare example does occur, as on baskets made by Walter Longabaugh (Pls. 4.43-a, b), which were constructed with a **soumak** weave near the top rim. Some of the lashing or handle treatments (detailed in later sections) may be considered decorative features of a basket.

A basket's shape, construction details, workmanship, and ornamentation all combine to link a basket to a particular basketmaker or region. Details of base constructions, methods of weaving, turndowns, rims, handles, feet, and lashings are specific to particular makers and often constitute regional "trademarks." Workmanship includes the preparation, shaping, and finishing of the basket materials, as well as how they are used together. One of the most evident aspects of workmanship is how a basket is woven; some makers take great care to make a tight, symmetrical basket, while others hastily "run up the sides." Another aspect is how the wood of a handle or rim is shaped; is the cross-section rounded, squared, or tri-angulated? Each detail of a basket must be taken into consideration when analyzing a basket for identification purposes.

Bases

1. Rectangular Bases

The simplest of the oak split baskets is a rectangular- or square-based basket. Square baskets have stakes of equal length, while rectangular baskets have long stakes for the length dimension and shorter ones for the width dimension. Baskets with a center overhead handle usually have an odd number of stakes on the sides where the handle is to be attached, to assure symmetrical placement and balance of the handle.

The most common base construction is plain weave (Pls. 4.16-a, b). Stakes of adjacent sides are kept at right angles, and small open spaces are left between the stakes. The spaces in the bottom of a basket often are left intentionally, to allow for air circulation and for dirt and debris to drop through.

If a closed base is preferred, the stakes sometimes are worked in twill weave, or often, after the base is completed, the spaces of a plain-woven base are filled in with short splits called **fillers**. Fillers are added to either the length or the width of the base. A rectangular-based basket attributed to southeastern Ohio (Pl. 4.20) has fillers woven along its lengthwise stakes, while baskets from Warren County, Tennessee (Pl. 4.17), have fillers

Pl. 4.16-a *(Above):* Elmer Knott, Athens County, Ohio, weaving the base of a hamper, 1988. Knott weaves an open plain weave base in his rectangular baskets. He says that it is important to have an uneven number of stakes (which he calls "ribs") on the side where the handle is to be placed. Both Elmer and his sister Nora Rutter learned basketmaking from their mother, Jane Rutter. As Nora recalled, "My mom could remember her grandmother and grandfather making baskets. It goes clear back as far as I can remember" (19 Aug. 1989). According to Elmer, his father was Welsh, and he believed that there was some Indian blood on his mother's side. Splitwork was the only type of basketmaking that they and all their relatives practiced. At the age of eighty, Knott continues to make rectangular-based baskets; he does not like to make round ones, although he made many in the past. "I talk them [customers] out of the notion of making them [round ones], if I can. They're *hard* to make. . . . You have to get down on your knees. . . . It takes about a half-hour or hour to get the bottom in them, the way you get that hump in them." Making bases of rectangular split baskets was much faster and did not hurt his back. When asked about the possibility of working at table height, Elmer replied, "You have to work the way you learned to work." Elmer had seventeen children, but only one, Elmer L. Knott, has learned to make baskets (Knott and Knott, 20 Aug. 1989). Photograph © by Christine Keith, used courtesy of Elmer Knott.

Pl. 4.16-b *(Opposite):* Weaving the sides. Elmer Knott weaves the sides of his baskets using the row-by-row method. He begins the sides using two weavers to help control the turned-up stakes. After these initial rounds, he splices each row on a different side from the previous row. In the background are several baskets awaiting top rims. Knott always lets the baskets dry before he turns down the stakes and adds either a single-notched overhead handle or double-notched ear handles, an inner and outer rim, and a crossed lashing (Knott and Knott, 20 Aug. 1989). Photograph © by Christine Keith, used courtesy of Elmer Knott.

Pl. 4.17   Rectangular split baskets with closed bases and skids, Warren County, Tennessee (Huddleston and Huddleston, 29 Nov. 1984). This closed base is created by weaving short stakes called "fillers" alongside the base stakes. The fillers are inserted into the baskets' sides to end. The carved feet on the base, known as "skids," protect and strengthen the bottom and sides as they overlay the base stakes and continue up the sides. See Pl. 4.40. Dimensions from left: 7″ x 10 1/2″ rectangular base, 10″ x 13″ top, 7″ s.h., 11 3/4″ o.h.; 8 1/4″ square base, 11 3/4″ x 12 3/4″ top, 8″ s.h., 12″ o.h. Collection of C.B. and Donna Huddleston.

woven alongside the short stakes, with the ends of the fillers worked up the basket sides. One ingenious maker crossed the fillers on the diagonal to produce an eye-catching cross-stitched base (Pls. 4.18-a, b).

Some basketmakers alter the weaving method in order to make a closed-bottomed basket. One method is to lay the stakes for one dimension of the basket side by side, while spacing the stakes in the other dimension farther apart. The edges of the closely spaced stakes usually are tapered at the base perimeter to facilitate weaving the basket sides. Another base construction alternates weaving stakes with fillers, until the base is completed (Fig. 4.8). These fillers form a structural part of the base, rather than being an addition after the base is woven. As each filler is woven, the ends are turned back upon themselves and tucked into the weaving. Although this base construction is not common, baskets with the stake-and-filler base have been found scattered throughout the central Appalachian region. The unusual oval-shaped basket with a framed foot, thought to be from Virginia (Pl. 4.19), is woven with fillers, as is the large storage basket found in Tennessee (Pls. 4.63-a, b).

Pl. 4.18-a Rectangular-based basket from Scott County, Virginia (King, 10 May 1985). The handle is painted green, but the rest of the basket is a deep brown, dark from years of handling. From the top, this basket appears to be a well-constructed but plain basket. Dimensions: 7″ x 9″ base, 9″ square top, 7″ s.h., 10 3/4″ o.h. Collection of Marcus Farthing King.

Pl. 4.18-b Base view of basket in Pl. 4.18-a. The filled-in base is unusual; the base fillers are woven on the diagonal to fill the spaces in the plain woven base, creating a crisscross pattern.

After the base is woven, a single row occasionally is woven around the perimeter to hold the bottom in shape (Pls. 4.20-a, b). This holding row makes the base a bit larger, but, more importantly, it helps in controlling the stakes while they are turned up for the sides.

Corners of rectangular baskets are sometimes modified in order to change the squared shape of the basket base into a more rounded form. Some makers round the corners by splitting the corner stakes (Pls. 4.2 and 4.12) or by adding corner bye-stakes. Baskets from southeastern Ohio and neighboring counties of West Virginia (although not solely baskets from those areas), often have one bye-stake added diagonally to the base at each corner before the sides are woven (Pls. 4.20-a, b). Occasionally baskets are begun with a rectangular base construction and then are made oval by adding several bye-stakes at each corner (Pls. 4.19 and 5.49).

One of the strongest, most beautifully shaped square-based baskets is one with a cross-braced bottom (Pls. 4.21-a, b) attributed to Craig

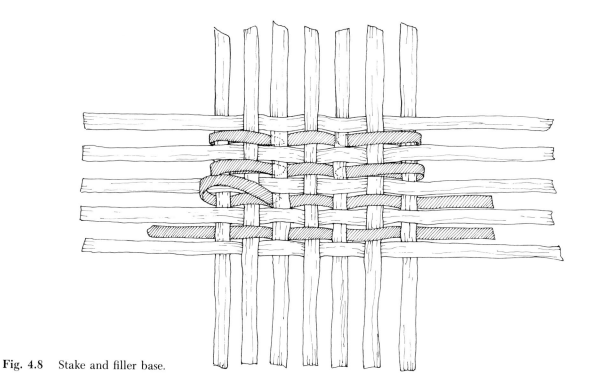

Fig. 4.8   Stake and filler base.

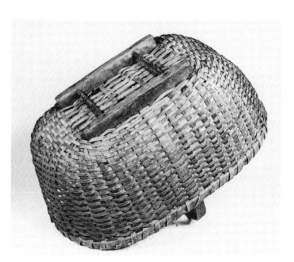

Pl. 4.19   Stake-and-filler base construction on basket attributed to Virginia (Doolin, 19 Feb. 1985). The stakes for the width of this basket are threaded through holes in a wooden frame, making the framed foot a structural part of the basket. The handle hoop also acts as a stake of the base and sides. Several bye-stakes are added at each corner, creating an oval-shaped basket. Dimensions: 7″ x 10″ frame foot, 14 1/2″ x 22″ oval top, 10″ s.h., 17″ o.h. Collection of Datha Doolin.

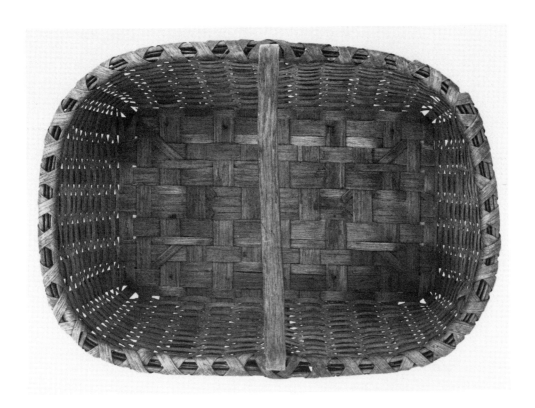

Pl. 4.20-a   Rectangular-based split basket with corner bye-stakes. The addition of a bye-stake at each corner is common in baskets of southeastern Ohio and neighboring West Virginia but is not confined to those regions. The bye-stakes allow for a tightly-woven corner and also give the basket body a more oval shape. The base is plaited in plain weave, and a holding row is worked around the base perimeter to help secure the stakes. Dimension: 15″ x 21″ base, 8″ s.h., 14″ o.h. Collection of Mr. and Mrs. Robert H. Schafer.

Pl. 4.20-b   Corner detail of basket in Pl. 4.20-a. As the holding row is woven, the weaver is given a half-twist at each corner. Bye-stakes then are inserted before the stakes are turned up for the sides. Also visible are the "fillers" which close in the spaces in the plaited base.

Pl. 4.21-a   Cross-braced, square-bottom split basket. Baskets with this base construction are known from Craig County, Virginia, and neighboring Monroe County, West Virginia (Moore, 20 June 1984; Nash and Nash, 10 May 1988). Because of the height created by the bottom bracing and skids, this basket appears to float above its base (Pl. 4.21-b). Dimensions: 4″ square base, 6 1/2″ top, 4″ s.h., 7 1/4″ o.h. Collection of Roddy and Sally Moore.

Pl. 4.21-b   Base view of basket in Pl. 4.21-a. The plain woven base is worked tightly, leaving very little space between the stakes. One of the diagonal braces has been split to give the odd number necessary for spiraling in plain weave. The fortified base construction certainly is not needed on a basket so small, but large bushel baskets of this construction are known (Nash and Nash, 10 May 1988). The carved outside single-notched handle has tails which extend into the base.

County, Virginia. At first glance, this basket is easily mistaken for a round-based one, because of the bulging sides and the nearly perfectly round top rim. Laid in just after the base is woven, the diagonally-crossed braces are tapered from each end to the corner of the base and become additional side stakes. The basket rests on the two thick parallel skids, which also add structural support to the base and sides.

2. Round Bases

Typical round-bottomed split baskets have stakes which intersect each other and radiate out from the center of the base, much like spokes of a wheel. Popular terms for round-base constructions include "spoked construction" and "spider base." Although nearly all round baskets are begun with a spoked construction, there is diversity in the number and shape of the stakes. Small baskets may have as few as four stakes while very large baskets may have as many as twenty-four. Round baskets often have stakes which are tapered to their center section, the part of the stake that forms the basket bottom. Tapering the stakes allows the base to be woven close to the center of the basket, creating a base stronger than those created by untapered stakes. Some baskets, particularly those made in southcentral Kentucky, central Tennessee, southeastern Ohio, and parts of Pennsylvania, have straight stakes (Pls. 4.22, 4.25, 4.61). Not tapering the stakes reduces significantly the time needed for material preparation and weaving.

The order in which stakes are laid out for round bases varies, but one general principle remains true, regardless of the number of stakes: stakes are laid out so that the weaver locks the positioned stakes in place on the first round. This effect is achieved by laying out half of the stakes equally spaced and then laying the second half in the spaces between the first stakes (Fig. 4.9).

Double-Bottom Base

The most common base construction found throughout the entire central and southern Appalachian region is the **double bottom**, made with sixteen stakes. The distinction of the double-bottom base is that it is made with two separate sets of stakes in two layers; the first set of eight stakes is laid out and woven for a few rows, and then a second set of eight stakes is laid into the spaces between the first set. The weaver from the first bottom locks in the added stakes by passing under the first stakes and over the second set (Fig. 4.10). The double-bottom base is woven to its completion with all sixteen stakes.

Two common layouts are the "right angle," used for both sets of bottom stakes (Fig. 4.9), and the "spiral," used most often for the second set of stakes only (Fig. 4.10; Pl. 4.23). Most double-bottomed baskets have only one bottom woven, with the second set of stakes laid to either the inside or the outside of the base. However, some makers weave both sets of stakes before joining them together. Compare two baskets, both with

Pl. 4.22 Basket merchant. "John Carter, who operates a stand at Munfordville [Kentucky], puts final touches on a basket to take eggs to market," reads the caption on this 1940 photo. His round basket clearly shows the wide, untapered stakes common in round split baskets of southcentral Kentucky. Both rib and split baskets with colored splits are being sold here. Photograph by Miller, reprinted with permission of the Louisville, Ky., *Courier-Journal* and the *Louisville Times*.

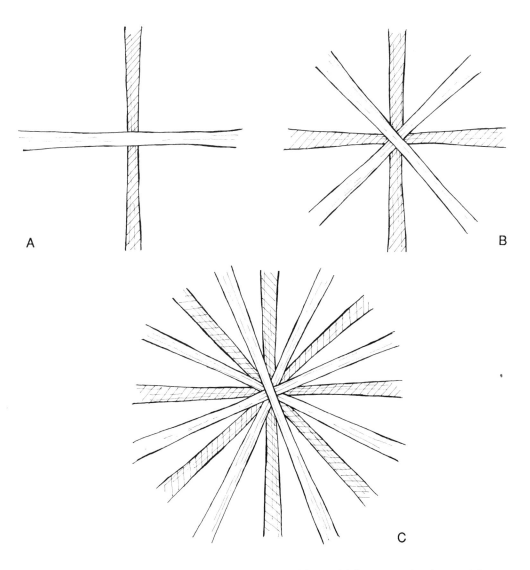

Fig. 4.9   Eight-stake right-angle layout for a round base: (a) first pair of stakes at right angles; (b) adding the second pair of stakes; (c) completed layout.

double-bottom constructions (Pls. 4.24-a, b; 4.25). The basket made by Sherman Luke of Noble County, Ohio (Luke, 22 Apr. 1985) (Pl. 4.24-b), has sixteen tapered stakes; the second bottom has been added to the inside of the basket, forming a high dome in the center. The basket made by Sarah Wayt Billetter of Belmont County, Ohio (Pl. 4.25), has only twelve stakes, and the second bottom, constructed of stakes with little taper, has been added to the outside; the base is fairly flat. Sarah Billetter taught

Pl. 4.23 Round double-bottomed basket with spiraled second bottom. The stakes of a second bottom often are added in a spiral when woven into the base. The most unusual feature of this basket is the number of stakes—fourteen, seven in each bottom. The narrow rims are tacked in several places with small square iron nails, which have left dark streaks in the wood. The stakes have been cut off at the top edge of the basket, and the figure-eight lashing is worked between and through the stakes, a finishing detail of many baskets from westcentral Virginia. This basket was found in a rural church in southeastern Kentucky, and the wear reflects its possible use as an offering tray. Dimensions: 6 1/2″ base, 9″ top, 3″ s.h. Collection of Cynthia W. and Michael B. Taylor.

Fig. 4.10 Laying a spiraled second bottom in a double-bottom base.

her son, Samuel E. Billetter, to make baskets with this same double-bottom construction. While Samuel used oak, he also made split baskets from other types of woods (Pl. 1.4) (Myers, 10 Oct. 1984; Horward, 4 Apr. 1951; Gladden, 28 Sept. 1984). S.E. Billetter and Sherman Luke were contemporaries who lived in adjacent counties. Their baskets, however, show the differences which can be found even within a small geographical region, because the makers were working within different basket traditions.

White-oak basketmakers describe the process of weaving a round base as "building," "plaiting," and, occasionally, "stitching" the bottom of the basket. The weaving begins close to the center and most often is worked in a continuous spiral technique that interlaces the stakes. The direction of the spiral may vary with the individual basketmaker's hand preference or method of working.

Pl. 4.24-a Double-bottomed round split basket made in the early 1900s by Sherman Luke (1870–1940), Noble County, Ohio. Luke dug coal for a living, but during the evenings and winters, he often worked on baskets for his own use or to trade or sell to neighbors (Luke, 22 Apr. 1985). The domed base, the low broad shape of the basket body, and the carved handle, with its squared shape (due to the long thick grip of the bow), are distinctive features of Luke's work. The splits in Luke's basket are extremely smooth, and, according to his son, he scraped the splits with glass from old bottles. He also used a shaving horse and drawknife, but he whittled the handle notches with his knife (Luke, 22 Apr. 1985). Dimensions: 10″ base, 12 1/2″ top, 7″ s.h., 11 1/2″ o.h. Collection of Bill and Glenna Luke.

Pl. 4.24-b Base view of basket in Pl. 4.24-a. Domed bases are not common on central and southern Appalachian baskets. The stakes of this basket are smoothed and tapered to a narrow point in the middle, where they form a definite peak in the center of the base. From the outside, the addition of the second bottom is barely detectable. The dome-shaped base allows air to circulate and gives the basket a level seat.

A skilled basketmaker at work is a sight to behold. The long stakes of the unfinished basket whirl around quickly while nimble fingers skillfully interlace the weavers (Pl. 4.26). Irskel Nicholson describes his method of laying out and weaving the first set of stakes of a double-bottom basket:

> Now this is a sixteen-rib [stake] one. Now always start with the split rib. The first rib you lay down is the split rib, you've got to use one. . . . You lay out the first ribs which would be half of whatever you use. Of course, you could use eight, twelve, sixteen, twenty, twenty-four, any even amount. . . . Criss-cross them. Always lay the last one [stake] down next to the split rib. Your first stitch

Pl. 4.25   Outside placement of the second bottom. Base view of basket made by Sarah Wayt Billetter (1835–1892), Belmont County, Ohio (Myers, 10 Oct. 1984) (Pl. 1.4). This double-bottom base construction and foot are common on baskets from central and eastern Ohio. While the stakes of the first bottom are tapered so that they can be woven near the center, where they cross, there is little taper to the stakes of the second bottom. The second bottom is woven into the base just before the stakes turn up. A thick foot is lashed to the base to allow the basket to sit level. Dimensions: 12″ top, 7 3/4″ s.h., 13 1/2″ o.h. Collection of Edith Billetter Myers.

helps to hold that one down. We always hold them with the thumb, just spin . . . go on around and keep on plaiting it, weaving it up. . . . You spin your basket to the left, stitch it to the right. Once you get that thing [the base] out to here you can go around just as fast as you can put them [the weaving splits] in. You are turning it all the time you are stitching it. (Nicholson and Nicholson, 16 Mar. 1985)

After the first bottom is woven, the second set of stakes is added (Fig. 4.10). Irskel Nicholson commented on some important points: the first base must be woven out far enough so that the stakes of the second bottom can go in between the stakes of the first bottom, and there also must be enough room to allow the weaving split to be worked snugly against the previously woven row. "Use these splits very thin when you start out. If you use them thin, they'll go in easy." If the weaving split is in the correct position, then the stakes of the second bottom are secured in place as the base is woven. Nicholson offers more advice: "When you lay the second bottom down, your [weaving] split has got to be to the underneath side of your split rib" (Nicholson and Nicholson, 16 Mar. 1985).

A typical Central Appalachian round split basket has only a slightly peaked center, unlike the exaggerated dome in Luke's basket (Pls. 4.24-a, b). While dome-based baskets are not common, they are stronger structurally, due to their convex curves. Most makers such as Lucy Cook of Page County, Virginia, just "punch in the bottom when we are finished to make it sit level" (Showen, 12 Mar. 1978).

Pl. 4.26   Oral ("Nick") Nicholson, Doddridge County, West Virginia, 1984, building a double-bottom round split basket. Having completed the base, Nicholson now begins weaving the sides. He holds the basket against his body to force the stakes to turn upward. Nicholson made baskets, and taught and demonstrated basketmaking at Fort New Salem, Salem, West Virginia. He learned basketmaking from relatives who left Virginia to settle in West Virginia (3 Oct. 1984). Nicholson is a descendent of Nicholson families who migrated from Madison and Page counties, Virginia, to Doddridge County, West Virginia, before the Civil War (Martin-Purdue 1983, p. 100).

Single-Bottom Bases

Single-bottom based baskets are defined as having a single layer of stakes in their base construction. Single bottoms may be made with any number of stakes, and the same weaving techniques used for double bottoms may also apply. Single bottoms, while used for all sizes of round baskets, are often used for small and miniature baskets where only a few stakes are sufficient for size requirements.

Large bushel and fireside baskets were made by Oscar Peters of Cabell County, West Virginia, using a sixteen-stake single base (Pl. 4.27-a). Peters carved the stakes, leaving a wide center section approximately four inches long, with sharply angled shoulders. The ends of the stakes were then tapered down to the shoulder. One stake was split so that the weaving could spiral, and then all stakes were laid out to begin the base (Pl. 4.27-b). The layout of the carved stakes makes a "medallion" center. Although Oscar is no longer living, this single base with a medallion center is being continued by his brother, John Peters of Wood County, West Virginia (John Peters, 1 Dec. 1989).

Lucy and William Cody Cook of Page County, Virginia, are well known for their baskets made using a single-bottom construction and split stakes (Pl. 4.28; Fig. 4.11). Lucy begins her large round baskets with eight wide stakes which taper to a narrow strip in the center. To spiral the weaving, she splits the stake laid down first and works the bottom diameter for several inches. In order to keep the weaving tight and increase the diameter of the base and the size of the basket, she then splits all the stakes, or "ribs," as she calls them, and she splits one a third time, to give the odd number of working ends (Fig. 4.11). Lucy claims that this method is her own invention and is much easier than the more typical traditional double-bottom construction (Cook and Cook, 14 Mar. 1985). Split-stake bottomed baskets are regional to the Virginia Blue Ridge, and many may have been made at the Cook home or by others in the vicinity who use the same method.

Single-based baskets made with bye-stakes are known in regions of eastern Tennessee and in neighboring areas of Virginia and North Carolina (Pls. 4.29, 4.30-a, b). Bye-staked bases typically begin with two to eight untapered stakes which are crossed at right angles. After the initial stakes are woven, bye-stakes are inserted into the weaving, in a manner similar to the way ribs are added in the sides of rib baskets (Fig. 4.12). The bye-stakes are the same thickness and often the same width as the initial stakes, but they are tapered at one end so that they can be inserted easily into the weaving. There is much diversity in bye-staked round-base

Pl. 4.27-a   *(Above):* Group of baskets made by Oscar Peters, Cabell County, West Virginia (George and George, 9 Jan. 1985). Peters learned basketmaking from his father, Frank Peters, who farmed and made baskets near Walker, West Virginia (John Peters, 1 Dec. 1989). Many of Peters' baskets found "new homes" through the Pancake Realty firm of Huntington, West Virginia, which gave one of his white oak baskets to each new owner (George and George, 9 Jan. 1985). Dimensions, clockwise from left: Bushel basket: 12″ base, 13 1/4″ s.h., 16″ o.h. Fireside basket: 11″ base, 21 1/2″ top, 4″ s.h., 11 1/2″ o.h. Rectangular basket: 7″ x 12″ base, 8 1/2″ s.h., 11 1/2″ o.h. Shopper: 4″ x 10″ base, 8 1/2″ s.h., 13 3/4″ o.h. Collection of Jane George.

Pl. 4.27-b   Round base detail of fireside basket in Pl. 4.27-a. One of the characteristics of Peters' work is the "medallion center" used on his round-based baskets. Sixteen stakes are carved identically and laid out to form this distinctive base.

Pl. 4.28 Lucy Cook, Page County, Virginia, 1985, with bushel baskets. Part of a winter's work is represented here in the Cooks' storage room. As the Cooks produce many baskets, they have adopted techniques which not only are functional but also save time. These baskets with a split-stake construction require less material preparation and are much quicker to weave than ones with the traditional double-bottom construction (Cook and Cook, 14 Mar. 1985).

Appalachian White Oak Basketmaking

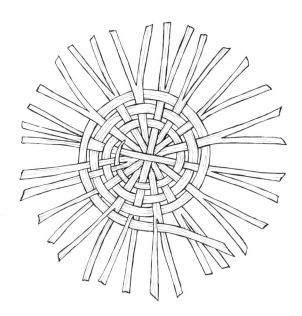

Fig. 4.11   Single-bottom split-stake round base.

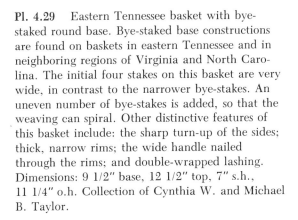

Pl. 4.29   Eastern Tennessee basket with bye-staked round base. Bye-staked base constructions are found on baskets in eastern Tennessee and in neighboring regions of Virginia and North Carolina. The initial four stakes on this basket are very wide, in contrast to the narrower bye-stakes. An uneven number of bye-stakes is added, so that the weaving can spiral. Other distinctive features of this basket include: the sharp turn-up of the sides; thick, narrow rims; the wide handle nailed through the rims; and double-wrapped lashing. Dimensions: 9 1/2″ base, 12 1/2″ top, 7″ s.h., 11 1/4″ o.h. Collection of Cynthia W. and Michael B. Taylor.

constructions, with variations in the number of initial stakes and bye-stakes and in the way bye-stakes are inserted. Bye-staked baskets may be woven with a split-stake spiral (Pl. 4.30-b), or spiraled by inserting an extra stake to make an uneven number of working ends (Pl. 4.29).

The bye-staked baskets tend to have a certain appearance which is quite different from that of other round-based baskets. The stakes often are quite thick, and sometimes there is an extra rim at or near the base. The basket sides are turned up sharply from the base, resulting in a shape resembling a bucket. The stakes often are tacked to the top rim rather than lashed, particularly if the stakes are thick.

4. Split Baskets   161

Pl. 4.30-a Handleless bye-staked round-based basket, purchased in western North Carolina; origin uncertain. Bye-staked round baskets tend to have similar appearances: the stakes are often thick (like "staves"), and the sides of the basket generally are turned up sharply, making a fairly straight-sided basket with a flat bottom. Dimensions: 13 1/2″ base, 17 1/2″ top, 8″ s.h. Collection of H. Wayne and Rachel Nash Law.

Pl. 4.30-b Base detail of basket in Pl. 4.30-a. The initial base layout uses eight thick stakes. One of the stakes is split to make an odd number of working ends, so that the base can be plain-woven in a spiral. After a few rounds of weaving, two tapered bye-stakes are inserted beside every other stake.

Fig. 4.12 Single-bottom bye-staked round base.

Ralph Chesney of Union County, Tennessee, makes an ornate and finely finished bye-staked round basket (Pl. 4.31). The initial stakes are quite thick and are whittled to a narrow width in the center. The bye-stakes are of the same thickness, and the ends are sharpened to a fine point. When the base is woven, a delicate star effect is created, a stunning contrast to the solid sides formed from the thick stakes and wide weavers. All of the materials of Chesney's baskets are scraped and sanded several times, making the baskets extremely smooth. The foot rim at the very outer edge of the base occasionally is seen on round baskets, but the decorative braids which cover the rims and handle are rare. As Ralph once said, "It's hard to imagine all the work that goes into making one of these baskets" (Chesney and Chesney, 26 Nov. 1984).

A last type of single bottom is reminiscent of base constructions typical of wickerwork baskets, where the stakes are laid out to intersect each other in groups of three or more (see chapter 5). In Lincoln County, West Virginia, Ethel Bias, daughter of oak basketmaker Claude Linville and willow basketmaker Emmer Linville, experimented with different construction techniques. She made lidded sewing baskets (Pl. 4.67) and straight-sided wastebaskets with wickerwork base constructions. Bias was quite innovative (Pl. 1.15), but she also copied requested baskets (George and George, 9 Jan. 1985). White oak split baskets with base layouts in wickerwork techniques are rare and may reflect the influence of foreign models, published literature, or perhaps basketmakers more familiar with wickerwork techniques.

3. Oval Bases

Oval-bottomed split baskets are by far the least common of all split baskets. Oval baskets present a dilemma intrinsic to no other base shape: how to regulate the varying distances between the stakes that produce its unique elliptical shape. Some oval bases are set up like double-bottomed round bases, but with the center weaving elongated to an oval (Pl. 4.32). Other bases use constructions more typical of rectangular bases, beginning with plaiting the stakes over and under each other and then adding bye-stakes at each corner to round out the ends (Pl. 4.19). A third oval base is made entirely of bye-stakes (Pls. 4.33-a, b). This particular basket is constructed with a handle hoop for a stake, with the bye-stakes always added alongside the handle hoop. The stakes of this basket vary in width in order to retain equal spacing after the turn up.

Pl. 4.31 Ralph Chesney, Union County, Tennessee, 1985. Ralph makes baskets of two types: round split baskets with bye-staked bases, identical to baskets made by his father, Carr Chesney (ca. 1875–1951); and rib baskets. Both Ralph and his father did carpentry work. Ralph built not only his house, but also many of its furnishings. The most impressive pieces of furniture were a table and a rocker, both with nicely turned legs. When asked about the furniture, Ralph commented that he had whittled the symmetrical spindles and "turnings" with his pocket knife. Sharing his philosophy, Ralph quietly said, "I look over every basket that I make and always say, 'What can I do to improve on that?' Every basket that I make, I try to make it a little better" (Chesney and Chesney, 26 Nov. 1984 and 4 Feb. 1985).

Pl. 4.32 Elmer Price, Shenandoah County, Virginia, 1985, building an oval split basket. Oval-based baskets are not common. Price uses eight stakes for the base but adjusts the taper and length of the stakes, as well as the angles where they cross in the center, to create an oval base. He is careful to keep the oval shape while he weaves the base and the sides. Occasionally Price makes large oval baskets: "I've made them clean up to hold two gallons, once in a while, like that." Price sometimes makes three or four differently-shaped baskets starting with the same base construction. Price is always thinking up new designs: "I get a lot of notions for some reason or another, I don't know why, I just try it" (Price, 14 Mar. 1985).

Pl. 4.33-a Oval basket with bye-staked base, found in a farmhouse in Culpeper County, Virginia; origin uncertain (Elder, 10 June 1983). The ends of the overhead handle are overlapped and joined, forming a continuous hoop which is flattened for the base of the basket (Pl. 4.33-b). The preformed handle hoop is an integral part of the basket structure, with the flattened section of the handle determining the base dimensions. The figure-eight lashing runs through holes pierced in the wide stakes, and much has remained intact despite the wear this basket has received. Dimen-

sions: 8″ x 9″ oval base, 11″ x 12 1/2″ oval top, 7 1/4″ s.h., 11 1/4″ o.h. Private collection.

Pl. 4.33-b Base detail of basket in Pl. 4.33-a. The vertical base stake is comprised of the overlapping ends of the handle hoop. All other stakes in this base construction are short, tapered bye-stakes which are added to create the oval base.

4. Plank Bases

The plank bottom, made from a wood board, is the simplest basket base. The origin of plank bottoms is unknown, but the use of a board bottom seems to appear wherever split basketmaking and woodland crafts are traditional. In West Germany's Hessen district, pack baskets were made with plank bottoms shaped from beech (Gandert 1963, p. 22), and, in the South Tyrols of Austria, plank bases for baskets were cut from birch (Will 1985, p. 38). In this country, different shapes of veneer baskets were made with plank bases. On Nantucket Island, Massachusetts, the making of plank-bottomed baskets was recorded in the mid-1850s (Seeler 1972, pp. 7–9). Plank-bottomed baskets are found in scattered instances throughout the Central and Southern Appalachians and do not seem to be confined to any specific region.

Plank bottoms are made from various woods and in all shapes and sizes. Once the plank is shaped, side stakes are either tacked along the edge (Cl. Pl. 13; Pls. 4.34-a, b) or inserted into holes bored in the base (Pl. 4.35). Baskets with plank bottoms often are made with the thick, wide side-stakes sometimes called "staves" (Irwin 1982, pp. 67–68), perhaps because of their resemblance in construction and appearance to barrel staves. These "staves" are often tacked to rims at the top to make a framework before the sides are woven. The use of plank bases allows the construction of enormous baskets, such as the basket sleigh from the eastern West Virginia Alleghenies (Pl. 4.35).

Pl. 4.34-a   Round plank-bottomed basket; origin unknown. Planks of varying shapes and sizes are found as bases on split baskets. Dimensions: 3 1/2″ base, 6 1/2″ top, 3 1/4″ s.h. Collection of Dianne and Kelly Mink.

Pl. 4.34-b   Base detail of basket in Pl. 4.34-a. The base is made of pine, and the side stakes are secured between the edge of the wooden base and a base rim hoop and fastened with small wooden pegs. Baskets with solid bottoms have varying numbers of stakes, depending on the size of the base and width of the stakes.

Pl. 4.35   Basket sleigh from eastern West Virginia (Haney, 14 Jan. 1986). It is painted blue and still has much of the original paint. Heavy stakes are inserted into holes in the plank base. The gracefully shaped body of the basket is approximately two by three-and-a-half feet at the base. The shape is reinforced by the heavy top rim and thick round rod, lashed in the figure-eight technique. Dimensions of entire sleigh: 73″ long and 46″ high. Collection of David Haney.

Turning Up and Side Weaving

After a base is completed, the basketmaker turns up the stakes to form the sides of the basket. The first few weaving rows determine the side shape of the basket. Weaving with a firm tension will cause the sides to be straight, while a more relaxed tension will give the sides more flare. Once these first rows are worked, the initial shape cannot be changed unless the weaving is removed and rewoven.

In round- and oval-based baskets, the side weaving is a continuation of the base weaving, and in most cases, the same weaving split is continued from the base up the sides. The basketmaker is careful to keep the distance between the stakes equal, as well as to work the weaving split at an even tension to turn all stakes up at the same angle. The symmetry of the basket depends on these skills. In rectangular baskets, where only the stakes are the base components, the stakes are usually turned up before any weaving splits are begun. The critical points for shaping these baskets are the corners. Controlled tension at the corners is needed to create a rectangular basket with even corners and the desired side shape.

Finishing Details

1. Turndown and Rims

When the basketmaker has spiraled the sides of a basket, the last weaver is generally tapered and woven to its end. Occasionally, one final wider weaving row is added at the top of the basket to make a definite row for the rim attachment. The ends of the stakes are turned down over the top weaving row and pushed down into the weaving alongside the stakes (Fig. 4.13). If the stakes are wide or thick, the ends are often narrowed or thinned so they can be folded and tucked more easily (Pl. 4.9). The turndown varies: some makers turn down all stakes, alternately turning to the inside and the outside of the basket, while others turn down every other stake and cut off the remaining stakes flush to the top of the basket. Baskets with nailed-on rims and those with lashings which pierce the stakes generally are not turned down; rather, the stakes are cut flush to the top rim (Pls. 4.23 and 4.57; Fig. 4.1-a).

Basketmakers refer to the process of finishing the basket edge as "rim the basket" (Nicholson and Nicholson, 16 Mar. 1985), "bind the basket" (M. Ross, 8 May 1985), or "put on the hoops and handles" (O. Nicholson, 3 Oct. 1984). The rims are prepared and constructed in the same manner as hoops for rib baskets: the ends are scarfed to form a smooth continuous band when joined (Fig. 4.14), but in this case usually only the outer edges are beveled. Each maker has a preference for a particular rim thickness and width and usually will use the same rim treatment on both round and rectangular baskets. Some makers add a **filler**, a piece of wood made to fit into the space between the basket rims. Cherokee split baskets often have a rounded rod used as a filler (Pl. 4.48) or a thin split which rests on top of the rims.

Most oak split baskets have both inner rims and outer rims. Cherokee splitwork typically is finished with a thick outer rim and a thin split for

Fig. 4.13   Turndown.

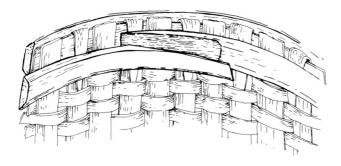

Fig. 4.14
Scarf join of an inner rim.

an inner rim. Baskets made by the Cooks, Nicholsons, and others from the Blue Ridge Mountains of Virginia, however, have only an outer rim and no inner rim (Pls. 4.28, 4.38-a, 4.39; Cl. Pl. 14). These Blue Ridge baskets have stakes turned down to the outside only, with the outside rim holding the turndown.

The shaping of the rim determines the shape of the top of the basket: round, square, oval, or rectangular. The rim is bent into shape while the wood is green and allowed to dry before it is lashed to the basket. The drying time allows the wood to shrink and makes it possible for the handles and the rims to fit better on the basket and the lashing to remain tight. Basketmakers who make many baskets of the same size make many rims at a time. Lucy Cook stores her curved rims inside a finished round basket in order to keep them shaped properly while they dry (Cook and Cook, 14 Mar. 1985). Irskel Nicholson has worked out a practical rim for his rectangular split baskets: he makes a rim in two sections, with each section bent into an open-ended rectangular shape. After completing the body of a basket, he fits the two dried rim sections to the basket by adjusting the overlap of the two pieces. In this way, he does not have to fit each rim to each basket, and the same rim pieces work for several different baskets (Nicholson and Nicholson, 16 Mar. 1985).

2. Handles

Handles are one of the most distinctive features of splitwork. Handles are either structural (woven as part of the basket body) or applied (attached after the basket is woven). The most common handle for split baskets is an **overhead handle**, made from a single piece of wood which spans the top of a basket. An overhead handle may be added after the basket body is woven or made first and incorporated into the base structure as a stake. Both large and small baskets often have **ear handles**, two small handles that most commonly are added to opposite sides of the basket for hand grips. Movable handles, known as **drop** or **swing handles**, are constructed with a **bail** attached to a pivot. Overhead, ear, and drop handles are quite diverse in workmanship and mode of attachment, ranging from a thick split, simply nailed or riveted to the rims, to elaborately carved notched handles. **Handle holes**, a type of structural handle, are made by leaving spaces in the weaving under the rim, so that the rims double as hand grips.

In making overhead, ear, or drop handles, the first step is the selection of wood that is straight and free from knots. The tough heartwood often is used for handles. However, if the handle has a tight bend, such as an ear handle or a small hinge for a swing handle has, then pliable, fine-grained sapwood is a necessity. Poor wood may crack or bend unevenly.

The dimensions of the handle billet vary with the type of handle. In most cases, the width of the handle billet is roughly equal to the width of the stakes. The thickness will depend upon the method of handle attachment. Thick billets are required for notched handles, while other handle types use thin billets. Except in the case of handle hoops, the length of the handle billet is measured to include the length of the **bow** (the length of the handle that spans the rims) plus the **tails** (the ends of the handle which are inserted down into the side weaving to help secure the handle). Many basketmakers work without rulers or tape measures, arcing a split across the top of a basket to determine the handle height and length of the bow. Handles may vary in height with the intended use of the basket: low handles provide better balance for a loaded basket, while high handles allow better access for getting items in and out of the basket.

Pl. 4.36 Cherokee twill-woven basket. A handle hoop with a lock join, a thick outer rim and a thin inner rim with a basic single lashing, and twill pattern work are details typical of Cherokee split baskets. The base of this basket is woven in a twill (2/2) with doubled stakes. The weaving splits were originally black and are woven one row at a time rather than spiraled. Woven patterns carried names and meanings special to the Indians. Martha Ross, Swain County, North Carolina, a contemporary Cherokee maker, calls this pattern "cross on the hill" (8 May 1985). Dimensions: 6 3/4″ x 11″ base, 7″ s.h., 12″ o.h. Private collection.

Overhead Handles

Structural overhead handles called "handle hoops" are preformed D-shaped hoops which are woven into the base and sides as a stake. In the case of this preshaped handle, the basketmaker determines the base size and also the side height of the basket by the shaping of the handle. In most cases, the ends of the handle are overlapped and secured in the same way as the ends of hoops in ribwork, and then are nailed, notched, and tied (Pl. 4.33-b), or they may be lock-joined (Fig. 3.2). The locked handle is a detail typical of rectangular split baskets made by the Cherokees (Pl. 4.36; Cl. Pl. 11). On the Qualla Reservation today, there are men who specialize in making these handles and provide them for other basketmakers who concentrate on weaving (M. Ross, 8 May 1985).

Nonstructural handles are shaped and placed on the basket before the rims are in place. A handle is centered on the basket and the tails inserted under the weaving splits along a stake. The tails of a handle may extend only down the basket sides or may continue into the base. If the tails continue into the base, the handle becomes an extra support at the bottom, adding strength. After the handle is in position, the rims are fitted to the top of the basket, and both handle and rims are lashed in place.

The "split-end" handle is one of the distinctive features of baskets regional to the Blue Ridge Mountains of Virginia (Pls. 4.38-a, b; 4.39; Cl. Pl. 14). This handle construction is quickly implemented. Split-end handles are made from a thick split with the ends shaped to conform to

Pl. 4.37 Irskel Nicholson, (b. 1925), Shenandoah County, Virginia, 1985, latching the ends of a split-end handle. He inserts the handle into his double-bottomed basket before the rim is cross-lashed in place. Irskel learned from his father Landon, who learned from *his* father, Thomas Jackson Nicholson (Nicholson and Nicholson, 13 and 16 Mar. 1985).

Pl. 4.38-a Virginia Blue Ridge Mountain baskets. These round split baskets are typical of those made for many generations by the Nicholson and Cook clan (see Martin-Perdue 1983, for family genealogy). Distinctive features of these split baskets are: only an outer rim, every other stake turned down to the outside, and split-end handles (Pl. 4.38-b). Dimensions, from left: 4″ base, 7″ top, 3 1/4″ s.h., 5 3/4″ o.h.; 4 1/4″ base, 7 1/2″ top, 3 1/4″ s.h., 6 3/4″ o.h. Collection of Benny Long.

Pl. 4.38-b Split-end handle detail of basket in Pl. 4.38-a. The end of the handle is split in half. One end is folded back toward the rim and tucked into the weaving, while the other end is slipped into the base.

Pl. 4.39 Rectangular lidded picnic basket. The split-end handle and the single outer top rim are identifying characteristics of this Virginia Blue Ridge basket. Another rim is lashed to the inside of the basket, about one-and-a-half inches below the top edge. This extra rim provides a ledge upon which the lid rests. The domed lid protects the contents and doubles as a tray. Dimensions: 9″ x 15″ base, 8 1/2″ s.h., 14 3/4″ o.h. Private collection.

the width and taper of the stakes. The ends are slipped under the weaving and alongside stakes on the outside of the basket (Pl. 4.37). The end of the handle is pushed out of the weaving at the base edge and then is split in half. Each split end is latched into place, one folded back toward the rim and the other end tucked into the bottom. Irskel Nicholson describes this technique as a "double latch handle" (Nicholson and Nicholson, 16 Mar. 1985), and Oral Nicholson descriptively calls it the "push-and-pull handle" (3 Oct. 1984). With the handle latched in place, it cannot be pushed down farther or pulled out, and, as it is held tightly by the weaving, there is little side-to-side movement.

One of the most common overhead handles is the notched handle (Fig. 4.15-a, b, c). Baskets are made with both double-notched handles (Pls. 4.24-a, 4.55, 4.27-a) and single-notched handles (Pls. 4.40; 4.41; 4.54-a, b; 4.62-a, b; Cl. Pls. 10 and 16). Notched handles often are carved with a thick center handgrip. The thick center does not bend and results in a square-shaped handle (Pls. 4.40, 4.24-a, 1.4). On baskets with finely crafted double-notched handles, the rims of the basket fit snugly into the carved notch, eliminating vertical or side-to-side handle movement. Single-notched handles have a greater tendency to slip sideways, and, if the ends of the handle do not extend into the base, there is always the possibility that the handle may be shoved down into the basket body. Many old baskets have breaks in the weaving where the notch has been pushed out of place.

To make a double-notched handle, the basketmaker first measures and cuts the handle billet to length. Then notches are marked on the tangen-

Pl. 4.40 Warren County, Tennessee, rectangular split baskets (Huddleston and Huddleston, 29 Nov. 1984). Both of these baskets have single-notched handles with a thick handhold in the center. The handles are bent to fit the inside of the basket. The side weaving is spiraled using a split stake to create an odd number of working ends. Other details of this regional style include: tapered stakes at the top edge which provide space for the wide lashing split, crossed lashings, and skids added to the base (Pl. 4.17). Collection of C.B. and Donna Huddleston.

tial surface of the billet to equal the width of the rim (Fig. 4.15-a). After the notches are cut out, the bow is carved, and the tails are shaved down below the shoulder of the notch to fit into the weaving (Fig. 4.15-b, c). The handle is bent to shape, fitted to the rims, and left to dry. Handles may be bent to fit either the inside or the outside rims of the basket. Inside placement is more common, as there is less tendency for the wood to crack or split at the notch when bent.

Some baskets are made with decorative woven overhead handles. Most woven overhead handles are formed by three or more heavy splits or rods which span across the top of the basket and then are woven with a thin weaving split. Often the center bow may be an overhead handle with two rounded rods added to either side (Pl. 4.56; Cl. Pl. 12). One rather unusual example is a shallow oval basket with a woven handle constructed from five heavy splits (Pl. 4.42). A woven and wrapped handle, as well as an unusual top rim treatment, was worked on the rectangular market basket made by Walter Longabaugh of Lancaster County, Pennsylvania (Steinmetz and Rice 1959, pp. 80–88) (Pls. 4.43-a, b).

Pl. 4.41 Round basket with single-notched over-head handle, ca. 1920s, attributed to Norman Lovell, a basketmaker who lived in Giles and Bland counties, Virginia (Arthur and Arthur, 11 Mar. 1985). The wood is left thick below the notch to support the rim of the basket, and the handle is fitted to the outside of the basket. The stakes have been cut below the rim to allow more room for working the basic single lashing. This double-bottom basket has both bases woven, and the weaving is spiraled by splitting a stake. Dimensions: 11 1/2″ base, 15″ top, 7″ s.h., 12 3/4″ o.h. Collection of Ralph and Sarah Arthur.

A

B

Fig. 4.15 Double-notched overhead handle:
(a) handle billet with notches marked to the width of the rim;
(b) carved handle;
(c) fitting a handle to a basket.

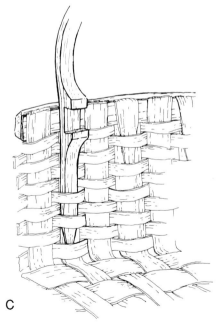

C

Pl. 4.42   Shallow oval basket with unusual woven handle; origin unknown. Five bows form this handle. The end and middle bows are slipped alongside a stake into the weaving, while the other two loop around the rim of the basket and are secured with the weaving of the handle. This basket has a triple-bottom base construction. The first base is woven slightly oval with six stakes, then a second bottom of six stakes is added in a spiral on the inside of the basket. After the second bottom is secured with a few weaving rows, a third bottom of twelve stakes is added to the bottomside in a spiral. Two sides of the basket are turned up to give the finished basket its shape. Baskets of this shape are commonly called "flower baskets." A sturdy lashed-on foot elevates the base. Dimensions: 9 1/4" x 10 1/2" oval base, 15" x 22" oval top, 7" s.h., 13" o.h. Collection of Susan D. Lott.

Pl. 4.43-a   Rectangular market basket of unusual design, attributed to Walter Longabaugh, Lancaster County, Pennsylvania. A photo showing Longabaugh carrying baskets he made appears in *Vanishing Crafts and Their Craftsmen* (Steinmetz and Rice 1959, p. 88); however, no information is recorded about how he learned to make this style. The shaping, top rim treatment (Pl. 4.43-b), and handle are unusual. Three handle bows are inserted alongside the three center side stakes, then they are woven separately close to the rim and gradually pulled together until they are wrapped as one piece. According to Steinmetz and Rice, Walter was a hermit, living in his log homestead in eastern Lancaster County, where he also made wreaths and bottomed chairs and earned a reputation as a "water-smeller" or "dowser" (1959, pp. 80–88). Dimensions: 8" x 11" base, 10" s.h., 18" o.h. Collection of Jeannette Lasansky.

Pl. 4.43-b   Rim detail of basket in Pl. 4.43-a. Two sets of rims reinforce the top edge. Between the rims, two rows of a decorative weave, known as *soumak* in fiberwork, are worked.

Ears and Wrapped Handles

Quite frequently, large heavy-duty split baskets are made with two side handles, called "ears," attached to opposite sides of the basket. A large, heavily-loaded basket is much easier to carry with ears than with a single overhead handle. While the more common ear handle has double notches (Pls. 4.44 and 4.1), single-notched ears are also known (Pls. 4.45 and 4.53-a). Pegged, nailed, wrapped, and split-end ears are other types of attachments used for ear handles. Occasionally, baskets have two leather or rope handles riveted to the rim, instead of carved wood ones. Factory-made baskets often had heavy wire ear handles.

Some baskets have small ears designed as finger holds, rather than hand grips. These handles are found on small baskets such as table and work baskets. Cherokee fish baskets (Pl. 4.45) and feed baskets (Pl. 4.3) were made with small ears for attaching a belt, a rope, or a shoulder strap. The strap not only freed the hands for gathering, but also supported the basket as an extended handle.

Making ear handles is somewhat more complicated technically than making overhead handles. As with overhead handles, the ear-handle billet is sized for both width and thickness. The length of the bow varies, depending on the height and shape of the handle. The ear is carved, working on both the radial and the tangential surfaces: the notches and tails are carved on the radial surface of the billet while the bow is worked on the tangential surface (Fig. 4.16-a, b, c). An ear often is tied to retain its shape and allowed to dry before inserting it into the basket.

Another type of handle used for ears or other small handles is the **wrapped handle**. A wrapped handle is begun with a foundation piece which is shaped and fitted to the basket. The ends of the foundation piece are tucked alongside a stake or secured by folding them back into the weaving. A split is wrapped around the foundation to fasten the handle to the basket. Wrapped handles are the weakest type of ear handle and therefore most often are used on baskets with light contents, such as feather baskets (Pl. 4.66) or small table baskets. Small wrapped handles also are made to be used as pulls on lids (Pls. 4.44, 4.65, 4.67).

Drop or Swing Handles

In today's marketplace, one of the most prized baskets is one with drop or swing handles. The handles are attached by a pivot and move conveniently out of the way, resting on the rim or alongside the basket body, when not in use. While members of the Eastern Cherokee group make swing-handled baskets, the authors have found that such baskets are sel-

Pl. 4.44 High ear handles allow this tall basket to be lifted easily. It was purchased in central Kentucky; the origin is uncertain (Doolin, 19 Feb. 1985). The double-notched ears are attached to the outer rim, while another wrapped ear makes a pull for the lid. It is unusual to find lids in good condition and still with their baskets. The well-constructed lid is hinged to the basket with a heavy folded split. The basket and the lid both have sixteen-stake double-bottom constructions and are woven with a split-stake spiral. Dimensions: 12″ base, 17″ top, 24″ s.h., 29″ o.h. with lid. Collection of Datha Doolin.

Pl. 4.45 Cherokee fish basket. This narrow-necked basket was designed to hold just enough fish for a daily ration. Cherokee basketmaker Martha Ross described the traditional fish basket: "The old ones were kind of narrow and not as big [as the larger curved-necked baskets made and sold today]. When you went fishing, you didn't catch a whole lot, just a mess at a time. You caught your limit, maybe six or seven, whatever your family needed" (8 May 1985). A leather shoulder strap is attached to the ear handles. Dimensions: 3″ x 8″ base, 13″ s.h., 15″ o.h. Courtesy of the Museum of the Cherokee Indian, Cherokee, North Carolina.

A

B

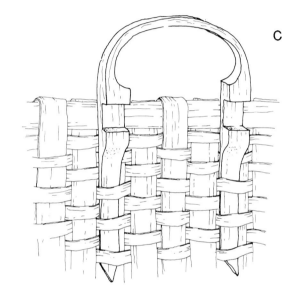

C

Fig. 4.16 Double-notched ear handle: (a) notches are cut from the radial surface while the bow is carved on the tangential surface; (b) completed ear handle before bending—the tails are shaved down on the radial surface below the notch; (c) ear handle bent to shape and fitted to a basket.

Pl. 4.46 *(Below):* Drop-handled basket attributed to Robert Henry (1898–1968), Centre County, Pennsylvania (Bohn, 16 Oct. 1984; Lasansky 1979, p. 49). Copper rivets are used to attach the drop handles directly to the rims of the basket. Metal hinges attach the lid to the basket rim. Robert and his father, Calvin Henry, used wooden molds for weaving their baskets (Lasansky 1979, pp. 40–41). Dimensions: 11″ x 18″ base, 6″ s.h. including lid. Private collection.

dom made by non-Native Americans in the Central Appalachians. In New England, however, drop-handled baskets are common, made by both native and non-native basketmakers. According to Wetherbee and Taylor, who describe the drop-handled baskets made by the Taghkanic basketmakers in New York State, "there are many other double bottom round bottom swing handle baskets; it is a common form" (1986, p. 29).

Two sources of non-native drop-handle baskets are the Henry family of Centre County, Pennsylvania (Pl. 4.46) (Lasansky 1979, pp. 40–41), and Elmer Price of Shenandoah County, Virginia (14 Mar. 1985). Both made rectangular picnic-style lidded baskets with drop handles riveted directly to the rims. Handles of this type also frequently are found on factory-made veneer baskets (Pl. 4.6).

More intricate swing handles consist of three parts, a bail—the movable part of the handle—and two **hinges**—the handle pivots. The hinges most often are carved like small ears. Two types of bails, both used by the Cherokees, pivot on ear hinges. A drilled-end bail is made by carving out the bow section, leaving thick ends so that a hole may be bored through the radial surface for the pivot (Pl. 4.47). On a laced-end bail, the ends are carved to a tail and then threaded back through small holes in the handle bow (Pl. 4.48). These handles are used on contemporary shopping and purse baskets by Cherokee makers. Usually men make the handles, while the women weave the baskets (M. Ross, 8 May 1985). The Cherokees often use hickory instead of oak for hinges and bails because of its fine grain, ease of carving, and pliability.

Handle Holes

Handle holes are created below the rim of the basket by turning down one or more stakes below the top edge of the basket and reversing the weavers on the stakes at the edge of the hole (Pls. 4.49 and 4.61). Quite often a wide weaving split, made the width needed for the handle hole, is woven at the top instead of reversing the weaving of several narrower splits (Pl. 4.61). As a handle construction, handle holes are strong and quickly made, and they require no additional materials.

Handle holes are constructed on all sizes of baskets. Large round and rectangular field baskets commonly have handle holes. On smaller baskets, the size of the holes is reduced significantly, so that they often serve as finger holds rather than as hand grips. A feed basket, possibly of Pennsylvania origin, uses small woven holes as a place where ropes are tied to the basket, so that the basket can hang around the animal's neck (Pl. 4.4).

Pl. 4.47 Cherokee swing-handled "shopping" or "purse" basket. The drop handles with drilled bails are attached with ear hinges. This basket uses dyed white oak for the stakes, maple for the weavers and the curlicue overlay, and hickory for the handles. The base is plain woven with fillers, and each stake is then split in half to double the total number of working ends before the sides are worked. The side weaving is worked row by row. Dimensions: 4 3/4″ x 11 1/2″ base, 10″ s.h., 16″ o.h. Courtesy of the Museum of the Cherokee Indian, Cherokee, North Carolina.

Pl. 4.48 Swing-handled basket with laced bail, made by John and Elenora Wilnoty. The handle and hinges were carved by John Wilnoty, a well-known Cherokee woodcarver; his wife, Elenora Wilnoty, wove the basket (Glass, 23 May 1983). The ends of the laced handle are whittled and laced through holes pierced in the bail. The handle of this basket is carved from hickory, a wood often selected for handles because of its pliability. An unusual feature is the center stake, which is carved on its ends to make hinges for the bail. The hinges are worked similarly to the laced bail: a long tail is carved and then threaded back through a hole bored in the thick shoulder of the hinge. Some of the stakes, as well as the weaving splits and the lashing, are dyed. The use of different colors and widths in the row-by-row side weaving adds a decorative element. The small round rod which fills in the space between the top rims is a detail also common in Cherokee work. Dimensions: 5″ x 7″ base, 4″ s.h., 9 1/2″ o.h. Private collection.

Pl. 4.49 Large field basket with handle holes, from Washington County, Ohio. Handle holes are made by leaving spaces in the weaving at the top edge, so that the rims can serve as hand grips. Heavy skids under the base protected the basket when it was dragged along the ground and also provided the structural support much needed in a basket this large. This basket had been used for harvesting produce near Marietta; when heavily loaded, it would have taken two people to lift the basket. Dimensions: 17 3/4" x 33 1/2" base, 24 3/4" x 38" top, 11 3/4" s.h. Collection of Cynthia W. and Michael B. Taylor.

Pl. 4.50 Fish creel bought in Buncomb County, North Carolina (Elkins, 9 May 1985). Holes are worked into the back for a strap and into the lid for dropping the fish into the basket. At the base of the strap holes, the weaving splits narrow and also turn back, a technique more common in rib-work (Fig. 3.3). The turnbacks create a higher back, allowing the lid to rest at an angle. Dimensions: 9" x 5" base, 9 1/2" back height. Collection of Edd and Peggy Elkins.

The same technique is used to make holes for straps or belts, as well as a hole in the lid of a split oak fishing creel (Pl. 4.50)

3. Lashings

Lashings or **bindings** are used to attach rims and handles to a basket body and, often, to attach a foot to a base. Lashings are both functional and decorative and fall into two categories, "single" and "crossed" lashings. Single lashings are those in which the lashing split is worked around a rim or foot in one direction only. Crossed lashings are those which are worked first in one direction and then are reversed to cross back over in the opposite direction. Both single and crossed lashings are used for feet and top rims.

Top lashings are wrapped around the rims and are worked through the spaces in between the stakes or through holes pierced in the stakes. If the stakes are close together, some basketmakers taper the ends to allow more room for the lashing split. The basketmaker holds or clamps the rims snugly to the basket body and pulls the lashing split tight. Basketmakers select a strong, flexible split for the lashing. A basket is only as good as the lashing, for, once the lashing is loose or breaks, the deterioration of the rest of the basket is close at hand.

When a lashing split runs out, a new one must be added. Lashing splices are made in many different ways. Some baskets show where the exhausted or new end was pushed down through the weaving on the basket sides and folded back up and under a weaving row (Fig. 4.17). Another splicing method overlaps the ends of the lashing splits and works them together for one or two wraps. A more unusual method simply knots the ends together.

A common method, the *basic single lashing* (Fig. 4.17), is demonstrated by Currence Dobbins of Glenville, West Virginia (Pl. 4.51). As a lashing split is laced a single time between each stake and around the basket rims, a diagonal line is created (Pls. 4.52-a, b). The diagonal line may go to the right (Pl. 4.30-a) or the left (Pl. 4.34-a), depending on the direction from which the lashing is worked. On most baskets with basic single lashings, the forward diagonal is interrupted at the handle. Here the lashing split is sometimes worked back across the handle, creating an "X" before continuing with the lashing (Pl. 4.18-a).

Another single lashing, the *double-wrapped lashing* (Fig. 4.18), loops the lashing split twice through each space between stakes. If the stakes are

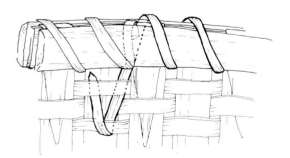

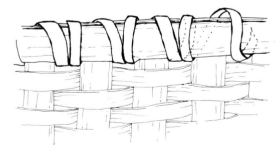

Fig. 4.17   Basic single lashing and splice.   Fig. 4.18   Double-wrapped lashing.

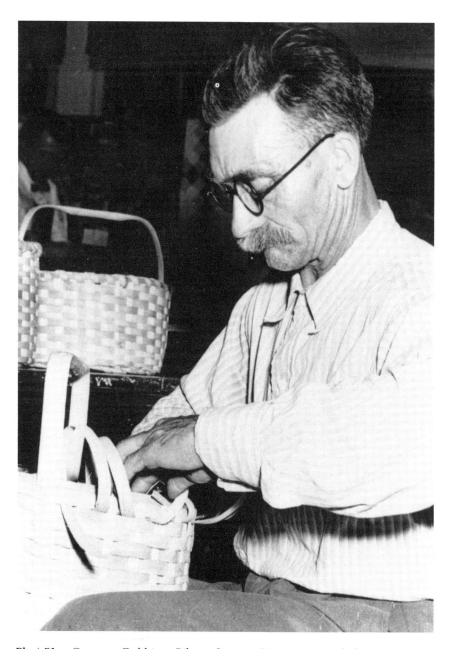

Pl. 4.51 Currence Dobbins, Gilmer County, West Virginia, lashing a round
split basket. He is loosely working the lashing split part of the way around the
rims and then will go back to pull it tight. His basket in the background shows
a carved handle with the thicker handhold in the center of the bow. He often
used grey-dyed weaving splits and added a foot to his double-bottomed baskets
by lacing a split through the base weaving (Laird ca. 1960). Photograph from
the Catherine Candace Irvine Laird Collection, used courtesy of Norman M.
and Dorothy Irvine.

Pl. 4.52-a Single-lashed foot and rims on a basket attributed to eastern Ohio. The thick, rounded rims are lashed with the basic single lashing. The tall pedestal foot is lashed onto the base weaving (Pl. 4.52-b). Dimensions: 6 1/4″ base, 10 3/8″ top, 4 3/4″ s.h., 8″ o.h. Collection of Marilyn Kemble.

Pl. 4.52-b Detail of foot on basket in Pl. 4.52-a. The single-lashed foot is worked around a thick foundation which is 3/4″ high.

wide apart, the first wrap tends to make a vertical line, while the second wrap makes a long diagonal as it travels to the space between the next two stakes. The second wrap adds more strength and can be quite decorative (Pls. 4.53-a, b; 4.29). A more complex and unusual single lashing appears as braiding on the top edge of the rims (Pls. 4.54-a, b). The lashing method is the same as that used in leatherwork to bind unfinished edges. This *laced lashing* is quite rare in oak work but appears as the finishing edge for some split pack baskets made from spruce roots from the Sudetenland in central Europe (Gandert 1963, pp. 124–27).

Pl. 4.53-a   Square-based basket with double-wrapped lashing. Purchased in Tennessee, origin uncertain (Rigsby, 18 Feb. 1985). The size of the rims is about the same as that of the core for the lashed foot (Pl. 4.53-b), a feature uncommon on rectangular baskets. The tops of the stakes have been tapered to allow for the double-wrapped lashing. The high rounded ear handles are single notched. Dimensions: 10 1/2″ square base, 5 1/2″ s.h., 7 1/2″ o.h. Collection of Bruce Rigsby.

Pl. 4.53-b   Foot detail of basket in Pl. 4.53-a.

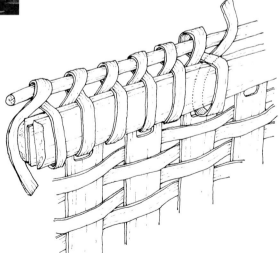

Fig. 4.19   Figure-eight lashing.

Pl. 4.54-a Rectangular split basket with laced lashing; origin unknown. The unusual lashing tightly binds and finishes the top of the basket (Pl. 4.54-b). The base is plain woven and the sides worked with a split-stake spiral. This basket has a closed base with the ends of the fillers continuing up the basket sides. The single-notched handle is attached to the outer rim and bound in place by the tight lashing. Dimensions: 10″ x 13″ base, 8 1/4″ s.h., 13″ o.h. Collection of Datha Doolin.

Pl. 4.54-b Laced lashing detail of basket in Pl. 4.54-a. The stakes have been pierced to allow the lashing split to pass through. The single lashing interlaces itself to make a braid on the top edge. A new lashing split is joined by overlapping the old and new ends and working together for several stitches. This lashing technique is used in leather-work to finish unbound edges and was used to finish certain central European pack baskets (Will 1985, pp. 126–28; Gandert 1963, pp. 124–27).

Other single lashings include the addition of a rod as part of the finished binding. On some baskets from Pennsylvania, a *wrapped-rod lashing* is worked: the lashing split is wrapped around the rod and the rims, then just around the rod for several turns before catching the rims again (Pls. 4.55, 5.44-a, b).

One decorative single lashing, the *figure-eight*, also incorporates a top rod above the basket rims. The lashing split is worked in a figure-eight configuration around the rims and the rod (Fig. 4.19). The appearance of the figure-eight lashing varies, depending on the shape of the rod, the width of the lashing split, the number of times the split is lashed between

Pl. 4.55   Basket with wrapped-rod lashing. This lashing is found occasionally on split and rod/split baskets (Pls. 5.44-a, b) from Pennsylvania. The round top rod acts as a filler closing in the space between the rims. Dimensions: 5″ base, 8″ top, 4 3/4″ s.h., 8 1/2″ o.h. Collection of Dianne and Kelly Mink.

Pl. 4.56   Basket made by Elmer Propst (b. 1901), Pendleton County, West Virginia. Propst, who also made rib baskets similar to those of the Eye family (Pl. 1.5), learned basketmaking from his father, Abraham Propst. Elmer constructed his baskets on a wooden mold, beginning with the handle and the top and bottom rims. He tacked the side and base stakes to these rims, unmolded the basket, and then filled in the base and sides. The top edge was finished with a figure-eight lashing which was repeated for the foot (Laird 1969–72). Besides making baskets, Propst also was well known for his cooperage of cedar buckets (Shobe, 29 July 1982). Dimensions: 7″ x 11″ base, 8 1/2″ x 11 1/2″ top, 6″ s.h., 11 1/2″ o.h. Collection of Annie Handley Shobe.

Pl. 4.57 Pete Ware, Bedford County, Virginia, 1985, demonstrating how he burns holes through stakes for the lashing. The iron piercing tool—forged by his father, Pete Ware, Sr., who made the same style split basket—is about three feet long and tapers to a point at one end. The pointed end is heated until red hot, and a hole is burned through the top of the stake, just below the nailed-on rims. The basket then is finished with a top rod and the figure-eight lashing (15 Mar. 1985). The distinctive figure-eight lashing through the stakes is quite common on many traditional baskets from central western Virginia.

the stakes, and whether or not the lashing is worked through the stakes. The lidded Tennessee basket (Pl. 4.65) has a wide lasher worked once between the stakes, while the basket sleigh (Pl. 4.35), a rectangular basket made by Elmer Propst (Pl. 4.56), and various rod/split baskets from western North Carolina (Pls. 5.47, 5.48, 5.49) have the lashing split worked several times between the stakes. This same lashing technique is the style used by Henry Beverley of Nelson County, Virginia (Sisto 1976).

In westcentral Virginia and neighboring West Virginia, the figure-eight lashing often is worked through a hole pierced in the stake. Pete Ware of Bedford County, Virginia, described how he and his father worked the lashing. First they nailed the rims to the top of the basket and cut off the ends of the stakes. Holes were then burned in the stakes, using a hand-forged piercing iron (Pl. 4.57). By setting the hot iron on the stake just below the rim, an oblong hole was burned through (15 Mar. 1985). Some baskets have holes which are chiseled or pierced through the stakes with a sharp tool (Pls. 4.60-a, c; 4.33-a; 4.13; 4.23; Fig. 4.1-a).

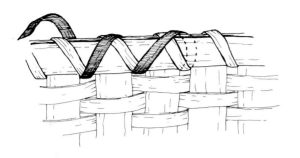

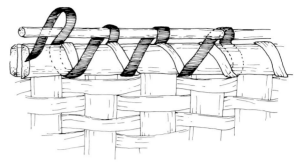

Fig. 4.20　Crossed lashing.　　　　　**Fig. 4.21**　Crossed figure-eight lashing.

A very common lashing used on white oak baskets is the *crossed lashing* (Fig. 4.20). This lashing is begun by working as for a basic single lashing. Upon completing the basket circumference, the split is reversed and worked around in the opposite direction, lashing the basket a second time. The crossed lashing tightly secures the rims and handle and is a stronger binding than the basic single lashing. Usually the lashing split is wrapped between every stake, but occasionally baskets show distinct separate crosses where the lashing split is worked between every other stake (Pl. 4.58).

While one occasionally finds a *crossed-figure-eight lashing*, not enough examples are known to ascertain if this may be a regional style (Fig. 4.21). A basic single lashing is worked, a top rod is added, and the lashing is then reversed. The rod is attached with a figure-eight movement as the lashing is worked through the spaces between the stakes. The rod is decorative and covers the space between the rims, but the rod is not secured as well as the single figure-eight lashing (Pl. 4.59).

4. Feet

Feet elevate and protect the base of a basket. The addition of a foot adds years to the useful life of a basket, guarding the base from excessive wear and moisture. Types of feet vary with the construction of the basket. Some are incorporated into the base or side structure as the basket is being built, while others are added after the basket body is completed. Added feet can be replaced when they become worn.

Common feet added to rectangular baskets are known as "slats," "skids," "slides," "skates," or "runners." These are made of thick heavy splits which are attached to run the length or width of the base (Pls. 4.60-a, b; 4.17). Elmer Knott of Athens County, Ohio, remembered the rectangular split

Pl 4.58 Round split basket with cross-lashed rims and foot, from southeastern Ohio. The lashing of the rims and foot gives a balanced appearance to this bowl-shaped basket. The lashing split is worked between every other stake, resulting in clear crosses. The basket is woven with chasing, and a wide single-notched overhead handle spans the top of the basket. The basket was used at the turn of the century as the family market basket (Malone, 22 Apr. 1985). Dimensions: 9 1/2″ base, 17″ top, 8″ s.h., 15″ o.h. Collection of Mary Ann and Max Malone.

Pl. 4.59 Basket with crossed-figure-eight lashing; origin unknown. This pot-shaped, double-bottomed basket is woven with chasing. Both bases are woven before being joined together. Dimensions: 9″ base, 10″ top, 5″ s.h. Collection of Datha Doolin.

baskets which his uncle used to make: "He made a lot of them baskets [with slats] for delivery people, delivering groceries. . . . He'd put slats on them [the baskets]—for where they'd pull them out of that wagon. . . . He'd run the slats up the side, he'd put about three—run them longways. . . . They could slide them [the baskets] out to the endgate" (Knott and Knott, 19 Aug. 1989). Slats are almost always present on large rectangular baskets intended for heavy use (Pl. 4.49). Added runners give essential structural support to a basket base and also make it easier for a basket to be dragged through the fields as crops are gathered. Skids also are found on small baskets, where structurally they may not be needed.

Pl. 4.60-a Rectangular-based split basket with skids, westcentral Virginia (Arthur and Arthur, 11 Mar. 1985). The overhead handle, nailed to the rims, extends into the base, completely covering the original center stake (Pl. 4.60-b). The corners of this basket are well protected by the added feet. The top edge is decoratively bound by tight figure-eight lashing, which is worked both between stakes and through holes in the stakes. Dimensions: 8″ x 9 3/4″ base, 7 3/4″ s.h., 12 1/2″ o.h. Collection of Ralph and Sarah Arthur.

Pl. 4.60-b Base view of basket in Pl. 4.60-a. It is unusual to have skids applied to both the length and the width of a base.

Pl. 4.60-c Lashing detail of basket in Pl. 4.60-a. Round holes have been pierced through the stakes for the lashing.

Pl. 4.61 Pennsylvania round split basket with skids. Twelve skids are run on top of stakes to support the base and protect the bottom edge. "H E A" is painted in blue on the side of this basket. Such round baskets were made in standard sizes, and many of them are either initialed or branded, perhaps to identify the user or maker. Dimensions: 9″ base, 16″ top, 12″ s.h. Courtesy of the Pennsylvania Farm Museum of Landis Valley, Pennsylvania Historical and Museum Commission.

The simplest skid is a heavy split nailed or lashed to the base of the basket. Other skids have carved ends that are bent up and slipped into the weaving alongside a stake. This type of skid strengthens the side of the basket and also protects the vulnerable corners. The ends of the skid may continue up to the top of the basket, or may extend only partway up the sides.

While skids are not as common on round oak split baskets because of these baskets' base structure, here too the same principle applies—skids are added on top of base stakes. Some skids protect the edge of the base by following the curve of the base and turning up before slipping into the weaving of the side (Pl. 4.61). Heavy skids which extend all the way up the sides and are nailed to the rims typically are found on large, commercially-made round split baskets. Such baskets still were used in the 1970s in some small rural post offices to hold mail for sorting. The heavy skids protected the base when the full baskets were dragged across the floor (Nash and Nash, 10 May 1988).

A less common foot on round baskets is a crossed skid made from two thick splits which intersect at right angles over the center of the base (Pls. 4.62-a, b). The feed basket (Pl. 4.4) also has thick crossed skids, which may help to account for its excellent condition.

A lashed foot is the most common foot found on round split baskets (Pls. 4.41 and 4.58), but it also is used occasionally for rectangular or

Pl. 4.62-a   Round split basket, Summers County, West Virginia. When the basket was bought from a home near Hinton, the seller said that it had been in the home as long he could remember and that it had been used as a storage basket for cloth (Arthur and Arthur, 11 Mar. 1985). Its unusual shape, heavily reinforced base, and massive single-notched handle indicate that the basket was built for heavy use and perhaps for a particular pur-

pose. Dimensions: 12 1/2″ applied foot, 17 1/2″ base, 12″ x 14″ oval top, 9″ s.h., 14″ o.h. Collection of Ralph and Sarah Arthur.

Pl. 4.62-b   Base view of basket in Pl. 4.62-a. The strongly reinforced base has both crossed braces and a lashed-on foot. The added structural support and protection offered by the feet would allow this basket to carry heavy loads.

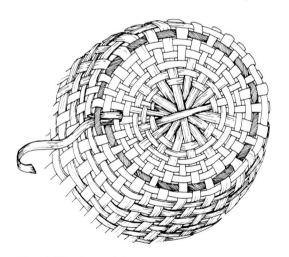

Fig. 4.22   Lashed foot.

square split baskets (Pl. 4.53-b). The lashed foot consists of a core (a rounded rod or thick split) shaped to fit the basket's base and bound onto the base with a split (Fig. 4.22). The split is wrapped over the core as it is threaded through the base weaving or around the base stakes. Lashings used for feet are: basic single, figure-eight, and crossed lashings. The shape and thickness of the core and the placement of the foot create differences in the sculptural appearance of the form. Some makers place a foot just outside of the base edge, causing the basket to appear straight-sided, while others bind the foot closer to the center, creating a low pedestal (Pls. 4.52-a, b). Round baskets which have the second bottom added to the outside of the basket, quite often have a foot lashed to the base, in order to give the basket a level seat (Pl. 4.25).

In the central and southern Appalachian region, baskets with legs are rare. Rectangular split baskets with four or more feet are known in New England, associated with wool washing (Ketchum 1974, pp. 14–15; Teleki 1975, p. 110). The legs elevate the basket and allow the water to drain from the wet wool. The addition of legs to any split basket allows for air circulation and also protects the base from ground moisture. The legs on a large oak storage basket found in central Tennessee were carved with a tail which is inserted into the side weaving and a shoulder for the corners of the basket to rest on (Pls. 4.63-a, b). A one-legged basket attributed to central Tennessee appears to be a one-of-a-kind piece (Pl. 4.64). A long rounded pole extends above the basket to make a handle, while below the basket, it becomes the walking stick.

5. Lids

Lidded baskets are not common. It is the special-purpose basket which requires a lid and merits the added effort needed for its construction. Lids are found on different types of storage baskets, such as feather baskets, sewing or work baskets, and the later purse and picnic baskets. A properly fitting lid requires the skill of an experienced basketmaker. Lids are made to rest either on top of the basket or inside the top rim (Pls. 4.65, 4.66, 4.67, 4.44, 4.46, 4.50, 4.63; Cl. Pl. 15). Domed lids create extra storage space but also take more materials for their construction. Elmer Price described making a basket with a domed lid as making two baskets, one upside down on top of the other (14 Mar. 1985). A rectangular picnic basket from the Blue Ridge Mountains, Virginia, has a domed lid fitted to

Pl. 4.63-a   Storage basket with legs, found in central Tennessee; origin uncertain. The legs would keep the contents dry and the bottom away from any moisture on the ground. The square base is worked with a stake-and-filler construction, while the sides are woven with a split-stake spiral. The basket has no rims, and the lid has an outer rim only. The lid has a small wrapped pull attached to the intersection of the stakes. Dimensions: Basket: 14″ square base, 16″ top, 29″ o.h. including lid and legs. Lid: 17″ base, 19″ top, 4 1/2″ s.h. Foot: 3 1/2″ from floor to basket base. Collection of Mayfield and Teresse Brown.

Pl. 4.63-b   Detail of leg of basket in Pl. 4.63-a. The legs are carved to create a shoulder which supports each corner of the basket. The long tail of the leg is inserted up through the weaving on the side of the basket. This closeup view also shows the stake-and-filler base construction.

Pl. 4.64   *(Opposite):* Basket cane. Purchased in Tennessee; origin uncertain (Hackley, 17 Feb. 1985). The cane goes through the center of the basket and extends another two feet beneath the base. Supports are inserted into the base and woven around the cane to help stabilize the basket. Two wrapped handles anchor the basket to the cane. This basket bears some similarity to funnel-shaped baskets on sticks which were made and sold through the Allanstand Cottage Industries as "garden baskets" (Pl. 1.8). Dimensions: 8″ x 13 1/2″ rectangular base, 13″ x 17″ oval top, 6″ s.h., 40″ overall height including cane. Collection of Larry Hackley.

Pl. 4.65 *(Right):* Lidded rectangular split basket, eastern Tennessee (Mink, 18 Feb. 1985). Lids fitted to the inside of rectangular split baskets are rare. The lid here has a small wrapped pull attached to one corner. The figure-eight lashing binds a wide flat split above the rim. The basket's sides are slightly flared and the corners sharply squared. Dimensions: Basket: 6 1/2″ x 9″ base, 6″ s.h., 11″ o.h. Lid: 8 1/2″ x 11.″ Collection of Dianne and Kelly Mink.

Pl. 4.66 *(Above):* Urn-shaped basket, attributed to Tom Cave, Page County, Virginia, ca. 1912. In Virginia, urn-shaped baskets are popularly known as "feather baskets" but also served as general storage containers (Arthur and Arthur, 11 Mar. 1985). The narrower top opening and flat lid were necessary parts of this functional basket. The lid is rimless and has a folded split for a handle pull. The side handles are made by wrapping a foundation split which has been shaped and anchored to the basket. The wrapped handles are not very strong, but they serve well to lift light loads. Dimensions: 13″ base, 13″ top, 22 1/2″ s.h. Collection of Ralph and Sarah Arthur.

Pl. 4.67   Lidded sewing basket made by Ethel Linville Bias, Lincoln County, West Virginia. Both basket and lid are made with a base construction similar to those used in round wickerwork. The bases are begun with two groups of three stakes intersecting each other, a layout which is unusual in splitwork. Bias liked to experiment with new designs, often drawing on her own ideas or requests from customers (George and George, 9 Jan. 1985). See Pl. 1.15. Dimensions: Basket: 12 3/4″ base, 13 1/2″ top, 4 1/2″ o.h. including lid. Lid: 14″ base, 7/8″ s.h. Collection of Jane George.

Pl. 4.68   White oak hat; origin unknown. The top of the hat is the oval base of the basket. The basket sides are shaped carefully as they are woven. The side stakes are bent approximately at right angles to form the brim. Dimensions: 4 1/2″ x 5 1/2″ top of hat, 2 1/2″ brim width, 5″ o.h. Collection of Roddy and Sally Moore.

the inside of the basket (Pl. 4.39), while a large storage basket has a round domed lid which covers the outer rims of the basket (Pl. 4.10). Often baskets with lids which are made to fit over the outside are made without outer rims, so that the lid can fit the top of the basket more easily.

Occasionally one finds hats woven of white oak. Whether they were made as functional items or merely as novelties is not known. This particular one shows quite a bit of style, with its menswear shape and additional hatband (Pl. 4.68). Hats are the ultimate lids.

Cl. Pl. 1　Tishie Caldwell, Bell County, Kentucky, 1983, holding melon-shaped rib baskets which she made from willow and honeysuckle collected near her home. Caldwell learned basketmaking from her mother, who had learned from a German relative. While Caldwell uses honeysuckle and willow for her baskets, her son uses white oak to make an identical form (25 May 1983). Their baskets are marketed through the Red Bird Mission, Beverly, Kentucky.

Cl. Pl. 2　Oval rib basket with very close ribbing and woven wrapping; origin unknown. This finely woven basket shows the dark coloring of the oak caused by age and use. Dimensions: 8 1/2″ x 13 3/4″ top, 6 1/2″ s.h., 9″ o.h. Collection of Larry Hackley.

Cl. Pl. 3　Cherokee lidded rib basket with black and red dyed splits. This basket is meticulously worked in every detail. The hoops have been joined with wooden pegs and the radiating ribbing worked into the framework. The swinging lids are attached by slipping the ends of the lid frame into two holes bored through the handle hoop. The dyed splits have been woven to create an overall design on both basket and lids. Dimensions: 8 1/2″ x 9 3/8″ top, 5″ s.h., 9″ o.h. Courtesy of the Museum of the Cherokee Indian, Cherokee, North Carolina.

Cl. Pl. 4 Large oval rib basket bought at the 1923 Shaker auction at Pleasant Hill, Kentucky (Hamilton, 18 Feb. 1985). Although this basket may have been used by the Shaker community, there is no evidence to indicate that it is Shaker made. The yellow-painted basket is constructed with a heavy rim and a spine which extends above the rim to make carrying grips. The woven four-fold-bond wrapping is worked around the rim and the spine. Baskets were often painted to freshen and brighten them. In many cases, paint has helped to preserve baskets, coating and protecting the wood. Dimensions: 13 1/2″ x 20″ top, 8″ s.h., 12″ o.h. Collection of Hazel Hamilton.

Cl. Pl. 5 Round rib basket with vertical ribbing. Purchased in Glasgow, Kentucky; origin uncertain. This rounded basket uses a combination of flat ribs on the base and round ribs on the sides. The first five ribs on either side of the spine are woven in with the wrapping. The ends of all the added ribs are either tucked under the top of the wrapping or folded over the rim hoop and secured to the inside of the rim under the weaving. Dimensions: 16″ top, 10″ s.h., 14″ o.h. Collection of Bill and Dot Van Corbach.

Cl. Pl. 8 Martha Jones, Warren County, Tennessee, finishing a "fan" basket. Martha and her husband Dan make two distinctive rib basket shapes which they call "fans" and "dollies." The fans, named for their resemblance to a fan, were invented when Dan had a short piece of timber that was only long enough for short ribs; using them resulted in the curved outline of the sides. Martha remembered helping her mother, Novella Freed, make baskets. Her mother would make the frames, and Martha would weave them in (7 May 1985).

Cl. Pl. 6 Rib basket with ring wrapping. The ring wrapping, the particular method of vertical ribbing, and the shape are notable characteristics of this rib basket, which is attributed to northwestern Virginia (Long, 14 Mar. 1985). The basket is woven with green and red dyed splits. Dimensions: 12″ top, 8″ s.h., 11 1/2″ o.h. Collection of Burt Long.

Cl. Pl. 7 "Kentucky egg" basket. The elongated handle hoop and the high placement of the rim create a deep basket. Baskets such as these were made in Knott County, Kentucky, by Bird Owsley for the Hindman Settlement School's "Fireside Industries" (Watts, 26 Nov. 1984). The hoops and ribs are made of hickory, as are those of other rib baskets from the eastern Kentucky region. The weaving splits have been dyed brown. Dimensions: 7″ top, 9″ s.h., 13″ o.h. Courtesy of the Hindman Settlement School, Forks of Troublesome Creek, Hindman, Kentucky.

Cl. Pl. 9 "Dolly" basket made by Dan and Martha Jones, Warren County, Tennessee. Martha named this basket after Dolly Parton, a well-known country music singer. Martha said that she keeps pulling and pulling the ribs out to form the two "knots" (bulges). She weaves the "dolly" with dyed splits, emphasizing the curves and creating the image of a figure with a bikini (7 May 1985). This basket and the "fan" (Cl. Pl. 8), modifications of the traditional rectangular "box" basket, are examples of innovative shapes devised by contemporary traditional makers. Dimensions: 8″ x 12 1/2″ top, 7 1/4″ s.h., 13″ o.h. Collection of Larry Hackley.

Cl. Pl. 10   Round split baskets attributed to Botetourt County, Virginia (Moore, 12 Mar. 1985). The color on the stakes and weavers was applied only to the outside of the materials and only to the sides of the baskets. The baskets are woven by chasing with one natural weaver and one red-stained weaver. The color and weaving technique create vertical blocks on the baskets' sides. These baskets have slightly domed centers and heavy single-notched handles. Dimensions, from left: 6 1/2″ base, 11″ top, 6 1/4″ s.h, 10″ o.h.; 8 1/2″ base, 14 3/4″ top, 7 1/2″ s.h., 13 1/2″ o.h. Collection of Roddy and Sally Moore.

Cl. Pl. 11   Cherokee picnic basket with lid. The strong vertical stripes on this split basket are created by alternating dark and light stakes and weavers in row-by-row plain weave. The lid is woven to continue the pattern from the basket sides. The lock handle is made from hickory and forms one of the base and side stakes. Dimensions: Basket: 8 1/2″ x 15 1/2″ base, 8″ s.h., 12 1/2″ o.h.; Lid: 8″ x 16″ x 2″. Collection of Robert S. Brunk.

Cl. Pl. 12   Twill split basket with red dyed splits, possibly from Tennessee (Hackley, 17 Feb. 1985). This basket is woven completely of over-two/under-two twill. The woven handle is made with two rods inserted into the weaving on either side of a wider single-notched handle. Dimensions: 9″ x 12″ base, 7 1/4″ s.h., 12 1/2″ o.h. Collection of Larry Hackley.

Cl. Pl. 13 Rectangular plank-bottomed split basket with blue and white paint, purchased in Hart County, Kentucky; origin uncertain (Van Corbach, 20 Feb. 1985). Plank-bottomed baskets were made in a variety of sizes and shapes; the size and shape of the plank determines the basket's size and shape. Stakes are usually nailed to the base and sometimes to the rims, creating a framework for the sides. This plank base is made of pine, but the handle, stakes, and weavers are of oak. Dimensions: 7″ x 14″ base, 10″ x 16 1/2″ top, 7″ s.h., 12 1/4″ o.h. Collection of Bill and Dot Van Corbach.

Cl. Pl. 14 Small round split baskets from the Blue Ridge Mountains, Virginia (Helsley and Helsley, 13 Mar. 1985). Rows of dyed weavers make a small chain design at the edge of the base and on the sides of the baskets. Like other baskets from this region, these round baskets have a double-bottom base construction, spiraled plain weave using a split stake, stakes turned down to the outside only, finished top edge with only an outer rim and crossed lashing, and overhead handle with split-end attachment (see Pl. 4.38-a). Dimensions, from left: 7 1/4″ base, 9 3/4″ top, 4″ s.h., 5 1/4″ o.h.; 5 1/4″ base, 7 1/4″ top, 4″ s.h., 7″ o.h. Private collection.

Cl. Pl. 15 Unusual lidded red-painted split basket rimmed with a wire edging; origin unknown. This basket is similar in design to flower-sellers' baskets used by street vendors in London (Wright 1983, p. 167). The lid becomes a tray for the display of merchandise. The wire edging is unusual, but it is similar to a border worked in white oak on a basket at the Pennsylvania Farm Museum of Landis Valley (Schiffer 1984, p. 11) and on the rims and sides of Pennsylvania rye straw coilwork (Lasansky 1979, pp. 38–39). The low squared handle has a large single notch under the outside rim. A wire has been attached to the handle and spanned across the top to help support the lid and probably to help the basket retain its shape. Dimensions: Basket: 13″ x 25″ base, 13″ x 23 1/2″ top, 9 1/2″ s.h., 14″ o.h.; Lid: 11 1/2″ x 23″. Collection of Datha Doolin.

Cl. Pl. 16   Square split baskets from Pulaski County, Virginia (Moore, 12 Mar. 1985), are woven by chasing. One weaver is dyed red and alternates with the plain weaver to make strong vertical lines of color. Alternate stakes are stained blue on only the outside of the basket. These distinctively shaped square-based baskets with high domed bases are the result of controlled weaving tension. These baskets are not typically Appalachian but are similar in shape to some New England ash splint baskets. While baskets with this "cat-head" shape were commonly made on molds by the Shakers and were named for the peaked corners of the bottom, which form "cat-ears" (Wetherbee and Taylor 1988, p. 108), the irregularities in this basket indicate that it was created freehand. Dimensions, from left: 6 1/2″ square base, 11 1/2″ top, 6 1/2″ s.h., 11″ o.h.; 8″ square base, 13 1/2″ top, 7 3/4″ s.h., 13 3/4″ o.h. Collection of Roddy and Sally Moore.

Cl. Pl. 17   Ohio oval rod basket with green stripes. Like many other baskets from southcentral Ohio, this basket is worked in basic techniques with thick rods. The oval bottom is begun with three lengthwise sticks inserted through five crosswise sticks and then paired. The upsett is made with a three-rod wale, and the sides are randed by chasing. The roped handle has a thick foundation rod which is wrapped with smaller rods. Dimensions: 7 1/2″ x 15″ base, 12″ x 19″ top, 8″ s.h., 12 1/2″ o.h. Collection of Cynthia W. and Michael B. Taylor.

Cl. Pl. 18   Rod sewing basket with wrapped handles. This small basket still has the pin and needle cushions attached and has scraps of fabric, pins, and snaps caught in the weaving. The combination border consists of a top scallop border with the stakes running back down through the weaving to the base, to make the foot border. The basket shape, combination border, and wrapped handles all indicate that this basket is probably of Pennsylvania origin. Dimensions: 7″ base, 9″ top, 4″ s.h., 5 3/8″ o.h. Collection of Cynthia W. and Michael B. Taylor.

Cl. Pl. 19   Large willow basket found in eastern Ohio. The checkered pattern on the basket sides is created by weaving peeled (light) and unpeeled (red) willow in four-rod wale (2/2). Willow for baskets, both cultivated and native, grew throughout the eastern United States. Willowwork's prevalence and its appearance, so similar to oak rodwork, often cause rod baskets to be mistaken for ones made of willow. Dimensions: 13″ base, 22 1/2″ top, 12 1/2″ s.h., 15″ o.h. Collection of Cynthia W. and Michael B. Taylor.

Cl. Pl. 20   Oak rod basket with high scallop border and side floats, Shenandoah Valley, Virginia (Hackley, 17 Feb. 1985). This style, with its high, scalloped, open border, is seen repeatedly in European and American willowwork. Groups of four stakes are worked into a top border and then threaded back through the side weaving to the basket base. At the base, three of the four stakes in each group are clipped short, and the remaining ones are bordered off for the foot. The base is randed, the upsett is three-rod waled, and the sides are randed except for two rows of waling in the midsection for attaching the floats. Dimensions: 9″ base, 12″ top, 8 1/4″ s.h., 12 1/2″ o.h. Collection of Larry Hackley.

Cl. Pl. 21   Rod basket with brown stripes, Hardy County, West Virginia (Shobe, 15 Jan. 1986). This basket shows many regional features of rod baskets of the Shenandoah Valley, Virginia, and the South Branch of the Potomac River Valley, West Virginia. Such characteristics include the flared shape, three-rod wale on both base and sides, and the roped handle, with its triangular-shaped attachment (see handle detail, Pl. 5.37). Dimensions: 8″ base, 11″ top, 7″ s.h., 11″ o.h. Collection of Annie Handley Shobe.

Cl. Pl. 22   Rod basket with blue and red dyed weavers, attributed to upper Shenandoah Valley, Virginia. This basket shows how fading often occurs on baskets which were once brightly colored. Blocks of blue alternate with red blocks on the basket sides. The base is fitched, beginning with a flat split and then changing to rods. A round of five-rod wale (4/1) is worked both as a foot and as the first upsett row, and then the sides are woven with three-rod wale. The handle is roped to the left over a slightly flattened foundation piece (see handle detail, Pl. 5.36). Dimensions: 7″ base, 10 1/4″ top, 6 1/4″ s.h., 10 1/4″ o.h. Collection of H. Wayne and Rachel Nash Law.

Cl. Pl. 23   Rod baskets made by Jacob Mentzer (worked 1875 to ca. 1930), Lancaster County, Pennsylvania (Lasansky 1984, p. 889). Mentzer is known for his use of rods painted with bright enamels, which were then woven into the three-rod waled sides of his baskets. The top edge is finished with a wide border, with the stakes ending to the inside. A low foot is added by inserting stakes into the weaving and then bordering off. Dimensions, clockwise from left: 7 1/2″ base, 9 3/4″ top, 4 3/8″ s.h., 6″ o.h.; 7″ base, 9″ top, 4 1/4″ s.h., 5 3/4″ o.h.; 5 1/4″ base, 8″ top, 4″ o.h.; 3 3/4″ base, 6 1/4″ top, 3″ s.h., 4 1/2″ o.h. Collection of Dr. and Mrs. Donald M. Herr.

Cl. Pl. 24   Rodwork basket with black dyed rods, probably from Pennsylvania. The base is fitched using dark and light rods which alternate to form blocks of color. Instead of the more typical three/three bottom-stick base layout, the bottom of this basket has a two/three bottom-stick layout. The sides are three-rod waled with one dark and two natural rods, over the twenty side-stakes, which causes the pattern to spiral. Dimensions: 6 1/2″ base, 11 1/2″ top, 4 3/4″ s.h., 5 3/4″ o.h. Collection of Cynthia W. and Michael B. Taylor.

Rod Baskets

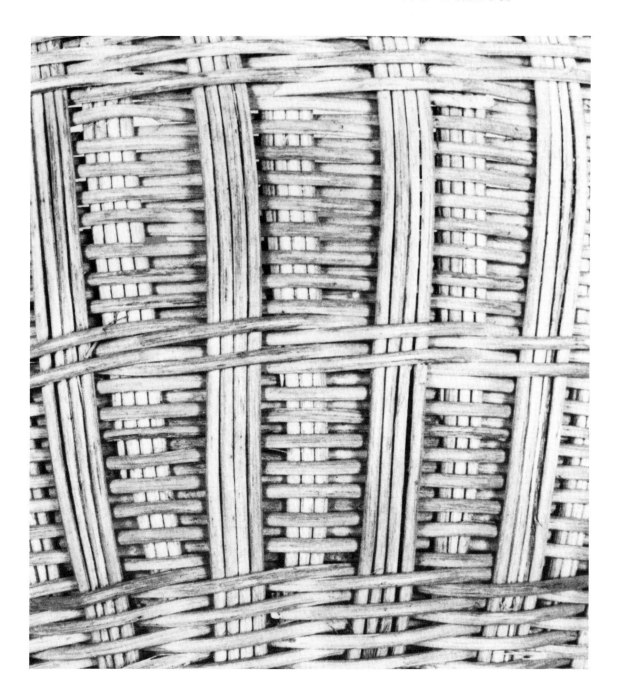

Introduction

A **rod basket** is a **wickerwork** basket woven from **rods** — round shoots or long slender sticks of wood. Oak **rods** (Pl. 5.3) are the key to identifying oak rod baskets (Pl. 5.1). These oak baskets often are mistaken for baskets made of willow (*Salix* sp.) (Pl. 5.4), round reed machined from the rattan palm (*Calamus* sp.) (Pl. 5.5), or other shoots or vines. For an untrained eye, it is difficult to distinguish among these rounded materials when they are worked into a basket, particularly into baskets made with a combination of materials. Rods from shoots are thick at the butt end and gradually taper to a narrow tip, while drawn wood rods and round reed are of uniform diameter. Shoots have leaf and bud scale scars clearly visible on the outer surface. Reed and oak have virtually the same outer appearance: the rods appear to have a lengthwise grain and are usually uniform in diameter for their entire length. In cross-section, oak and other hardwoods show growth ring divisions, willow and other shoots have a center pith, and reed reveals many small pores. Another identifying characteristic of rod baskets is their weight; the solid wood basket is much heavier than one made of willow or reed.

Each material has its own characteristics, then, with differences in length, diameter, flexibility, and density; consequently, each material is handled differently in basketmaking. The techniques of constructing oak rod and willow baskets are similar, but there are also differences because of the characteristics of the two materials. In many ways the working of oak rods is more similar to reedwork than to willowwork, because of the uniform diameter of both materials.

The forerunner of American rod basketry is European wickerwork (Pl. 5.2). In Europe, cultivated willow has been the mainstay of wickerwork basketmaking for centuries, but other native plant species, as well as imported materials, such as reed (starting in the mid-1800s), also have been used. In rural areas of the Central and Southern Appalachians, settlers made wickerwork baskets from uncultivated native willows, vines, and shoots of wood such as osier dogwood, elm, and maple.

Here is where the puzzle begins — someone began making wickerwork baskets from hardwoods, including hickory, maple, and, most commonly, white oak. The wood is split into long squared splits and used as splits or further finished into rods, by pulling the square billets through a metal

Pl. 5.1 Oval oak rod basket with lid, Union County, Pennsylvania (Bohn, 16 Oct. 1984). Oak rod baskets often are mistaken for baskets made of willow, vines, or round reed. Like this basket, many oak rodwork forms closely resemble European wickerwork. Many characteristics of central European willow wickerwork are evident in this oak basket: the shape, the domed lid, the high foot, and the decorative floats (Turtschi, Sept. 1989). Dimensions: 9″ x 12″ base, 13 1/2″ x 18″ top, 9″ s.h., 16″ o.h. Private collection.

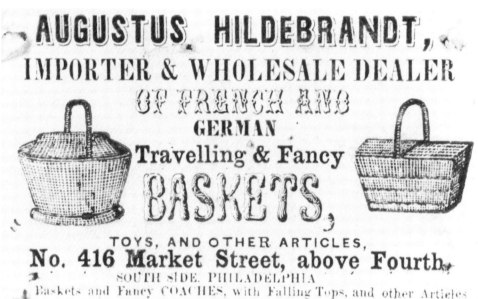

Pl. 5.2 Trade card of Augustus Hildebrandt, Philadelphia merchant; dated 1862. Willow baskets not only were made in the United States, but also were imported by dealers such as Hildebrandt. Made of both rod and split willow, a lidded, medium-sized basket with overhead handle was known as a "traveling" basket. The basket illustrated on the left is similar to some Pennsylvania oak rod baskets (e.g., Pl. 5.1). Private collection.

die (Fig. 2.18; Pls. 2.10-a, b) or whittling (Fig. 2.16). There is no known precedent in Europe for making whittled or die-shaped rods for basketmaking. However, the technology used in making round rods is similar to that in making round pegs for furniture work or drawing wire.

The authors surmise that suitable basket willow was not as available in the central Appalachian region as it was in Europe and that, consequently, immigrant basketmakers turned to other plants in the search for materials for wickerwork baskets. Oak, being readily available and known for its splitting properties, made a likely choice. As the cultivation of willow takes much time and effort (Heseltine 1982, pp. 7–12; Fitzrandolph and Hay 1926, pp. 1–87) and imported willows would have required cash expenditures, the year-round availability of white oak, a relatively "free" resource, also may have contributed to its selection for rodmaking. Once discovered, the durability of the oak wickerwork basket, compared to its willow counterpart, may have made the oak a preferred material. The thick rods and wickerwork techniques make oak rodwork the most durable of white oak basket forms.

Unknown in New England and the Deep South, oak rodwork is a basket type made primarily in the Central Appalachians. Although not as common or widespread as split and ribwork, rodwork seems to have been the dominant basket tradition in some areas. Of all white oak basket types, oak rod baskets are the most complicated technically, reflecting the skills of trained basketmakers. Oak rod baskets are more prevalent in areas settled by German groups, and many rod basket styles and their constructions are tied closely to central European wickerwork (Thierschmann, Sept. 1987; Turtschi, July 1986 and Sept. 1989) (Pls. 5.6 and 5.14-a; Cl. Pl. 20).

Concentrations of rod baskets are evident in southeastern and central Pennsylvania and in the Shenandoah Valley of Virginia, areas of dense German settlement. Other areas of extensive rodmaking are southcentral Ohio and the South Branch of the Potomac River Valley in West Virginia. Rodwork is also evident in eastern Tennessee, western North Carolina, central Kentucky, and as far west as Indiana.

Looking at the location of rodwork and the names of rodmakers, and analyzing the technical details of rod baskets, the authors believe that oak rodwork originated with German immigrant basketmakers, possibly as early as the eighteenth century. Many Germans settled early in southeastern Pennsylvania. Later groups either joined the established settlements or migrated southward to the Shenandoah Valley and the

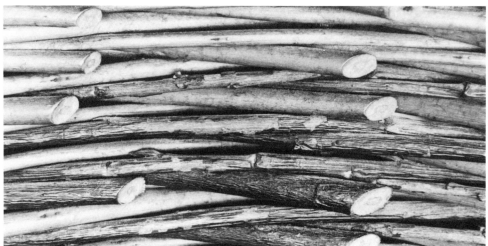

Pl. 5.3 *(Above):* Detail of oak rods. These oak rods are only slightly rounded. Wood grain is apparent on the sides of the rods, and distinct grain lines (growth-ring divisions) are visible on the cut ends. Other clues to identify the material as oak are the weight and density; oak rods are much heavier and harder than either willow or round reed.

Pl. 5.4 *(Below):* Detail of willow. Lower section is unpeeled willow, upper section is peeled willow. The triangular-shaped leaf and bud scars are visible on the surface, but the most noticeable characteristic of willow is the large pith in the center. Another identifying characteristic of willow rods is their natural taper from the large butt end to the small tip.

 Some native species of willows were available to the early settlers for basketmaking, but an 1848 article in the *American Agricultural* indicated that willow cultivation was quite minimal and that sizable amounts of willow were being imported from Germany and France (Allen 1848, p. 45). There are accounts of later willow cultivation in America (Teleki 1979, pp. 67–69; Lasansky 1979, pp. 25–27). Henry Mercer reported visiting

A. Bethtrain of Dublin, Bucks County, Pennsylvania, on 2 August 1919. Having immigrated in 1883, at the age of twenty, from Saxony, Germany, Bethtrain continued to make willow baskets in America. From 1884 to 1885, he worked for a seventy-five-year-old willow basketmaker, Michael Frohman, and afterwards Bethtrain continued to make willow baskets, cultivating his own German basket willows. Bethtrain described willow nurseries in Pennsylvania, New York, Maryland, and Illinois (Mercer 1926, 192–93). Apparently the cultivation of basket willow was strongly encouraged by the federal government, for in 1914 the U.S. Department of Agriculture issued a Farmer's Bulletin devoted entirely to basket willow culture (Lamb 1925).

Pl. 5.5 *(Above):* Detail of round reed. Round reed, machined from the rattan palm vine, is a very evenly rounded material. Another notable feature of reed is the many pores clearly visible in the cross-sections of the cut ends. Reed is quite easy to handle as a material and can be worked into a basket very quickly. Some reed baskets are indistinguishable from oak rod baskets from a distance, but the reed's light weight is a giveaway. Reed will darken with use and age, but the surface never gains the patina so often associated with well-used oak baskets.

   In the nineteenth century, reed was extensively imported into Europe and used in commercial basketwork. Thomas Okey noted the use of reed in England by commercial basketmakers, who used it for wicker furniture and luncheon and other baskets, either by itself or in combination with willow. He mentioned its easy manipulability for use by children, women, and home workers ([1912] 1986, p. 11). By the early 1900s, a number of supply houses in the United States, such as Louis Stoughton Drake and Milton Bradley, were advertising reed and other basketmaking supplies for home, school, and commercial use (Louis Stoughton Drake ca. 1918; Milton Bradley Co. 1923). A number of basketry books also gave step-by-step descriptions for working many different forms (James 1903, 1904, and n.d.; White 1901; Turner 1909).

Pl. 5.6   Willow baskets from Franklin County, Virginia (Moore, 12 Mar. 1985). The makers of these willow baskets had much expertise in handling the material. The bases, upsetts, and top side sections are waled, and the side midsections are woven with a combination of French randing and mock waling. The basket on the right shows a wide, waled ledge which once supported a lid. While the floats on these baskets appear similar to those found on oak rod baskets with combination borders, the working technique for floats on willow baskets can be different. In this case, the outside stakes were probably added at the upsett and worked in as the basket sides were woven to the top of the basket. The handles are carved from white oak, and the lid pull is an oak split. Dimensions, from left: 7 1/2″ base, 8 1/2″ top, 9″ s.h., 14″ o.h.; 7 1/2″ base, 8″ top, 7 1/2″ s.h., 12 1/2″ o.h. Collection of Roddy and Sally Moore.

Cumberland Plateau or across Pennsylvania into the Ohio Valley (Thernstrom 1980, pp. 502–505; Aurand n.d.).

Rod basketmaking was ongoing well into the twentieth century in several areas of the Central and Southern Appalachian Mountains. According to Jeannette Lasansky, "Most often the basketmaker's skill was passed on to younger family members and neighbors, in effect creating dynasties of round-rod oak basketmakers such as the Shively-Olmstead-Boop clan of Union County, the Mentzers of Lancaster County, the Shaffer-Moyer family of Clinton County, and the Zong-Moad group of Juniata County" (1984, p. 893).

Large numbers of rod baskets found in the Shenandoah Valley of Virginia and in the South Branch of the Potomac River Valley of West

Virginia also indicate one-time strong traditions. Analysis of the details of the work indicates not only regional distinctions but also significant variations—most likely evidence of family traditions or particular variations used by individual makers or communities of makers. However, at this time, little work has been done to record the names of rodmakers or their families.

In southcentral Ohio, Rosemary O. Joyce has done extensive research documenting the work and knowledge of one oak rod basketmaker, Dwight Stump (Pls. 5.10 and 5.21), of Hocking County, Ohio. Stump remembered the names of over fifty individuals who were involved in rodwork around Hocking and Fairfield counties and talked about a whole community of oak rod basketmakers who lived out on Tar Ridge, known as "basket country" (Joyce 1989, pp. 125–32, 209–211). According to Stump, most of the makers on Tar Ridge made big two-handled baskets: "You couldn't have got one of these kind of little baskets, like the Easter egg, fer any kind of money then. And they specialized in the two-thirds bushel. You couldn't get 'em t' make anything less. That's what they started in on and learnt, and that's what they'd make. They was easier made, too, didn't take s' long t' make" (Joyce 1989, p. 127). Dwight indicated that the years 1916 and 1917 marked the height of basketmaking in that region, resulting in the consumption of most of the good basket timber in the area (Joyce 1989, p. 131).

Rod basketmaking has also been documented in regions of Kentucky and Tennessee, although there is no indication of a continuing tradition in those areas. In a 1903 article, Jennie Lester Hill records that the Rector and Moore families were making two different styles of round rod baskets in central Kentucky (Hill 1903, p. 212). In the late 1800s, Jim Meadows, living in the Cumberland mountains in Coffee County, Tennessee, was making oak rod baskets (Irwin 1982, pp. 58–59); and in the 1920s and 1930s in Knox and Jefferson counties, Tennessee, the Hickey family made and peddled baskets throughout the area (Faulkner and Faulkner, 28 Nov. 1984; Thompson 1977, pp. 76–78) (Pl. 5.7).

Today, the tradition of making oak rod baskets has nearly died out. Few rodworkers are making baskets. Dwight Stump of Hocking County, Ohio, has given up making baskets himself, but his son Bobby occasionally makes a few (Joyce, 24 Aug. 1989). In 1983, Homer Summers of Kanawha County, West Virginia, started making rod baskets in the tradition of his wife's relatives, and when his health is good, he continues to make them. By 1989, he had made over four hundred baskets (Summers and Summers, 15 Sept. 1989). Although a number of individuals remember members of

Pl. 5.7   Group of oak rod baskets made by the Hickey family. In Jefferson and Knox counties, Tennessee, in the 1920s and 1930s, Hickey made his living by basketmaking, with his children helping (Faulkner and Faulkner, 28 Nov. 1984). Many Hickey baskets are still in existence, showing both very fine, tight work and coarse, loose work—perhaps indicating different family makers. The features of the Hickey baskets include: graceful flaring shape, tall foot, fitched base, waled and randed sides, trac borders, and roped handle with V-shaped handle attachment. The Hickey family made several different styles, including round, small and large oval, and wall baskets. Dimensions, from left: Oval: 7″ x 11 1/2″ base, 9 1/2″ x 15 1/2″ top, 8 1/4″ s.h., 13 1/2″ o.h. Wall: 4″ x 7 1/4″ plank base, 6″ x 9″ top, 4 3/8″ s.h., 10 1/2″ o.h. Round: 11″ base, 13 1/2″ top, 9″ s.h., 16 1/4″ o.h. Private collection.

their family making rod baskets, these potential basketmakers have not taken up rodwork. It is quite possible that this distinctive American basketry form may reach extinction.

Many of the technically complex rod forms are not being made by today's rodmakers, and the makers who once knew how to make them are deceased. The baskets themselves have been analyzed and are described in great detail in this chapter, but the technical descriptions of rodwork have been generalized from terminology used in willow basketmaking. As it is not possible to know the rodmakers' technical vocabulary, the authors have chosen terms used in German and English willow basketmaking (see Okey 1912, Will 1985, Wright 1983, Knock 1970, Heseltine 1982).

Structure and Materials

There are different types of oak rod baskets, with all the basket types having shaped rods as the primary weaving material of the basket body. Most rod baskets are constructed using rounded rods for both the foundation and the weavers. These rod baskets are made in round and oval shapes. Although rectangular willow baskets were made in both Europe and America, the authors have yet to see a rectangular basket made from round oak rods. Other rod basket forms have a structural foundation like splitwork or ribwork, but use round rods as the weaving materials. The authors have termed these basket types **rod/split** and **rod/rib** baskets, respectively, and these types are treated in a separate section at the end of this chapter, along with a most unusual **rod/coil** form.

The overall structure of a rod basket (Fig. 5.1) begins with the construction of the basket bottom. The bottom of a basket consists of **bottom-sticks** interlaced with weaving rods. When the base is completed, the ends of the bottom-sticks are trimmed, and **side-stakes** are inserted alongside

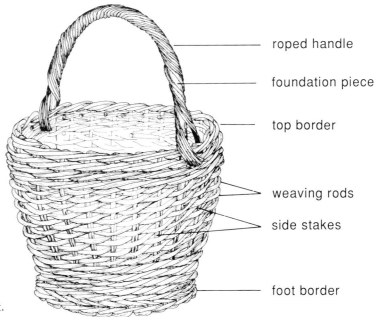

roped handle

foundation piece

top border

weaving rods

side stakes

foot border

Fig. 5.1   Structure of a rod basket.

Pl. 5.8 Small rod sewing baskets, Shenandoah Valley, Virginia. Often bits of fabric, rusted pins, and other small notions remain caught in the weavers in the bottom of small two-handled baskets, evidence of their use as sewing baskets. These small baskets most likely were made by the same maker (unknown) and show refined skills in both weaving and material preparation—the weaving rods are only 3/32″ in diameter. The bases are begun with pairing which changes to waling, while the entire side is worked with three-rod wale. The shape and weaving techniques are almost identical to those seen in large feed baskets from the same region (Pl. 5.9). Dimensions, from left: 6 1/2″ base, 10 1/4″ top, 4 1/4″ s.h., 5″ o.h.; 6 1/4″ base, 9 3/8″ top, 3 3/4″ s.h., 4 1/2″ o.h. Collection of H. Wayne and Rachel Nash Law.

each bottom-stick and turned up to form the uprights for the basket sides. An **upsett,** the first rounds of side weaving, holds the side-stakes upright. The sides are woven, and the ends of the side-stakes are laid down around the top edge to make the **border.** Rod baskets are constructed with both carved and **roped handles** and occasionally without handles. A rod basket may have a **foot** added to protect the basket base.

Rods of varying lengths and diameters are the chief material for all rod baskets. The size of the rods in a basket is influenced by the intended size and use of a basket—from small two-handled sewing baskets with rods 3/32 inches in diameter (Pl. 5.8) to large bushel feed baskets with rods a quarter-inch in diameter (Pl. 5.9). Large baskets use large diameter rods, and often the rods are left rough (sometimes still square in cross-section). Within any one basket, several different sizes of rods may be used, depending on the basket form and the working methods of the maker. The rods used for bottom-sticks most often are the rods largest in diameter (often two or three times as thick as the weaving rods), as they are the main support of the basket. Side-stakes sometimes are slightly thicker than weaving rods, but often they are the same diameter. The foundation

Pl. 5.9 Oak rod "feed" basket made by Hugh Wratchford (d. 1914). Wratchford lived and worked in Hardy and Grant counties, West Virginia, through the early 1900s. He is said to have made hundreds of oak rod bushel baskets for local farmers to use as "corn" or "feed" baskets (Pack, April 1979; Ratsford, 15 Jan. 1986; Shobe, 15 and 21 Jan. 1986). Weaving rods in this basket are 1/4″ in diameter. Both large and small baskets, such as these with three-rod waled sides, a flared shape, and two ear handles, are common through the northeastern counties of West Virginia and in the north and central Shenandoah Valley of Virginia. Dimensions: 13 1/2″ base, 25″ top, 11″ s.h., 13″ o.h. Collection of Annie Handley Shobe.

piece for roped handles is a thick split or rounded rod which is wrapped with small rods.

As with other basket forms, the work was often divided according to the skill required. It took experienced hands to split the wood down to a square billet close to the desired size of the rod, but drawing rods through a metal die could be done by less skilled labor. Bertha Fridley of Fairfield County, Ohio, recalled helping her grandfather:

> When we were kids at home, Ann and I especially, we had to poke the rods through [the die plate]. It was the most boring job in the world! We had to poke them through the holes in that little metal thing on a board, so then he'd pull 'em through. We were pretty small and couldn't pull through ourselves. Then that pulling 'd shave 'em off, make 'em round. There's a lot of work to it. I remember Grandpa would sit by the hour and do them. (Joyce, 10 Mar. 1986)

Similarly, in the 1920s, Nellie Grabill of Shenandoah County, Virginia, helped her foster father, John Funk, a rodmaker in Tom's Brook. During the day Funk split the oak into long squared billets, and after Nellie got home from school, she pulled them through the die (Helsley, 31 Mar. 1989; Helsley and Helsley, 16 Mar. 1989).

While material preparation was often a joint effort, current evidence indicates that the weaving of rod baskets was more often associated with men than with women. Of the more than fifty rodmakers in Ohio recorded by Joyce, only five were women. And according to Dwight Stump (Pls. 5.10 and 5.11), if women made rod baskets, they tended to make the small baskets (Joyce 1989, pp. 209–11; Joyce, 24 Aug. 1989).

Pl. 5.10 Rodmaker Dwight Stump, Hocking County, Ohio. In his workshop, Stump has two or three die boards with several metal dies mounted on them, for making various sized rods. The dies are made from the hard steel knives of mowing machines: first the steel is heated and then, using variously sized bolts, it is hammered "til you get kind of a bubble on there and then it kind of breaks through and you sharpen that. . . . Just take a file and just kind of touch up the edge real light" (Stump and Mansberger, 16 May 1984). After setting the chosen board into brackets mounted on posts, Stump uses a pair of pliers to draw the rods, beginning from the butt end because the wood does not splinter off as easily when pulled in that direction. He also likes to use wood that is cut in the summer, because the bark strips off more easily (Stump and Mansberger, 16 May 1984).

Pl. 5.11 Oak rod "egg" basket made by Dwight Stump, Hocking County, Ohio. Stump makes many sizes of round baskets, including a small Easter egg basket; an egg basket; a sewing basket; baskets of peck, half-bushel, two-thirds-bushel, and bushel dry volume; clothes basket; hamper; an apple bushel basket; and a popular new form, the apple basket or tray (Joyce 1989, pp. 62–63). Stump varies the size of the rods and the weave depending on the intended use of the basket; for example, while he makes a two-thirds-bushel basket for both a clothes basket and a corn basket, the latter uses heavier rods and has a denser weave (Stump and Mansberger, 16 May 1984). Like many other Ohio rod baskets, Stump's basket is woven of large rods and has no foot. Another characteristic often associated with Ohio rodwork (Cl. Pl. 17) is the band of three-rod wale used as an upsett, followed first by a wide section of randing and then by another waled section below the border. Stump uses the term "braiding down the top" for working the top border, and he often adds an extra crossed binding at the top. As Stump explained, "I put that there to draw it down tight, so it'll stay tight. You can take that off but a lot of 'em leaves that on" (Stump and Mansberger, 16 May 1984). Stump is left-handed and weaves left-

handed as well, working all movements from right to left. The left-slanting diagonals of the waled sections are evidence of Dwight's hand preference. Dimensions: 7 1/2″ base, 6 1/4″ s.h., 10 1/4″ o.h. Collection of Elizabeth Harzoff.

Weaves and Splices

Many different weaves are used in rodwork, with some weaves best suited for particular construction steps. A single basket may use several different weaves, with each weave giving its own distinctive appearance. Each weave is executed in a different manner; there are differences in the number of weaving rods and in the **strokes**—the over/under movement of each rod. If appropriate, the stroke movements are indicated in parentheses after the name of the weave. Typically, all weaving strokes are worked from left to right. In formal European training, students are taught to weave right-handed, regardless of their natural hand preference. In American oak rod baskets, however, the strokes are occasionally worked left-handed (right to left). Left-handed weaving is particularly evident in examining baskets which are waled or French randed, because the angle of the weaving slants to the left.

Weaves which form the basis for wickerwork constructions are worked either with or without twisting the weaving rods. **Randing, French rand-ing**, and **mock waling** are worked over and under without twisting the weaving rods. **Pairing, fitching**, and **waling** use several weaving rods which twist around each other while consecutively moving over and under. Twisted weaves often are used as holding weaves, to secure the positioning of bottom-sticks or side-stakes.

Round materials, because of their shape, are spliced differently than flat materials. The weave illustrations here also show the usual splicing tech-nique for each weave. As rods are spliced, the ends of the weavers are left long enough that they can be trimmed diagonally to lie snugly against a stake or rod. If a rod is trimmed too short, the end will pop out of place, leaving a hole. Trimming ends is known as "picking off." Usually the base is picked off after it is woven, and the sides are picked off after the borders are completed.

Randing (Fig. 5.2) — the over-one/under-one stroke — is technically the simplest weave in wickerwork and uses minimal materials. It must be ex-ecuted carefully, with even rod tension, to prevent the side-stakes from drawing together and to create smooth basket sides. Randing uses either one rod which is worked in a spiral around an odd number of working ends, or two weaving rods which chase around an even number of work-ing ends. In oak rodwork, bases are occasionally randed, but this tech-nique more often is used for side weaving (Pls. 5.12 and 5.11; Cl. Pl. 17). In Ohio rodwork, randing is the most common side-weaving technique.

French randing (Fig. 5.3) is commonly seen on oak rod baskets made in central Kentucky and Pennsylvania, although as a wickerwork technique it is universal. On close inspection, one can see the diagonal slant of the weaving rods, characteristic of French randing, a very fast weaving method which uses multiple rods of equal length. One weaving rod is placed behind each side-stake, and then each rod is woven over-one/under-one in succession. The rods are woven to their ends (usually ending on the inside of the basket), to complete a French-randed section. The height of a French-randed section depends on the length of the rods: the longer the rods, the higher the section. This weave is worked on the sides of rod baskets and is often bound by rows of waling placed above and below a French-randed section (Pl. 5.13). French randing is not used as a bottom weave on oak rodwork, although it is found as a bottom-weaving technique on some central European willow baskets (Wright 1983, p. 59).

Another untwisted weave is *mock waling* (Fig. 5.4). Mock waling has the appearance of waling, a twisted weave; however, it is not twisted. This weave is begun like French randing, with one weaving rod behind

Fig. 5.2 Randing.

Pl. 5.12 Handleless rod basket with randed sides, purchased in central Pennsylvania; origin uncertain. The side-stakes are clearly visible on a basket with randed sides. Extremely well executed, this basket could be a textbook example of different weaving techniques: the base is fitched, the upsett waled, the sides randed, and the top capped off with another waling section. The top edge is worked in a three-rod plain border (u1/o2/u1), while the foot is a three-rod plain border (u2/o2/u2). The absence of handles is probably intentional, for this basket may well have been made for its present use as a wastebasket. Dimensions: 8 1/2″ base, 10 3/4″ top, 8 3/4″ s.h. Private collection.

each stake; the weaving stroke is over-two/under-one. Occasionally mock waling is worked as the first and last rows of a French-randed section. It also is used on baskets with side floats, where it functions as a holding row for the **floats** (Pls. 5.14-a, b).

Pairing (Fig. 5.5) and *fitching* (Fig. 5.6), also known as "twining" in fiberwork (Adovasio 1977, p. 20), use two rods which twist around each other as the bottom-sticks or side-stakes are woven. In pairing, working left to right, two rods are worked over and under with a clockwise movement, creating an "S-twist." In fitching, the two rods are worked with the reverse movement, twisting alternately under and over each other in a counterclockwise fashion, creating a "Z-twist." While both weaves often are used for constructing bases (Pl. 5.15), fitching locks the bottom-sticks in place more securely (Turtschi, Sept. 1989). Pairing is worked occasionally as a side weave and sometimes as a narrow band for holding side-stakes in place beneath the border.

5. Rod Baskets   217

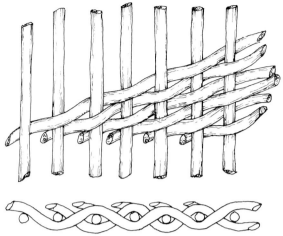

Pl. 5.13 Four-handled Pennsylvania rod basket. The sides of this basket have two sections of French randing capped off by rows of three-rod wale. In shape and size, this basket is reminiscent of European baskets made for laundry use. Four-handled baskets are not common. The ear handles, all with twisted roping-rods (Pl. 5.41), are thicker and longer than those on the sides. The large size suggests that two persons may have been needed to carry it when full. Dimensions: 14" x 24" base, 22 1/2" x 30" top, 13" s.h., 16" o.h. Collection of Cynthia W. and Michael B. Taylor.

Fig. 5.3 French randing.

Waling uses three or more rods which twist around each other as they interlace bottom-sticks or side-stakes, forming a wide ridge or "wale." In the most common wales, the weaving rods are worked over a set number and then under one; however, there are many variations in the weaving strokes, and here the specific over/under movement is indicated in parentheses. The wales most common in oak rodwork are discussed below. Waling is a very strong, dense weave which uses more weaving materials than any of the techniques described previously. When woven on the sides of a basket, waling makes a thick-walled basket with a smooth surface. Single rows of waling are used in side weaving, serving both functional and decorative roles.

Three-rod wale (2/1) (Fig. 5.7) is the most common wale used in rod basketmaking. Using three rods which consecutively move over-two/under-one, three-rod wale is used for both base and side construction. Three-rod wale commonly is used for the upsett weave, in conjunction with baskets which are randed or French randed on the sides (Pls. 5.7 and 5.13). It is a

Pl. 5.14-a   Pennsylvania oval rod basket with side floats and mock waling. The stakes are worked into a loosely scalloped top border and then drawn back through the rows of mock waling to make decorative side floats and also foot-stakes for the bottom of the basket. Although this basket shows many similarities to the one in Cl. Pl. 20, the different weaving techniques indicate that the basketmakers were working in different traditions. An overhead handle was once present on this basket. Dimensions: 4 1/2″ x 7″ base, 6″ s.h. Collection of Jeannette Lasansky.

Pl. 5.14-b   Aerial base view of oval basket in Pl. 5.14-a. This basket has a typical base begun with three lengthwise bottom-sticks crossed with five shorter bottom-sticks. The flat split lashing the bottom-sticks together is a technique often used in German willowwork (Turtschi, Sept. 1989).

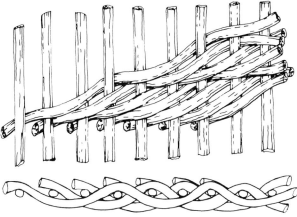

Fig. 5.4   Mock waling (2/1).

dense weave which completely covers the side-stakes on its "right" side, where the weavers float over *two* stakes, usually the outside of the basket. The "wrong" side looks similar to plain weave, in which the weavers cross over only *one* stake, with the side-stakes visible. Three-rod wale is a weave common in baskets made in the Shenandoah Valley, Virginia (Pls. 5.16-a,

Pl. 5.15 Paired base. Detail of sewing basket in Cl. Pl. 18. Half of a snap and a button remain caught in the rods, showing its previous use as a sewing basket. The base of this round basket is begun with three bottom-sticks inserted through two bottom-sticks, instead of the more common three/three configuration. The bottom-sticks are first bound with a flat split (Figs. 5.10-a, b) and, at the point of opening out, the weavers change to round rods. The two rods are woven alternately over and under the bottom-sticks, while twisting around each other. Pairing, a technique usual for weaving the bases of baskets, is not commonly worked on basket sides. Dimension of base: 7″. Collection of Cynthia W. and Michael B. Taylor.

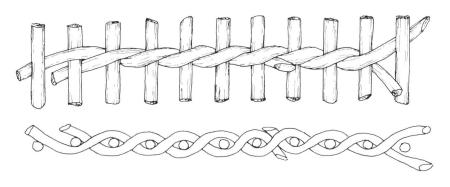

Fig. 5.5
Pairing (S-twist).

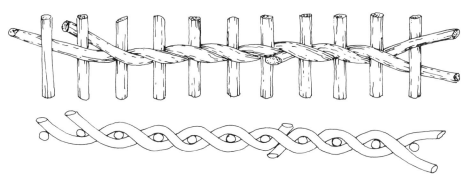

Fig. 5.6
Fitching (Z-twist).

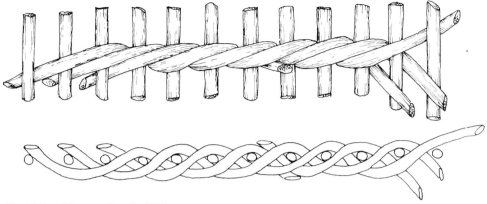

Fig. 5.7   Three-rod wale (2/1).

Pl. 5.16-a   Three-rod waled basket, Shenandoah Valley, Virginia. Characteristics of this basket are typical of many oak rod baskets from the same region: the shape (a wide basket body flaring from a relatively small base), waled base and sides, two-rod plain top border, added foot-stakes worked in a three-rod plain foot border, and the roped handle with the triangular-shaped attachment. Waled baskets are quite heavy and sturdy, due to the amount of materials used for the weaving technique. Dimensions: 9 1/2″ base, 16 1/2″ top, 8″ s.h., 15″ o.h. Collection of Cynthia W. and Michael B. Taylor.

Pl. 5.16-b   Base view of basket in Pl. 5.16-a. The domed base is constructed with a four/four bottom-stick configuration bound with very fine rods. As the base is woven, the diameter of the weaving rods increases until they are roughly the same size as the stakes. The foot-stakes are inserted into the waling of the side weaving, giving a distinctive appearance to the basket side. One row of waling is woven around the foot-stakes before they are bordered off with a three-rod plain border (u2/o2/u1).

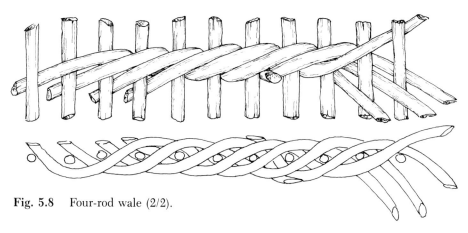

Fig. 5.8   Four-rod wale (2/2).

b; 5.8); in the South Branch of the Potomac River Valley, West Virginia (Pl. 5.9); and in southeastern and central Pennsylvania (Pl. 5.18).

Four-rod wale (Fig. 5.8) is used less commonly than the three-rod wale. It takes more weaving materials and creates a weightier basket with essentially the same outward appearance and results as three-rod wale. It is sometimes used for an entire basket, but most often it is used only as the finishing weave, to tighten the top of a basket before the side-stakes are woven into the border. The four rods move either over-three/under-one or over-two/under-two. The four-rod wale (3/1) appears similar to three-rod wale, with "right" and "wrong" sides. The four-rod wale (2/2) looks exactly the same on both sides, completely covering side-stakes inside and outside (Pl. 5.17).

Five-rod or six-rod wales are used occasionally to create a foot for the basket (Pl. 5.22) or to make a ridge on the inside, below the top rim, for a lid rest (Pl. 5.42).

Decoration and Signatures

Many features of a rod basket appear decorative but in fact are an integral part of the basket structure. Alternation of weaves on a basket's sides, borders, and handle attachments all may be considered ornamental. Other decorative elements of some rod baskets are *floats*, rods which "float" over the surface of a basket's sides. The floats can be either structural or nonstructural, and the techniques involved are discussed in the section on borders.

A purely decorative feature on some rod baskets is the use of color. Color is not common in rodwork, and only a few rodworkers who used color have been documented. Jacob Mentzer (who worked from 1875 to around 1930) of Lancaster County, Pennsylvania, colored selected rods with enamel paint and worked them into his baskets (Lasansky 1984, p. 889; Herr and Herr, 18 Oct. 1984) (Cl. Pl. 23). William Shaffer (1869–1943) of Clinton County, Pennsylvania, used a variety of techniques to accent the colorwork in his Easter baskets (Lasansky 1984, p. 889; Lasansky 1979, p. 21). When baskets are worked with colored rods, the structure and choice of weaving techniques is critical in creating the desired design (see Wright 1983, pp. 65–66). The manner in which the colored rods are worked into the basket can create a variety of color effects, such as blocks of color (Pl. 5.22; Cl. Pls. 19, 22, 24), horizontal bands (Cl. Pls. 17 and 21; Pl. 5.27), or spirals (Cl. Pl. 24).

Many distinctive features of rodwork help identify a basket as a product of a particular maker or region. Some clues to look for are: the shape of the basket, the shaping of the rods, the size of the rods used in each section of the basket, the layout of the base, the particular weaves worked in the basket base and sides, the method of working the borders, and the handle and the way it is attached to the basket. Even with two "identical" rod baskets, often there are noticeable differences which are not clearly visible at first glance, such as slight variations in weaves, border treatments, splicing methods, or the way a handle's roping-rods are tucked into the basket.

Bases: Round and Oval

Rod basket construction begins with the base. The length of the bottom-sticks and their layout are determined by the base shape—round or oval. The **slath** is the central bottom formation, made by interlacing the bottom-sticks to the point of "opening out"—that is, the point at which the weavers are worked around each bottom-stick (Pl. 5.15). The first base weavers are either flat splits, very small rods, or rods split in half—any appropriate material which can be worked tightly into the small beginning spaces. As the base weaving progresses, the weaving rods may be made thicker to support the bottom-sticks as the spacing between them becomes wider. In rodwork, the base most often is paired or fitched but also may be waled or randed. After the formation of the slath, the bottom-sticks continue to be interlaced with weaving rods to complete the basket base.

1. Round Bases

The most common rod basket is round (Pl. 5.18). Round bases (Figs. 5.9-a, b, c; 5.10) typically are begun with six bottom-sticks of equal length. Three of the bottom-sticks are split in the center, to make a space through which the other three are inserted (Fig. 5.9-a). The bottom-sticks are left in groups of threes, and the weaving is begun with a flat split (Fig. 5.10; Pl. 5.15) or small rod (Fig. 5.9-b). After two or three weaving rows, the bottom-sticks are "opened out"—each bottom-stick is separated and woven individually (Fig. 5.9-c). Care is taken to keep the spacing of the bottom-sticks even and the base round throughout the weaving.

As a base is worked, the weaving often is controlled so that the base shape will be domed. In rodwork, the weaves most often used for domed bottoms are waling or fitching. These weaves have a tight rod tension which allows the bottom sticks to be drawn up and held in place. After the bottom is completed, it is turned over so that the dome is to the inside of the basket (Pl. 5.16-b). The domed bottom makes a much stronger base than a flat one and will not allow the base to pull away from the basket sides under heavy use (Turtschi, July 1986).

2. Oval Bases

Oval bases are constructed with two lengths of bottom-sticks, longer ones for the length and shorter ones for the width. The number of bottom-

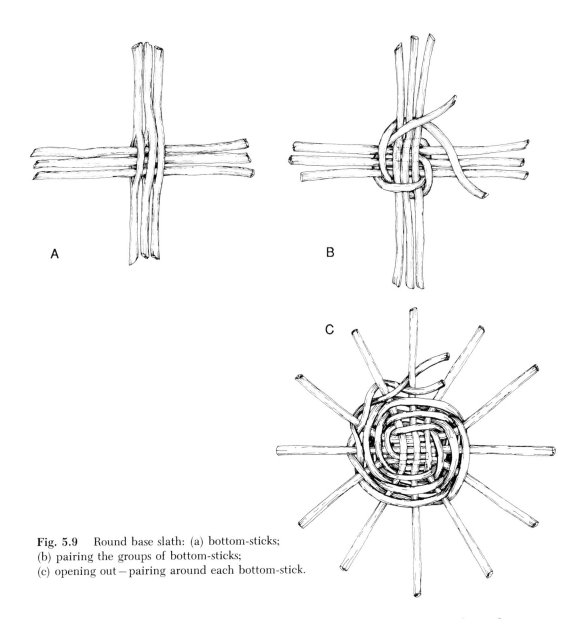

A   B   C

Fig. 5.9   Round base slath: (a) bottom-sticks;
(b) pairing the groups of bottom-sticks;
(c) opening out—pairing around each bottom-stick.

sticks varies, but a typical layout uses three lengthwise bottom-sticks and
five crosswise bottom-sticks. The most common base is similar to the
round bases in which the crosswise bottom-sticks are split in their centers
and the lengthwise sticks are inserted through (Fig. 5.11; Pl. 5.14-b). Another base also uses crosswise bottom-sticks which are split, but the
lengthwise support is a wide slat with its ends whittled into three or more
separate rods (Fig. 5.12; Pl. 5.19). The crosswise bottom-sticks are evenly
spaced on the slat and the base woven.

A number of unusual oval-based rod baskets from westcentral Virginia

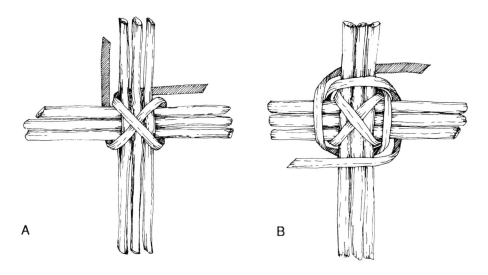

A   B

Fig. 5.10   Round base begun with flat splits:
(a) the first split is folded in half and crossed over bottom-sticks;
(b) each split weaves over/under, with a half twist between each group of bottom-sticks.

Pl. 5.18   Rod baskets made by Martin Mastle (b. 1907), Lebanon County, Pennsylvania (Lasansky 1979, p. 57; 15 Oct. 1984). The bases are chased and the sides waled with alternating bands of light sapwood rods and bands of darker heartwood rods. Mastle made both rib and rod basket forms (Lasansky 1979, pp. 33, 57). Dimensions, from left: 8 1/2″ base, 14″ top, 9 1/2″ s.h., 12″ o.h.; 7″ base, 11 1/2″ top, 8″ s.h., 14″ o.h. Collection of Jeannette Lasansky.

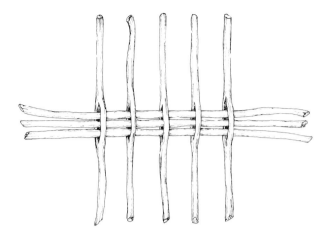

Fig. 5.11   Layout of bottom-sticks for oval base.

Pl. 5.19   Pennsylvania rod basket made by the Shively family. The base is begun with a solid lengthwise slat which is carved into three rods at each end. Five crosswise bottom-sticks are slit in the center and slipped onto the slat to complete the configuration of bottom-sticks. The handle of this basket is shaped into a D-ring, and the handle ends are tapered and slipped on each side of the center crosspiece — becoming both bottom-sticks and side-stakes. The preformed handle helps control the shape and size of the basket. The Shivelys lived in Union County, Pennsylvania, and made baskets up through the late 1940s (Lasansky 1979, p. 55; 15 Oct. 1984). Characteristics of the Shively baskets include: slat in the base, D-ring handle, randed base and sides, and combination top/foot border. Dimensions: 9″ x 12″ base, 12 1/2″ x 17″ top, 6 3/4″ s.h., 13″ o.h. Private collection.

Fig. 5.12   Oval base with solid slat.

(Pl. 5.20) combine details of rodwork and splitwork. There are no bottom-sticks in these baskets; the base is constructed with long foundation rods which are crossed over each other and bound in place with strips of tin. These rods are woven with randing to form the base, and then they are curved up to form the sides of the basket. The foot, handle, and top rim treatments are more typical of splitwork than rodwork.

Pl. 5.20 Unusual oval rod basket with features of both rodwork and splitwork. A number of baskets of this type have been found in westcentral Virginia; this one came from a home in Augusta County, Virginia. The base is laid out with long cross rods sandwiched between two layers of lengthwise rods held together by riveted aluminum straps. The whole basket is woven by randing, with the shaping completely controlled by the tension of the randing rods. Details of splitwork include a heavy outer rim that is cross lashed to the top of the basket, and a single-notched handle fitted to the inside of the basket. A thick rod is lashed onto the base for a foot. Dimensions: 6″ x 10″ base, 15 1/2″ x 12 1/2″ top, 7 1/2″ s.h., 13″ o.h. Private collection.

Side-stakes, Upsett, and Side Weaving

When a base is completed, the bottom-sticks are cut off flush to the weaving, and side-stakes are inserted. In round-based baskets, the number of side-stakes is equal to twice the number of working ends of the bottom-sticks. The end of each stake is tapered and pushed in close to the center. Two side-stakes are inserted at the end of each bottom-stick, one on either side. In oval-based baskets, the number of side-stakes can vary, depending on the shape of the basket and the number of crosswise bottom-sticks in the initial layout. In oak rodwork, oval baskets typically have two side-stakes added alongside each of the bottom-sticks on the ends of the base, and either one or two beside each of the crosswise bottom-sticks on the sides of the base. Baskets with two side-stakes added to each working end of the bottom-sticks tend to flare, with the top dimensions becoming much larger than the base dimensions (Pl. 5.26-a).

After the side-stakes are inserted into the woven base, they are turned up. In willowwork, this step is known as "pricking up." To facilitate bending and prevent cracking of the willow, an awl or knife is placed on the side-stake at the base edge and pushed into the side-stake as it is bent upward. It is unknown whether a similar technique is used to turn up oak side-stakes. After the side-stakes are turned up, they are held upright with the help of a hoop or a string.

An upsett is immediately woven to secure the side-stakes in an upright position (Pl. 5.21). The upsett is critical for shaping, as it determines the

Pl. 5.21 Dwight Stump, Hocking County, Ohio, 1984, weaving the upsett of a basket. Stump has tied the side-stakes (he calls them "stay-rods" or "side-rods") together at the top, to help shape the basket as he weaves (Stump and Mansberger, 16 May 1984). Stump makes a very sturdy basic basket. The round base slath is begun with what he calls the "bottom cross": two bottom-sticks inserted through three bottom-sticks, all secured with pairing. When the base is completed, he inserts two stakes alongside each of the bottom-sticks, forming what he recalls rodmakers calling a "web of stays," "spider," or "spider web" (Joyce, 24 Aug. 1989). Stump is weaving a three-rod wale for the upsett and will follow up by randing with two weavers, one chasing the other. At the top of the basket, three-rod wale will cap off the randing before the top border is worked.

Pl. 5.22 Red and white rod sewing basket, Shenandoah County, Virginia (Helsley and Helsley, 16 Mar. 1989). The maker of this basket wove the sides in three-rod wale with one dyed rod and two plain rods, to make blocks of color. Weaving with one dyed rod allows a basketmaker to alternate blocks of color up the sides of the basket by changing the sequence of the dyed rod in the weaving pattern. The top part of this basket is worked with a four-rod wale (2/2) using two dyed rods and so making wider blocks of color. The base of the basket is begun by fitching with a flat split, and then changes to fitching with rods. The foot is woven as the first row of the upsett, using a five-rod wale (4/1) which creates a small ridge at the edge of the base, upon which the basket rests. Dimensions: 7 5/8" base, 12" top, 4 1/4" s.h., 5 1/2" o.h. Private collection.

angle of a basket's sides. Once the upsett is woven, the basic shape cannot be changed. The first upsett row usually covers the angle of the bent side-stakes and the ends of the bottom-sticks. In some baskets, the first upsett row also serves as a foot, and on such baskets, the wide ridge is worked in a five- or six-rod wale (Pl. 5.22). One row is woven with the thick wale, and then enough rods are dropped to continue with a three-rod wale for the remainder of the upsett.

After the upsett is established, the basket shape is controlled further by the tension of the weaving rods and the spacing between the side-stakes. Most baskets flare gradually from the base to the top, but others are straight-sided (Pl. 5.23). Occasionally one sees bulbous rodwork forms which close in to a small top diameter (Pl. 5.24) and baskets which flare significantly at the top, like those made by the Hickey family of Tennessee (Pl. 5.7).

In willowwork, to keep the weaving tight so that no gaps appear in the basket sides, the weaving periodically is pounded with a small iron bar called a "rapping iron" or with the side of the basketmaker's hand. The basketmaker hits the weaving in between each stake all the way around every few rows or after a section of weaving is completed. This packs the willows down and helps to keep the weaving level. It is unknown whether oak rod basketmakers used a rapping iron, but the idea of packing the weaving by pounding certainly was known by Dwight Stump, who from time to time would pause to rap the basket sides with his hands as the side weaving progressed (Stump and Mansberger, 16 May 1984).

Pl. 5.23 Lidded basket woven with rods and splits; origin unknown. This basket flares slightly from the upsett but soon straightens to become almost vertical in shape. It is randed in sections with both flat split and round rod weavers, with each section being capped off by a row of three-rod wale to help hold and level the weaving. The basket has small ear handles set into the sides and a roped ear lid pull. The flat lid is fastened to the basket by a wire hinge. Dimensions: 14″ base, 21″ top, 25″ s.h., 26″ o.h. with lid. Private collection.

Pl. 5.24 Urn-shaped rod basket, Shenandoah Valley, Virginia (Helsley and Helsley, 13 Mar. 1985). Few rod baskets are seen with such an exaggerated shape. The basket's sides are upsett with waling to establish the wide flare, and then the basket is French randed to the widest point, where the weaving changes to three-rod wale. The three-rod wale is continued and woven with more and more tension, to draw in the sides to the small top opening. Dimensions: 11 1/2″ base, 11″ top, 12″ s.h., 16 1/2″ o.h. Private collection.

Top and Foot Borders and Floats

Borders are worked on the top edge of rod baskets to finish the rim, as well as on the base edge to form a foot. Top borders are made by laying down the ends of the side-stakes. If a side-stake is broken, a replacement is inserted alongside the broken one, and the new stake is used to weave the border (this technique is often used to repair baskets with worn top or foot borders). Foot borders often are made by turning the basket upside down and inserting short **foot-stakes** into the side weaving, at the edge of the base. The foot-stakes are then "bordered off." "Combination top/foot" borders are worked from the same stakes: the side-stakes are laid down forming the top border, and the ends of these side-stakes continue down the basket sides, emerging at the edge of the base, and are bordered off to form the foot. The length of the side-stakes required for a border is determined by the type of border to be worked. Basic edgings such as "trac" and "plain" borders require far shorter side-stakes than the more intricate combination top/foot borders.

Borders may be decorative as well as functional and range from a simple woven edge to elaborate and complicated braids. Well-made borders have evenly spaced side-stakes and are woven with tension to create a tight, even finish. When the border is completed, the ends of the border-stakes are trimmed on a diagonal (as in splicing).

The simplest border is the *trac border* (Fig. 5.13). Trac borders are worked with one stake at a time. Each stake is laid down in turn, following an established stroke pattern. The most basic trac is one woven with an over-one/under-one (o1/u1) stroke, but longer trac stokes are more common in rodwork. The beginning movement may be either over or under. West Virginia rodmakers Ogel Higginbotham, Rome Philips, and Homer Summers work a trac top border with an under-one/over-one/under-one (u1/o1/u1) stroke and then secure the ends of side-stakes into the weaving about an inch below the top border (Pls. 5.35-c, d). Other rod baskets (Pls. 5.25-a, b) have trac borders with longer weaving strokes; the longer the stroke, the higher the edging. A trac used by the Hickey family for both top and foot borders was woven with an over-one/under-one/over-two/under-one (o1/u1/o2/u1) sequence, with the side-stakes ending on the inside of the basket (Pl. 5.7). The over-two movement appears as a row of waling on the outside of the basket.

The tightest and strongest borders used in rodwork are the *plain borders*. These borders are worked with two or more side-stakes at a time, in several steps depending on the intricacy of the technique. Names for

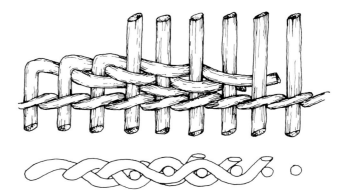

Fig. 5.13   Trac border (ul/ol/ul/ol/ul).

Pl. 5.25-a   Unusual basket with a trac border, from eastern Tennessee. The structural framework of this basket is made from hoops and round rods, but the weavers are flat splits. Just below the top trac border is a thick hoop, into which holes have been drilled for each stake to pass through. The handle also pierces the wide top hoop and is secured by a nail. This basket is quite sturdy, due to its unusual construction. Dimensions: 12 5/8″ base, 13″ top, 8″ s.h., 13″ o.h. Collection of Kathleen and Ken Dalton.

Pl. 5.25-b   Base view of basket in Pl. 5.25-a. The unusual base construction shows the thick center crosspiece. Holes are drilled in the crosspiece, through which the long foundation rods for the base and sides are threaded.

plain borders are derived from the number of initial side-stakes laid down in the first step and are further defined by the entire weaving movement of each stake. In rodwork, there are many types of plain borders, with differences in the number of initial rods (ranging from two to five) and their weaving strokes. The more rods used, the wider and thicker the border (the same principle applies to waling; in fact, plain borders often look like waling).

A common border used for top edgings as well as foot borders is the three-rod plain border (u1/o2/u1) (Fig. 5.14). It begins with three side-stakes, each folded down under the next one (Fig. 5.14-a). The first laid-down stake is woven over two stakes and behind one, exiting to the outside. The next upright stake is then laid down so that it lies alongside the first stake (Fig. 5.14-b). Working from left to right, the process of weaving the laid-down stake and laying down the next stake is repeated until all side-stakes are worked (Fig. 5.14-c). At the completion of the border, the ends of the final stakes are threaded under the initial side-stakes, keeping in pattern (Pls. 5.9, 5.34, 5.42).

A border used on the top edge of many baskets from Virginia's Shenandoah Valley is the two-rod plain border (u1/o1/u1/o1) (Fig. 5.15; Pls. 5.26-a, b; 5.16-a). This border begins with two side-stakes, each folded down behind the next consecutive stake (Fig. 5.15-a). The first laid-down stake is then woven o1/u1, and the third stake from the beginning is laid down beside it, so that the ends of both the first and the third stakes exit from behind the fourth stake (Fig. 5.15-b). The second stake repeats the o1/u1 movement and comes out behind the fifth stake, with the fourth stake bending down to align with the second (Fig. 5.15-c). As indicated by the weaving stroke, ends of the side-stakes on this border are worked to the inside (Fig. 5.15-d), where they lie flat under the edge of the woven border and are neatly clipped off, remaining almost completely hidden (Pl. 5.26-b).

After the top border is worked, a foot may be added. An added foot is constructed by inserting *foot-stakes* into the basket, either alongside the side-stakes or, if the basket is waled, up through the weaving itself, where the weavers float over two side-stakes (Pl. 5.16-b). Foot-stakes may be inserted only a few inches into the weaving or nearly to the top of the basket, strongly reinforcing the basket sides. This type of foot can be replaced, and foot repairs are seen on some rod baskets. The foot-stakes may be worked down into the border after insertion, or, if a higher foot is desired, a row or two of waling is woven before the border is worked (Pls. 5.7 and 5.34).

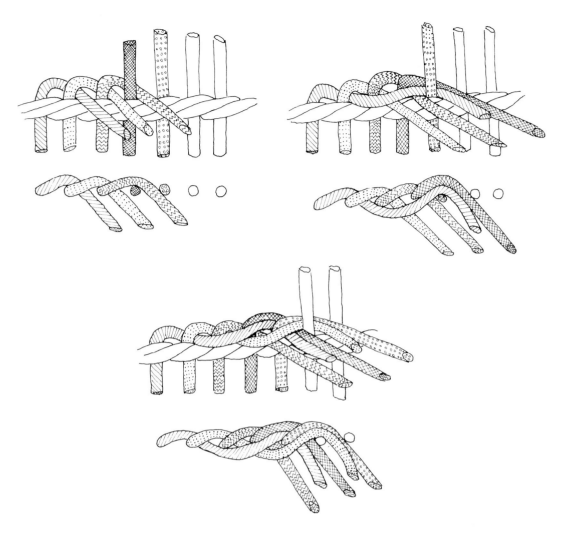

Fig. 5.14   Three-rod plain border (u1/o2/u1).

A border often used for feet is the three-rod plain border (u2/o2/u1) (Fig. 5.16). This border is a useful one for working foot- or side-stakes which are spaced close together or for working thick rods. While used for top borders as well, this is often the border used for feet on Shenandoah Valley rodwork (Pls. 5.16-b and 5.26-a). Foot-stakes almost always are spaced much closer together than the top side-stakes, due to the smaller base circumference. In baskets with a tight base curvature, the longer under-two stroke makes this border easier to work than one beginning with under-one.

There are many variations of *combination top/foot borders*, but they all

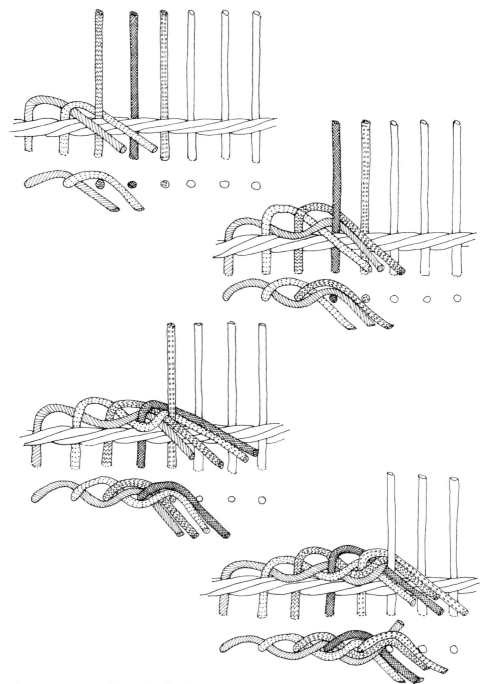

Fig. 5.15 Two-rod plain border (ul/ol/ul/ol).

Appalachian White Oak Basketmaking

Pl. 5.26-a Oval rod basket, Virginia. A number of oval baskets of this type have been found in Rockingham and Page counties of Virginia, although at this time the maker or community of makers is unknown. Typical of that region of the Shenandoah Valley, the base is begun with pairing and changes to three-rod wale, and then the sides are upsett and woven with the three-rod wale to the top. The top edge is worked in a two-rod plain border, a border often used on both round and oval baskets from this region (Pl. 5.26-b). Stakes are inserted through the waling and then laid down for a foot. The wide, thick handle is slipped alongside a stake and attached by nails hammered through the weaving and the handle ends. Dimensions: 7″ x 10″ base, 10″ x 14 1/2″ top, 7″ s.h., 11″ o.h. Collection of Cynthia W. and Michael B. Taylor.

Pl. 5.26-b Border detail of basket in Pl. 5.26-a, inside view. The two-rod plain border (u1/o1/u1/o1) appears as a wide, evenly twisted edging.

use the same general working method: the stakes which weave the top border are continued down the side, exiting at the bottom to make the foot-stakes. The stakes may be drawn down through all of the side weaving or only part of it, floating over sections of the sides and adding a decorative element to the basket. These continuous stakes are then bordered off around the base to make the foot of the basket.

Combination top/foot borders sometimes are worked on baskets which are three-rod waled on their sides (Fig. 5.17). A plain top border is worked, and then the side-stakes are threaded down through the weaving rather than alongside an adjacent stake (similar to the placement of stakes inserted for foot borders in Pl. 5.16-b). The stakes end below the base and are either bordered down immediately, or additional rows are woven for a higher foot and then finished. Stakes which are inserted through the

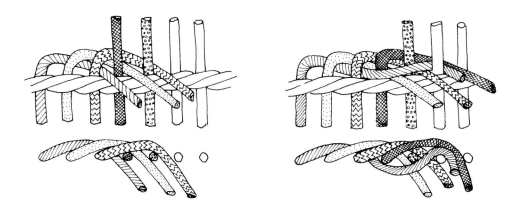

Fig. 5.16 *(Above):* Three-rod plain border (u2/o2/u1).

Fig. 5.17 *(Below):* Combination border with plain top border and unwoven foot. A three-rod plain border (u1/o2/u1) is first worked around the entire top edge. The ends of each stake then move over two stakes and are worked down through the side weaving, exiting at the base edge to form the foot border. The movement for each stake is u1/o2/u1/o2.

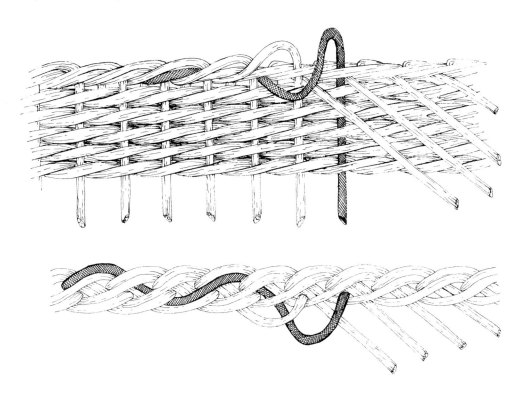

Pl. 5.27   Pennsylvania basket with green and red horizontal stripes and a combination top/foot border. The basket sides are worked in a three-rod wale (2/1). The top border is made by first working a three-rod plain border (u1/o2/u1), and then each stake is worked across two stakes and drawn down through the weaving to the base edge. The basket is finished with a three-rod plain foot border (u1/o2/u1). The stakes are visible on the outside of the basket, where they are threaded back down through the weaving, making the waling appear quite different from its usual smooth-sided, dense weave. The inside and the outside of the basket look exactly the same, with the vertical stakes showing through the weave. Baskets with this type of combination border are known mainly in Pennsylvania. Dimensions: 8 1/2″ base, 13″ top, 6 1/2″ s.h., 7 1/2″ o.h. Private collection.

Pl. 5.28   Rod basket with combination top/foot border made by Emby Shelly, Whitley County, Kentucky (S. Ross, 5 Apr. 1986). Working in a manner similar to that of the Rectors of Rockcastle, Garrard, and Madison counties, Kentucky (Pl. 5.34), Shelly began his baskets with a D-shaped handle hoop, wove the base, and then added the handle and used it as a guide to help shape the basket sides. After the sides had been woven, the stakes were worked into a low scallop top border, and the ends were threaded back through the weaving alongside adjacent stakes. He made a high foot by weaving three rows of waling before finishing with a three-rod plain foot border. The high foot allowed for the thickness of the handle overlap, which spans the underside of the basket. Dimensions: 8″ x 12″ base, 9″ x 15″ top, 6 1/2″ s.h., 12 1/2″ o.h. Collection of Smith G. Ross.

waling give the basket a very different appearance, almost as if an unusual weaving technique has been used. Instead of the dense wale weave which characteristically covers the stakes, side-stakes can be seen clearly on both the right and wrong surfaces. This combination top/foot border treatment is found on some Central Pennsylvania rod baskets (Pls. 5.27, 5.39-a, 5.1).

Some combination borders feature a *scallop border* (Fig. 5.18; Cl. Pl. 18) worked for the top edge. Among these are the rod baskets made by Emby Shelly of Whitley County, Kentucky (Pl. 5.28) (S. Ross, 19 Mar.

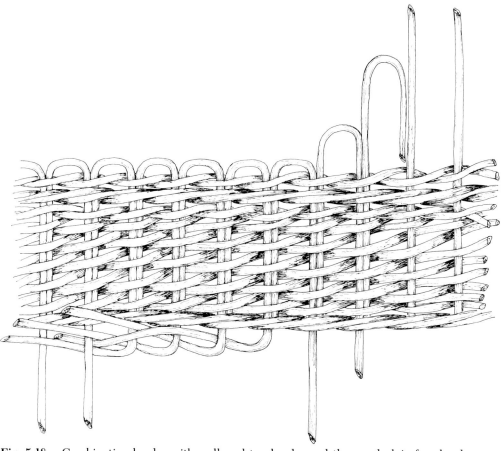

Fig. 5.18   Combination border with scalloped top border and three-rod plain foot border (u1/o2/u1). The top border is worked first, then the basket is turned over and the foot border worked.

1985 and 5 Apr. 1986). Shelly made both oval and round baskets and used the same combination border for both forms. His baskets have a low scallop top border in which the ends of each side-stake have been worked down the basket side alongside the next stake. It almost looks as if no border is present and the side-stakes are doubled. The stakes exit at the base, forming the foundation for the high foot, and are ended with a three-rod plain foot border.

Occasionally rod baskets with combination top/foot borders have scallop borders for both the top edge and the foot (Pls. 5.29-a, b; 5.30). Combination borders in which the stakes are worked into a tall scallop top border require long side-stakes, because of the significant height added to the basket side. Additional rods often are inserted alongside the stakes and woven with the original stakes to give the scallop more width and to reinforce the border (Pl. 5.14-a; Cl. Pl. 20).

The major characteristic of Madeira-style rod baskets is their high,

Pl. 5.29-a Oak rod basket with Madeira-style border; origin unknown. The base and the sides of this basket are three-rod waled. In addition to the intricate scallop top and foot borders and side braid, this basket was once very colorful; traces of red and blue dye are evident on the weaving rods. Dimensions: 7 3/4″ base, 11 1/4″ top, 5 1/2″ s.h. Collection of Cynthia W. and Michael B. Taylor.

Pl. 5.29-b Detail of basket in Pl. 5.29-a, showing the scallop border and finishing braid. After the long stakes are worked into a tall, scalloped edging, they are threaded through the side waling to the base, and a foot scallop is worked. The ends are then threaded back up through the weaving and finished with a braid.

scalloped, open-worked border (Pls. 5.29-a, b), which occasionally forms the entire side of the basket. Madeira work, also called "drawnwork," is thought to have originated in the Portuguese islands of Madeira and the Azores (Stephenson 1977, p. 28; Thierschmann, Sept. 1987). In 1901, Mary White wrote instructions for "one of the sturdy Fayal [Fayal is an island of the Azore group] baskets that the masters of sailing vessels used to bring home to our grandmothers in the good old times" (1901, pp. 130–33, 136, 138–39). According to Sue H. Stephenson, Madeira work was common in the Appalachian region after 1880 (1977, p. 28).

One of the features of some combination borders in oak rodwork is the incidence of *floats*, rods which for some portion of their length are not attached to a basket body, on the outside of the basket. Baskets with floats usually are constructed with a combination of two side weaves, such as French randing capped off by a row or two of three-rod waling or mock waling. In a three-rod waling stroke, the weaver skips over two stakes and under one; the long skip creates a space through which the floats can be drawn. At this time, oak rod baskets with decorative side floats have been attributed to the southeastern and central Pennsylvania counties of Montgomery, Union (Pl. 5.1), and Snyder (Lasansky 1984, pp. 886–94), and to the Shenandoah Valley of Virginia (Moore, 12 Mar. 1985 and 16 Mar. 1989; Hackley, 17 Feb. 1985) (Cl. Pl. 20). Baskets with crossed floats have been found in the Shenandoah Valley and in northeastern West Virginia

Pl. 5.30   Rod basket with crossed floats. Baskets with the high scallop border, in which the stakes are worked back through the weaving at the top and cross as they float over the center side section, occasionally are found in the Shenandoah Valley, Virginia, and northeastern West Virginia. This basket has an intricately worked scallop foot as well. The thick rods on this basket make the sharply curved border even more obvious. The sides are upsett and ended with three-rod wale and the middle section paired. Dimensions: 8″ base, 12″ top, 9″ s.h., 12 1/2″ o.h. Collection of Larry Hackley.

Pl. 5.31   Oak rod basket with serpentine floats, found in Rockbridge County, Virginia. Three rods are threaded through the weaving to make the lacy serpentine floats, which are strictly decorative. A variety of wales are used in this basket: the base is three-rod waled, the upsett and top are four-rod waled, the section where the scalloped edgings are visible is three-rod waled (1/2), and the midsection is five-rod waled (3/2). These varied walings made it possible to attach the decorative floats to the outside of the basket, while the inside remains the densely woven waled surface. The bottom looped floats are threaded through the waling to the base and then become the foot-stakes for the three-rod plain (u2/o2/u1) foot border. Dimensions: 7″ base, 11″ top diameter, 5 1/2″ s.h., 6 3/8″ o.h. Collection of H. Wayne and Rachel Nash Law.

Pl. 5.32   Oak rod coal scuttle from Pennsylvania. The inside of the basket is blackened, testifying to its use. Both an ear and an overhead roped handle are worked on this basket to make it functional. The base is constructed of a wide slat with its ends whittled into three bottom-sticks. The solid slat is crossed by six short bottom-sticks. The sides are woven left-handed with a three-rod wale, while the top and foot borders are worked right-handed. Dimensions: 9 1/2″ x 14″ base, 13 1/2″ x 21 1/2″ top, 9 1/2″ s.h., 15 1/2″ o.h. Collection of Cynthia W. and Michael B. Taylor.

(Pl. 5.30). Some regional German willowwork is constructed with floats (Will 1985, pp. 91, 122, 125), although the working method may be different from that typical of oak rodwork. In many cases, the floating stakes in willowwork are worked into the sides as the basket is woven rather than drawn from the top down, due to the less pliable nature of the willow (Thierschmann, Sept. 1987).

Floats on rod baskets most often are associated with combination borders, but not always. A most unusual basket with wavy floats has been found in Rockbridge County, Virginia (Pl. 5.31). The top serpentine float is strictly surface decoration—the rods are not a part of the border, but are extra rods threaded through the weaving. The looped floats at the bottom, however, also serve as the foot-stakes.

Handles: Overhead and Ears

Both overhead and ear handles are common in rodwork, with the handle choice often depending on the intended use of the basket. The coal scuttle (Pl. 5.32) has an overhead handle for lifting the basket and an ear handle for tilting to allow the coal to pour out.

1. Overhead Handles

Overhead handles may be incorporated as part of a basket's base and side structure or may be added after a basket body has been completed. Added handles may be attached by pegging (Pls. 5.33-a, b), nailing (Pl. 5.26), or

Pl. 5.33-a Pennsylvania rod basket made by David "Pappy" Moad (d. 1937). Moad's rod baskets have a carved overhead handle attached with a wooden peg (Pl. 5.33-b). He worked in Juniata, Mifflin, Perry, and Snyder counties, Pennsylvania. Moad used willow when it was available, and when it was not, he made oak rod baskets (Lasansky 1984, p. 893). The upsett of the basket is three-rod wale, the midsection is French randing, and a wide section of waling is worked at the top. The top border is worked in a plain border, with the ends of the rods tucked into the weaving of the top wale section (see detail, Pl. 5.33-b). Foot-stakes are added and several rows of waling worked before the plain foot border is laid down. Dimensions: 9″ x 12″ base, 9″ s.h., 15″ o.h. Collection of Jeannette Lasansky.

Pl. 5.33-b Solid handle attached with wooden peg, detail of basket in Pl. 5.33-a. Pegs or, more commonly, nails or wire are sometimes used to attach carved handles securely to a basket body. On this Pennsylvania basket, the thick, wide handle is inserted beside a stake and is fastened in place with a long peg which catches under a weaving rod.

roping. Structural handles usually are made in a D-shaped hoop, as in splitwork. Roped handles are the most common overhead handles.

A structural handle often is constructed before a base is woven, as was done by Kentuckians Emby Shelly of Whitley County (S. Ross, 19 Mar. 1985 and 5 Apr. 1986) and the Rector family of Rockcastle, Garrard, and Madison counties (Rector, 5 Apr. 1986). Both the Rector family and Shelly produced baskets with a handle made from a thick piece of white oak shaped into a D-ring (Pls. 5.34 and 5.28). The length of the flattened part of the handle predetermined the size of the basket base, and the arc of the handle controlled the shape of the basket sides. Centered underneath the woven base, the handle was treated as two stakes in the side weaving.

Baskets made by the Shively family of Pennsylvania (Pl. 5.19) and by

Pl. 5.34 Rod baskets made by the Rector family, who lived and worked in Rockcastle, Garrard, and Madison counties, Kentucky. Ed Rector, who still lives in Berea, Kentucky, remembers his father, two uncles, and grandfather Ike Rector making oak rod baskets. "They mostly made just a round basket . . . in peck, half-bushel and bushel [sizes]." As a child, Ed helped pull the rods, which he calls "rounded splits." His father often would stay up late finishing baskets which he peddled the next day (5 Apr. 1986). The Rector baskets are distinguished by the thick D-ring handle which spans the underside of the base, the high waled foot made from foot-stakes, and French-randed sides capped off by several rows of waling. Dimensions, from left: 11″ base, 14 3/4″ top, 9 3/4″ s.h., 15″ o.h.; 7 1/2″ base, 11 1/2″ top, 7 3/4″ s.h., 13″ o.h. Collections of H. Wayne and Rachel Nash Law; Cynthia W. and Michael B. Taylor.

Homer Summers and his relatives, Rome Philips and Ogel Higginbotham (Pl. 5.35-d), of Kanawha County, West Virginia, are worked along the same principle, but the handle is incorporated into the slath structure and used both as a bottom-stick and as side-stakes (Pls. 5.35-a, b, c, d). The ends of the handles in these baskets are carefully scarfed so that they fit together.

The roped overhead handle is started with a foundation piece which arcs across the top of the basket and forms the core of the handle. Foundation pieces may be round or slightly flattened, and their length is determined by the size and height of the handle. Small roping-rods are wrapped around the foundation, completely covering its surface and securing it to the basket body.

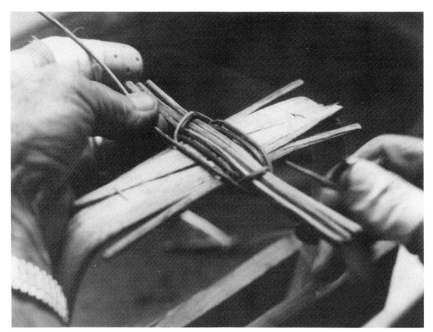

A

B

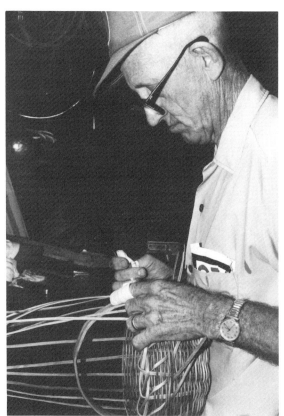

C

Appalachian White Oak Basketmaking

D

Pl. 5.35-a *(Opposite, top):* Rodmaker Homer Summers, 1984, beginning the base slath. Summers uses a vise attached to his workbench to hold the handle while he binds the bottom-sticks. Summers makes a D-shaped handle hoop in the same manner as his wife's great-uncle, Ogel Higginbotham: he scarfs the ends with tapers and notches so that the ends lock together, making an even width. Using roughly rounded bottom-sticks, Summers inserts three onto the handle and adds one on either side of the handle to create the base configuration. He then fastens the handle together with heavy staples and begins randing the base. Summers uses three sizes of weaving rods; the smallest are used to begin the base, and the larger ones are worked in as the spacing between the bottom-sticks and stakes becomes greater (Summers and Summers, 24 Aug. 1984).

Pl. 5.35-b *(Opposite, left):* Weaving the sides. Having inserted two flat stakes alongside each bottom-stick and the handle. Summers continues to use the vise to hold the basket while he rands the sides. He depends on the tension of his weaving rods and the preformed handle to turn up the basket sides (Summers and Summers, 24 Aug. 1984).

Pl. 5.35-c *(Opposite, right):* Bordering off. Summers lays down a simple trac border (ul/ol/ul) and then threads the ends of the stakes through the sides of the basket, leaving short floats. The floats help secure the stakes, as well as adding a decorative treatment to the top of the basket (Summers and Summers, 24 Aug. 1984).

Pl. 5.35-d *(Above):* Rod baskets made by Homer Summers and Rome Philips, Kanawha County, West Virginia. Summers learned to make baskets by looking at one made by his wife's great-uncle, Rome Philips, who lives nearby. Philips had learned basketwork from tearing apart a basket that had been made by Rome's wife's uncle, Ogel Higginbotham. The uncle did not make baskets for a living, only occasionally for his own household use or for family or neighbors. He farmed and also had a small forge for blacksmith work. Philips had made his die from an old forged hoe blade and gave a spare blade to Homer to make a die. Homer figured the rest out for himself (Summers, 24 Aug. 1984 and 3 July 1985). The two baskets differ only slightly: the uncle's basket has a row of three-rod wale at the base and halfway up the sides. Other than the waling, the baskets are identical. In 1983, Summers began making baskets in two sizes—small, with a 7 1/2″ base, and large, with a 9 1/2″ base. By 1989 he had made over four hundred baskets and was making five different sizes (15 Sept. 1989). Collection of Homer and Juanita Summers.

Pl. 5.36   Continuous roped handle attachment, detail of basket in Cl. Pl. 22. The roping on this handle is formed of long rods which are worked back and forth across the foundation piece two or three times before ending. In this case, the roping-rods are passed through the basket side under the same weaving row.

Fig. 5.19   Roped overhead handle.

Pl. 5.37   Roped handle using short rods, detail of basket in Cl. Pl. 21. Each roping-rod is worked only once across the handle core and is then ended. The attachment of this roped handle makes a triangular-shaped configuration as each rod is ended under consecutive rows of weaving. In this detail, just to the right of the handle attachment, the ends of the roping-rods are visible as small diagonal floats which do not quite follow the weaving pattern. Collection of Annie Handley Shobe.

Pl. 5.38 Virginia rod basket with V-shaped handle attachment. The whole basket is worked in a three-rod wale with very fine rods, and the base is highly domed. The foundation piece for the overhead handle is flattened rather than round, but most distinctive is the handle attachment. Dimensions: 8″ base, 11 1/2″ x 13″ top oval, 7″ s.h., 12″ o.h. Private collection.

Overhead handles may be roped in one of two ways, either with a long continuous rod or with several short rods (Fig. 5.19). The typical handle begins with a foundation piece centered on the basket, with tails inserted into the weaving alongside opposite stakes. All roped handles are wrapped with the same basic movement. The wrapping may begin from the left or the right-hand side of the foundation (as observed from the outside of the basket), and then the roping-rods are wound around the foundation, usually three to five times, keeping equal distance between the wraps. The roping-rods usually are threaded through the basket's side weaving from the inside to the outside, and then either are continued back across the foundation piece (Pl. 5.36; Cl. Pl. 22) or ended. The ends of the roping-rods are secured by threading into the weaving on the basket sides.

Handle attachments are often very distinctive. The roping-rods of some roped handles are worked to form a triangular-shaped configuration where they attach to a basket's sides. The ends of the roping-rods are threaded under consecutive weaving rows, creating diagonal lines (Pl. 5.37). This handle attachment is often found on baskets from Pendleton and Hardy counties in West Virginia (Cl. Pl. 21) and the Shenandoah Valley of Virginia (Pl. 5.16-a). A longer V-shaped attachment also is found in Tennessee (Pl. 5.7), where it was used by the Hickey family, and in the Shenandoah Valley, Virginia (Pl. 5.38). One oval Pennsylvania rod basket

Pl. 5.39-a Pennsylvania lidded rod basket, purchased in Union County (Bohn, 16 Oct. 1984). Lidded baskets are rare in rodwork. The basket is tightly woven in three-rod wale and has a combination top/foot border. The handle attachment is an unusual feature of this basket. Dimensions: 6″ x 11″ base, 8 1/2″ x 14 1/2″ top, 5 3/4″ s.h., 10″ o.h. Private collection.

Pl. 5.39-b Handle attachment, detail of basket in Pl. 5.39-a. The handle is notched and lashed to the basket body in a fashion similar to an ear wrapping in ribwork.

Pl. 5.40 Eight-eared basket from Shenandoah County, Virginia (Helsley and Helsley, 13 Mar. 1985). This unusual rod basket has evenly spaced ears worked around the top edge. Another detail of the basket is the looped foot-stakes that are inserted through the three-rod waling, forming tight scallops just under the top border. Remnants of white paint are evident. Dimensions: 7 1/2″ base, 10 1/4″ top, 5″ s.h., 6 3/4″ o.h. Private collection.

has a very unusual handle attachment: the handle is notched and secured to the basket body with small rods which are worked like an ear wrapping in ribwork (Pls. 5.39-a, b).

2. Ear Handles

Large field baskets (Pls. 5.9 and 5.18), as well as small utility baskets (Pls. 5.8 and 5.31; Cl. Pl. 24), have ear handles. Baskets with two ears have the advantage of being easy to stack. On small baskets, the ears often are made for finger-holds rather than hand-holds. In southeastern Pennsylvania, a number of both large and small baskets with four ear handles have been found (Pl. 5.13), and an unusual eight-eared basket is attributed to Shenandoah County, Virginia (Pl. 5.40).

Ear handles are most commonly roped with rods, but sometimes they may be wrapped with flat splits (Cl. Pl. 18). Roped ears (Fig. 5.20) are worked in a manner similar to the style of overhead roped handles. There are variations in the number of wraps, the type of attachment, and the direction in which an ear is wrapped. The following description of making an ear is based on the Shenandoah County, Virginia, sewing basket (Pl. 5.22). A foundation piece is inserted alongside two stakes. The roping-rod typically is begun from the left side of the foundation (facing the outside of the basket) and is wound from the inside of the basket around the foundation two or three times. The end of the roping-rod is threaded through the weaving from the inside of the basket to the outside and returns to the left following the pattern established by the first wrap. When the second wrapping is finished, the end of the rod is threaded

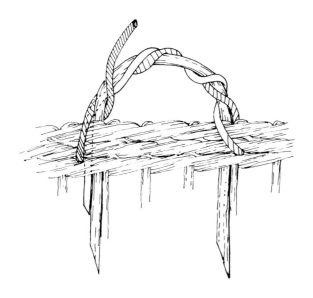

Fig. 5.20   Roped ear handle.

Pl. 5.41   Twisted roping on ear handle, detail of the four-handled basket in Pl. 5.13.

through the weaving from the outside to the inside of the basket on the left side of the handle bow, and the wrapping is continued back to the right. The previous two wrapping movements are continued until the foundation piece is covered.

In willowwork, the rods which wrap the ear handle bow always are twisted tightly to give the willows more strength and flexibility (Cl. Pl. 19). While not common, twisted roping-rods are worked on both ear and overhead handles on oak rod baskets (Pls. 5.41 and 5.17). In willowwork, the twisting is accomplished by first inserting one end of the roping-rod in place alongside the foundation piece. Holding the roping-rod firmly with the left hand, about a foot from its free end, the basketmaker cranks the end with the right hand. As the rod becomes twisted, the left hand moves down the rod, while the right hand continues to crank until the whole length of the wrapping rod is tightly twisted (Wright 1983, p. 36; Heseltine 1982, pp. 24–25). The twisted rod then is worked across the foundation piece. It is not known if there are any differences in the working method of twisting oak and willow.

Lids

Lids sometimes are made to cover rod baskets. In rodwork, lids are made to fit down inside the top rim (Pl. 5.42) or to cover the top of the basket (Pl. 5.43). If the lid is made to fit inside the basket opening, an extra ledge is often woven by waling to create a resting place for the lid. Lids for rod baskets are both flat and domed. A flat lid is made by simply working a basket base and bordering it off when the desired diameter is reached. Domed lids (Pls. 5.1 and 5.39) are a bit trickier to make, as the lid shaping and size must remain exact in order to fit the basket. Small ear handles often were attached to the top of the lid to aid in lifting (Pls. 5.43 and 5.23). Occasionally, basketmakers hinged the lids to the basket to keep them in place or prevent their loss (Pls. 5.42 and 5.23).

Pl. 5.42 Lidded rod basket from Shenandoah County, Virginia. Possibly made by the Day family (Helsley and Helsley, 13 Mar. 1985). Both the base and the lid are begun with flat splits which are fitched. The weaving material changes to rods, and the weave to three-rod wale. Many different wales are worked on this basket, with each best suited to its distinct function: the foot is created by a five-rod wale (4/1) at the upsett; the top two inches of the basket sides are worked with a four-rod wale (2/2); and a small ledge for the lid is woven with a six-rod wale (2/4). The outside edge of the lid is partially banded by a thick rod lashed on with a flat split. The lid pulls and hinge are made from a flat split wrapped into a ring and secured with another wrapping split. Dimensions: Basket: 6 1/2″ base, 9 1/4″ top, 6 1/4″ s.h., 10 1/2″ o.h. Lid: 8 1/2″ base. Private collection.

Pl. 5.43   Lidded hamper attributed to Rocking-ham County, Virginia (Moore, 12 Mar. 1985). The size and shape of this basket indicate that it was probably used as a storage basket. The high domed lid fits the basket tightly, following and emphasizing the widely flared shape. This waled basket has two large roped ear side handles and a small roped ear as a lid pull. Attaching the handles to the sides of the basket allows space for the lid to fit over the top of the basket. Dimensions: 15″ base, 25″ top, 15 1/2″ s.h., 24″ o.h. Collection of Roddy and Sally Moore.

Rod/Split Baskets

Rod/split baskets are attributed to North Carolina and Pennsylvania, although the occurrence of rod/splitwork may be more widespread. Rod/split baskets are those built with a foundation of flat splits, over which rods are woven. As in splitwork, the same base stakes are bent up to form the foundation for the sides of the basket. Finishing details include a variety of handles, rims, and top lashings, with these details often reflecting regional styles. Both the bases and sides of rod/split baskets are randed.

A round rod/split basket attributed to Pennsylvania clearly shows a typical round splitwork base construction (Pl. 5.44-a) with one split stake; the base is woven with slightly rounded rods (Pl. 5.44-b). The top rim treatment with wrapped-rod lashing has been found on other Pennsylvania split baskets (Pl. 4.55). Double-notched ear handles are common on split baskets, but these ear handles with multiple notches which catch the side weaving are quite unusual.

Another rod/split basket attributed to southeastern Pennsylvania is a large rectangular grain riddle (Pl. 5.45) (Mercer Accession Ledger). At one time there were probably many such baskets used for harvesting, but few have survived. This basket and the round rod/split basket (Pls. 5.46-a, b), also from Pennsylvania, have an unusual laced two-rod lashing (Fig. 5.21). The wide stakes of the round basket are pierced many times, allowing the lashing split to be worked closely and evenly around the top of the basket.

Pl. 5.44-a   Round Pennsylvania rod/split basket. Rod/split baskets have the structural framework of splitwork but are woven with oak rods. As in split-work, the stakes on this basket are turned down to the inside and heavy inner and outer rims fitted to the top edge. The basketmaker has used a nut and bolt to secure the outer rim overlap. The wrapped-rod lashing is worked around the rims two or three times and then around the filler rod several times before catching the rims again. One unusual feature of this basket is the carved ear handles with long handle tails which are notched eight or more times. The tails are slipped alongside stakes and the notches caught under the weaving rods holding the handles very securely. Dimensions: 16″ base, 21″ x 23 1/2″ top oval, 12 1/2″ s.h., 15″ o.h. Courtesy of Durell Street of Yesteryear, Center of Science and Industry, Columbus, Ohio.

Pl. 5.44-b   Base view of basket in Pl. 5.44-a. Clearly visible are the flat split foundation and the rim and lashing treatment. The double-bottomed basket is constructed with two sets of six flat stakes. One stake is split to make an uneven number of working ends, and the base and sides are randed with rods.

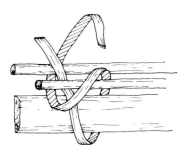
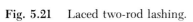

Fig. 5.21   Laced two-rod lashing.

Pl. 5.45 Grain riddle. According to the Mercer Accession Ledger, the basket was bought from A.H. Pennypacker, Pennsburg [Lehigh County, Pennsylvania], for five dollars in 1921. This huge rod/split basket most likely was used by two persons. The bottom is made with heavy flat splits, but the sides are woven with rough rods. The large spaces in the base were left intentionally, to allow the grain to sift through, while the larger leaves and stalks remained in the basket and were dumped after sifting. There is one heavy skid on the base, but it probably had two. The ear handles, made from thick flat splits which have been split at the end and woven back into the basket body, originally were wrapped with a flat split. This basket has the same unusual two-rod laced lashing as the one in Pl. 5.46. Dimensions: 26 1/2″ x 36″ base, 9 1/4″ s.h. Courtesy of the Mercer Museum, Bucks County Historical Society.

Pl. 5.46-a Pennsylvania rod/split basket. This round basket is very heavy, due to its thick split foundation and tightly woven body. The basket has no rims; the stakes are cut off at the top, and the tightly laced lashing is worked around two top rods and through slits pierced through the thick stakes. There is evidence of an overhead handle. Dimensions: 7 1/2″ base, 13″ top, 7″ s.h. Private collection.

Pl. 5.46-b Aerial view of basket in Pl. 5.46-a. This view clearly shows the top lashing and the base construction of flat foundation stakes. The stakes are laid out in a manner more typical of some wickerwork base constructions. Instead of all stakes crisscrossing as in splitwork, three stakes are laid out side by side and then crossed with other groups of threes laid out in the same manner. The top view of the lashing shows the tightly braided finished edge and the broken, loosened lashing where a handle once was present.

Pl. 5.47   Round rod/split basket from western
North Carolina (Moore, 12 Mar. 1985). The base is
begun with four flat stakes crossed in the center.
One bye-stake is added to make an odd number, so
that the basket can be spiraled with one weaver.
Other bye-stakes are added in as spacing allows, to
complete the base. Dimensions: 10″ base, 13 1/2″
top, 9″ s.h., 15″ o.h. Collection of Roddy and Sally Moore.

Pl. 5.48   Base view of oval rod/split basket, western North Carolina. This oval basket is begun by

laying out one long stake and crossing it with five
shorter stakes. The base oval is further shaped by
adding bye-stakes to round out the corners. The
base and sides are randed by spiraling with one
rod woven over an uneven number of working
ends. The sides alternate bands of flat split and
round rod weavers. The top is finished with a
single-notched handle fitted to an inner rim and
lashed with a wide split in a figure eight. Dimensions: 8″ x 14″ base, 13″ x 19″ top, 7 1/2″ s.h., 13
1/4″ o.h. Collection of H. Wayne and Rachel Nash
Law.

The base of this basket reflects wickerwork techniques—tapered stakes are
grouped together at the center, and a flat split binds the groups first,
before they are separated into individual stakes. Most of the base is woven
with a flat split, but the weaver changes to a round rod toward the edge,
and round rod weavers continue up the sides.

Both round and oval rod/split baskets are found in western North
Carolina made in various shapes and sizes, including large and small oval,
tall round, and low-sided round pie baskets and flower baskets. Many
North Carolina round and oval rod/split baskets have bye-staked base constructions (Fig. 4.12; Pls. 5.47, 5.48, 5.49). Some oval rod/split forms are
begun in a manner similar to that used in oval wickerwork baskets: the

Pl. 5.49   Oval rod/split hamper. This basket also shows features associated with other baskets from western North Carolina: thick flat stakes and figure-eight lashing. The lid and base are constructed in the same way—the stakes are woven into a narrow rectangle, and additional bye-stakes are added at the corners as spacing allows. It is doubtful that this large basket was used to carry heavy loads as the wrapped handles are small and weak for the basket size. Dimensions: Basket: 14 1/2″ x 23″ base, 11 1/2″ s.h.; Lid: 16″ x 28 1/2″ x 2″ Collection of Kathleen and Ken Dalton.

base is laid out with a single long bottom stake, crossed by three to five stakes (Pl. 5.48). A large oval lidded rod/split basket (Pl. 5.49) from western North Carolina begins with interlaced stakes, as in the construction of rectangular split baskets. Bye-stakes are added at the corners to give the oval shape. This basket has wrapped ear handles at each end. A number of North Carolina rod/split baskets are finished with a single notched overhead handle, an inside rim, and a figure-eight lashing (Pls. 5.47; 5.48). There are other rod/split baskets from western North Carolina with variations in construction features, indicating that more than one group of makers were working in the rod/split tradition in that region.

Rod/Rib Baskets

Oak rod/ribwork is scattered throughout the Central and Southern Appalachian Mountains, with rod/rib baskets attributed to central Kentucky (Hackley, 17 Feb. 1985; Hill 1903, p. 212), central and eastern Tennessee (Irwin 1982, p. 59), western North Carolina (Elkins, 9 May 1985) and westcentral Virginia (Irwin 1982, p. 60). In 1903, Jennie Lester Hill, teacher of domestic art at Berea College, Kentucky, mentioned a "melon-

Pl. 5.50-a Rod/rib basket. Purchased in Georgetown, Kentucky; origin uncertain. This basket is constructed with radiating ribbing, a technique common to rod/ribwork. The first ribs are the longest and are inserted into the wrapping; these long ribs determine the width of the basket body. Other ribs are added as needed, both under the rim and along the basket spine. The weaving rods are only slightly rounded. Dimensions: 14 1/2″ top, 8 1/2″ s.h., 14″ o.h. Private collection.

Pl. 5.50-b Splicing, detail of basket in Pl. 5.50-a. The ends of the weaving rods are slipped into the weaving alongside ribs.

Pl. 5.51 Rod/rib basket with flat split wrapping and radiating ribbing, western North Carolina (Elkins, 9 May 1985). The shape of this basket with the extended pouches is typical of rod/ribwork in western North Carolina. Dimensions: 12″ top, 7″ s.h., 11″ o.h. Private collection.

Pl. 5.52-a Oak and straw coiled baskets. These two baskets are similar in appearance because of their construction technique, but the basket on the left is worked completely with oak, while the basket on the right has a foundation of straw and is wrapped with an oak split. In Europe, straw coilwork was evident wherever grain crops constituted a major part of rural life; however, not much is known about oak rod coilwork. Dimensions, from left: 8″ base, 9 1/2″ top, 4″ s.h.; 7 1/2″ base, 11 1/2″ top, 4 1/2″ s.h. Private collection.

Pl. 5.52-b Detail of oak rod/coil basket in plate 5.52-a. The foundation rods are rounded just slightly and the wrapping splits worked very closely.

shaped basket . . . made of round splints" that had been made by the Moore family of Madison County, Kentucky, for at least three generations (1903, p. 212).

Rod/rib baskets are simply rib baskets woven with rods instead of flat splits (Pls. 5.50-a, b; 5.51). Historically, this type of work is an old form and technique. In Europe, ribwork is well known, with both flat splits and round rods.

Almost all oak rod/rib baskets use radiating ribbing (Fig. 3.13), the same technique used in most European willow ribwork. The weaving rods usually do not show the same evenly rounded shaping as other oak rod baskets. In many rod/rib baskets, the oak weaving rods are split out and left squared or only roughly shaped to form a slightly rounded rod. When one weaving rod ends and a new one begins, the ends typically are tucked alongside a rib (Pl. 5.50-b).

Rod/Coil Baskets

Rod/coil baskets constitute a real unknown. Not much information is available on these except that they do exist and are made completely from oak. Coilwork is a type of basketry which uses a center foundation secured with a wrapper. It is an extremely ancient basket form and is found mainly where plant materials are limited to grasses and shrubs. There is no concrete evidence as to the provenance of this type of rod oak basket. Sue Stephenson has seen examples around Danville, Virginia, but has little information regarding their history (15 Mar. 1985). The similarity of this one to straw coilwork, in size and appearance, is quite striking (Pl. 5.52-a, b).

Glossary

Awl A small, sharp-pointed tool for making holes.

Bail The movable part of a swing or drop handle.

Bark The outermost covering of a tree.

Basket body The simple containing structure of a basket, consisting of the base and sides.

Bastard splits (n.) See **tangential splits**.

Billet A sized blank of wood for making basket materials such as splits, rods, hoops, etc. Also called a "slat" and a "flitch."

Binding See **lashing**.

Board splits (n.) See **radial splits**.

Border In ribwork, several ribs added above or alongside the rim hoop, modifying the top basket edge. In rodwork, the top or bottom edge of wickerwork baskets, formed by weaving the ends of stakes in a particular sequence.

Bottom-sticks In rodwork, foundation materials for the base of a basket.

Bow In ribwork, a type of wrapping (see figure 3.6). In splitwork and rodwork, the length of an overhead or ear handle that spans above the rims.

Braid Decorative surface weaving which may cover the rim or handle of a basket. Most common in ribwork.

Brake A holding method or a device for securing the end of a piece of wood while it is being split.

Brash A description of wood that is brittle, cracking, or breaking when bent.

Butt log The part of the tree trunk from the ground to the first knot or limb, also known as a "pole" or "stick" of timber.

Bye-stakes In splitwork, short stakes which usually are added into a base structure. Bye-stakes can alter the original base shape and size. See figure 4.12.

Cambium The layer of cells in a tree, where the new sapwood and bark are formed. See figure 2.3.

Chasing Plain weave using two weavers that alternately work over and under an even number of working ends. Chasing is a spiral weave. See figure 4.7.

Curlicue overlay A decorative technique in which extra splits are threaded through the weaving of the basket body to form curls on the outer surface.

Die A metal tool used for cutting and shaping. In oak rodwork, a die is most often used to form evenly rounded rods. However, some basketmakers used dies for scraping splits. See figures 2.17 and 2.18.

Double bottom In splitwork, a round base made of two separate sets of stakes, in two layers. See figure 4.10.

Drawknife A two-handled cutting tool used to shave wood. See figure 2.12.

Dress (v.) To size a billet by shaving it. See figure 2.14.

Drop handle   A movable handle attached to a pivot, often consisting of a bail and two small ears for hinges. Also called "swing handle."

Ear   In ribwork, a type of wrapping (see figure 3.8). In splitwork, ribwork, and rodwork, an attached side handle, most often placed on opposite sides of a basket rim (see figures 4.16 and 5.20).

Earlywood   Also called "springwood." A thin weak layer of wood cells, formed in the first part of a tree's growing season and used as guidelines for making tangential splits. See **grain lines**.

End checks   Radial cracks on the end of a log, caused by loss of moisture and resultant shrinkage.

Feet   Added protections or supports on the base of a basket. Feet are also known as "slats," "slides," "shoes," "runners," "heels," "cleats," and "skids."

Fillers   In splitwork, extra splits to fill in a space, such as the fillers used to close in the bases of rectangular splitwork baskets or the fillers used to close the space between top rims.

Fitching   A wickerwork weave using two rods which twist around each other as they interlace the bottom-sticks or stakes, creating a Z-twist. Also known as "twining" in fiberwork. See figure 5.6.

Flitch   See **billet**.

Floats   In rodwork, structural or nonstructural rods which, for some portion of their length, are unattached to a basket body and "float" over a basket's side weaving, adding a decorative element.

Foot-stakes   In rodwork, rods which are bordered off for a foot.

Foundation   Basket materials which form the skeletal supporting structure of a basket body, to a large extent determining the basket's final size and shape.

French randing   A wickerwork weave which employs one weaving rod for each side-stake. Weaving rods of equal length are worked in plain weave, moving diagonally up the basket sides. See figure 5.3.

Froe   An L-shaped tool consisting of a wooden handle attached to a metal blade which is beveled on its lower edge. The froe is used to split wood apart by leverage and is used in conjunction with a wooden maul. See figures 2.7–2.11.

Gluts   Wooden wedges for splitting, made of tough dense wood such as dogwood or hickory.

Grain lines   The dark lines of earlywood cells, as seen in a tree's cross-section. Basketmakers call these earlywood layers "grains" and use them as guiding lines when making tangential splits.

Grains   See **grain lines**.

Grain splits   See **tangential splits**.

Growth ring   The annual ring made of layers of earlywood and latewood cells.

Handle   See **overhead handle**, **ear**, **drop handle**, **swing handle**, **roped handle**, **wrapped handle**, **woven handle**, **hoop**, and **handle holes.**

Handle holes   In ribwork and splitwork, a type of handle made by working spaces into the sides of a basket directly under the rims, so that the rims double as hand grips. See figures 3.1-b and 3.17.

Heartwood   The darker wood in the center of the tree, surrounding the pith (see figure 2.3). In basketwork, heartwood frequently is used for handles, hoops, rims, or ribs.

Hexagonal weave   A splitwork weave which interlaces over-one/under-one at oblique angles without twisting, creating hexagonal spaces. See figure 4.4.

Hinge   A type of pivot for the bail of a drop or swing handle, most often made like small ears.

Hoop   In ribwork, a shaped length of wood with its ends overlapped and joined together to form a continuous band. Hoops are the foundation of rib baskets, forming the handles, spines, and rims. Hoops typically are round or oval, but they also may be made in other shapes, including the square and the D shape. In splitwork, traditional basketmakers often use the term "hoop" for "rim."

Lash (v.)   To bind.

Lashing (n.)   In splitwork, the method of binding rims or feet to a basket body. Also called "binding." See figures 4.17–4.22.

Latewood   A dense layer of thick-walled wood cells, formed in the second stage of a tree's growing season. Also called "summerwood."

Maul   A heavy wooden hammer or mallet for striking a froe, a glut, or wedges to force wood to split. See figure 2.7.

Mock waling   A wickerwork weave which begins in the same way as French randing, with one weaving rod for each side-stake. The weaving rods often are worked in a twill (over-two/under-one) pattern. The finished weave looks like waling. See figure 5.4.

Movement   The entire working pattern of a weave or border. For example, the movement in plain weave is over-one/under-one (1/1).

Overhead handle   A handle that spans across the top of a basket, from rim to rim.

Pairing   A wickerwork weave using two rods which twist around each other as they interlace the bottom-sticks or side-stakes, creating an S-twist. Also known as "twining" in fiberwork. See figure 5.5.

Pith   The central core of a tree. See figure 2.3.

Plain weave   Interlacing of weaving materials, usually at right angles and without twisting, in an over-one/under-one pattern. Also called "checkerwork" and "simple plaiting" in splitwork and "randing" in rodwork. See figure 4.2.

Plaiting   A synonym for weaving.

Pole   See **butt log**.

Radial splits   Divisions made in line with the rays. Wood is split along the rays (radially) to achieve width. Also known as "board splits." See figure 2.8.

Randing   In rodwork, the term used for plain weave. See figure 5.2.

Rays   Lines of wood cells which radiate out from the pith through the wood to the bark. See figure 2.3.

Reed   A basketry material cut from the core of the rattan palm (*Calamus* sp.), which grows in Southeast Asia.

Rib   In ribwork, a curved foundation piece which is inserted into the hoop framework to form the sides of a rib basket. Ribs may be either flat or rounded and are anchored at the basket's wrapping. In splitwork, the term "rib" is commonly used by traditional basketmakers instead of "stake."

Rib baskets   Baskets made with a framework of hoops and ribs, which are filled in by weaving splits. See figure 3.1.

Ribbing   In ribwork, the method of inserting ribs into the sides of a basket. See figures 3.13–3.16.

Ribwork   The baskets and techniques of rib basketry.

Rim   In ribwork, a foundation hoop determining the top opening's shape and size. In splitwork, rims are made from thick splits to encircle the top edge of the basket body. Rims reinforce the basket and are bound in place by a lashing.

Rive (v.)   To split or tear apart.

Riving (n.)   Splitting.

Rod   A long slender stick, either growing naturally, as with willow, or shaped from wood by whittling or using a die.

Rod baskets   Wickerwork baskets using rods as the chief weaving material. See figure 5.1.

Rod/coil baskets   Baskets constructed with white oak rods for the coil foundation and bound with flat splits.

Rod/rib baskets   Baskets constructed with a framework of hoops and ribs and woven with rods.

Rod/split baskets   Baskets using flat splits as foundation materials and rods as weavers. These baskets share features of both rodwork and splitwork.

Rodwork   The baskets and techniques of rod basketry.

Roped handle   In rodwork, an overhead or ear handle consisting of a foundation piece wrapped with small rods which also attach the handle to the basket body. See figures 5.19 and 5.20.

Row-by-row   In splitwork, a method of weaving using an even number of working ends to build the sides of a basket. Each row is woven separately and stacks on top of the previous one.

Sapwood   The light wood in between a tree's cambium layer and heartwood. In basketwork, used mostly for making splits. See figure 2.3.

Scarf (v.)   To make a scarf join. (n.) A type of join made by cutting away two pieces so that they correspond to each other and then securing them together to form one continuous piece. See figure 4.14.

Season (v.)   To dry wood.

Shaving horse   A clamping device typically consisting of a bench with a block or head attached to a post and foot pedal. See figure 2.13.

Side-stakes   In rodwork, the foundation rods added into the base weaving to make the uprights for a basket's sides.

Single bottom   In splitwork, a round base made of one layer of stakes. See figures 4.11 and 4.12.

Slat   See **billet**.

Slath   In rodwork, the central bottom formation made by interlacing the bottom-sticks with weavers to the point of opening out. See figure 5.9.

Soumak   In splitwork, a decorative weave which moves first forward and then backward, wrapping around a vertical element before continuing forward.

Spine   In ribwork, the central bottom support of the basket. See figure 3.1.

Spiraling   Any method of continuous weaving to build a basket's base and sides. See figures 4.5–4.7.

Splice   To add a new weaver in order to continue weaving or lashing.

Split (n.)   The thin flat pliable wood strip prepared by riving a log. Also known as "splint." (v.) To divide or rive.

Split baskets   Baskets made chiefly from flat splits used for both foundation and weaving materials. See figure 4.1.

Splitwork   The baskets and techniques of split basketry.

Springwood   See **earlywood**.

Stakes   In splitwork and rodwork, stakes are the foundation materials for the base or sides of the basket. Also called by traditional split basketmakers "ribs," "staves," "standards," or "splits." See also **bye-stakes**, **side-stakes**, and **foot-stakes**.

Stick   See **butt log**.

Stroke   In rodwork, a term used to denote a complete unit of the weaving movement or pattern. In randing, over-one/under-one is a complete stroke.

Summerwood   See **latewood**.

Swing handle   See **drop handle**.

Tails   The ends of a handle which are inserted into the side weaving to help secure that handle.

Tangential splits   Splits made approximately at right angles to the wood rays, and in line with the growth rings. Also called "bastard" or "grain" splits. Oak is split tangentially to achieve thickness.

Turnback   In ribwork and splitwork, the reversing of a weaver back around a rib or stake. Turnbacks create short rows which either fill in a section of a basket body or leave a space in the weaving (such as handle holes). See figures 3.3 and 3.4.

Twill   Interlacing of foundation and weaving materials without twisting, in which the elements work over and under each other in movements greater than 1/1. The most common twills in oak splitwork are 2/2 and 3/3. See figure 4.3.

Twining   A term used in fiberwork, synonymous with "pairing" and "fitching."

Upsett   In rodwork, a term used to describe the rows of weaving used to "set up" the side-stakes.

Waling   Wickerwork weave using three or more rods which twist around each other as they interlace the bottom-sticks or stakes. See figures 5.7 and 5.8.

Weavers   See **weaving materials**.

Weaving materials   Splits or rods, which interlock by twisting or interlacing to secure the foundation and fill in the basket body. Also known as "weavers."

Wedges   Tapered pieces of metal or wood which are used for splitting wood. See figure 2.6.

Wickerwork   Baskets made chiefly of round materials, as well as the techniques used to construct these baskets.

Working ends   In splitwork and rodwork, a term to describe the total number of ends of foundation materials.

Woven handle   In ribwork and splitwork, a construction consisting of a central handle with extra ribs or splits added to either side. All pieces are interlaced with weaving splits.

Wrapped handle   In ribwork, splitwork, and rodwork, a handle consisting of a foundation piece wrapped with splits or rods. See also **roped handle**.

Wrapping   In ribwork, the configuration used for binding the junction of the handle and the rim hoops, forming the anchoring point for the ribs. See figures 3.5–3.12.

Bibliography

I. Published Sources

A. *Books, Government Publications, and Video Recordings*

Adovasio, J.M. *Basketry Technology: A Guide to Identification and Analysis.* Chicago: Aldine, 1977.

Alexander, John D., Jr. *Make a Chair From a Tree: An Introduction to Working Green Wood.* Newtown, Conn.: Taunton Press, 1978.

Allen, Barbara, and William Lynwood Montell. *From Memory to History: Using Oral Sources in Local Historical Research.* Nashville, Tenn.: American Association for State and Local History, 1981.

Aurand, A. Monroe, Jr. *Early Life of the Pennsylvania Germans.* Lancaster, Pa.: Aurand Press, n.d.

Barratt, Mary. *Oak Swill Basket-making in the Lake District.* Cumbria, England: Published by the author, 1983.

Bobart, H.H. *Basketwork Through the Ages.* New York: Oxford University Press, 1936.

Boggs, Elsie Byrd. *A History of Franklin: The County Seat of Pendleton County, West Virginia.* Staunton, Va.: McClure Printing Co., 1960.

Boyce, John Shaw. *Forest Pathology.* 2d ed. New York: McGraw-Hill, 1948.

Bullard, Helen. *Crafts and Craftsmen of the Tennessee Mountains.* Falls Church, Va.: Summit Press, 1976.

Camp, Charles, comp. and ed. *Traditional Craftsmanship in America: A Diagnostic Report.* Washington, D.C.: National Council for the Traditional Arts, 1983.

Campbell, John C. *The Southern Highlander and His Homeland.* Russell Sage Foundation, 1921. Reprint ed. Lexington: University Press of Kentucky, 1969.

Curry, Roger, and Betty Curry. *From Oak Trees to Baskets.* Salem, Mo.: Gibson Curry Baskets, 1986. Video recording, self-produced.

Duchesne, R., H. Ferrand, and J. Thomas. *La Vannerie.* Vol. 1, *Le Travail de L'Osier.* Paris: J.B. Baillière et Fils, 1963.

Eaton, Allen H. *Handicrafts of the Southern Highlands.* New York: Russell Sage Foundation, 1937. Reprint ed. New York: Dover, 1973.

Eller, Ronald D. *Miners, Millhands, and Mountaineers: Industrialization of the Appalachian South; 1880–1930.* Knoxville: University of Tennessee Press, 1982.

Fitzrandolph, Helen E., and M. Doriel Hay. *The Rural Industries of England & Wales: A Survey Made on Behalf of the Agricultural Economics Research Institute, Oxford,* pt. 2, *Osier-Growing and Basketry and Some Rural Factories.* 1926. Reprint ed. East Ardsley, England: EP Publishing, 1977.

Fowells, H.A., comp. *Silvics of Forest Trees of the United States.* Agriculture Handbook No. 271. Prepared by the Division of Timber Management Research Forest Service, U.S. Department of Agriculture, 1965. Reprint ed. Washington, D.C.: U.S. Government Printing Office, 1975.

Gandert, August. *Trägkörbe in Hessen.* Kassel, West Germany: Erich Roth Verlag, 1963.

Gettys, Marshall, ed. *Basketry of Southeastern Indians.* Idabel, Okla.: Museum of the Red River, 1984.

Gibson, Henry H. *American Forest Trees.* Edited by Hu Maxwell. Chicago: Hardwood Record, 1913.

Glassie, Henry. *Patterns in the Material Folk Culture of the Eastern United States.* Philadelphia: University of Pennsylvania Press, 1968.

Goodrich, Frances Louisa. *Mountain Homespun.* New Haven, Conn.: Yale University Press, 1931.

Grant, I.F. *Highland Folk Ways.* London: Routledge & Kegan Paul, 1961.

Hartley, Dorothy. *Made in England*, 4th ed. London: Eyre Methuen, 1974.

Heidingsfelder, Sharon. *Baskets.* Cooperative Extension Service, University of Arkansas Division of Agriculture, and U.S. Department of Agriculture, circular 527, 1977.

Hepting, George H. *Diseases of Forest and Shade Trees of the United States.* Agriculture Handbook no. 386. Forest Service, U.S. Department of Agriculture. Washington, D.C.: U.S. Government Printing Office, 1971.

Heseltine, Alastair. *Baskets and Basketmaking.* Shire Album 92. Aylesbury, Bucks, England: Shire Publications, 1982.

Irwin, John Rice. *Baskets and Basket Makers in Southern Appalachia.* Exton, Pa.: Schiffer, 1982.

Ise, John. *Our National Park Policy: A Critical History.* Baltimore, Md.: Johns Hopkins University Press, 1961.

James, George Wharton. *Indian Basketry, and How to Make Indian and Other Baskets.* 3d ed., revised and enlarged. Two books in one volume. Pasadena, Calif.: Published by the author, 1903, 1904. Reprint ed. Glorieta, N.M.: Rio Grande Press, 1975.

———. *Practical Basket Making.* Enlarged and revised ed. Boston: J.L. Hamett Company, n.d.

Jenkins, H. Geraint. *Traditional Country Craftsmen.* 2d ed. London: Routledge & Kegan Paul, 1978.

Joyce, Rosemary O. *A Bearer of Tradition: Dwight Stump, Basketmaker.* Athens: University of Georgia Press, 1989.

Ketchum, William C., Jr. *American Basketry and Woodenware: A Collector's Guide.* New York: Macmillan, 1974.

Knock, A.G. *Willow Basket-Work* 8th ed. 1970. Reprint ed. Leicester, England: Dryad Press, 1979.

Lamb, George N. *Basket Willow Culture.* U.S. Department of Agriculture, Farmers Bulletin 622. Revised edition of 1914 bulletin. Washington, D.C.: U.S. Government Printing Office, 1925.

Lasansky, Jeannette. *Willow, Oak, and Rye: Basket Traditions in Pennsylvania.* University Park: Pennsylvania State University Press, 1979.

Leftwich, Rodney L. *Arts and Crafts of the Cherokee.* Cullowhee, N.C.: Western Carolina University, 1970.

McMullen, Ann, and Russell G. Handsman, eds. *A Key into the Language of Woodsplint Baskets.* Washington, Conn.: American Indian Archaelogical Institute, 1987.

Mason, Otis Tufton. *Aboriginal Indian Basketry.* Reprint of "Aboriginal American Basketry: Studies in a Textile Art Without Machinery," in *Annual Report of the Board of Regents of the Smithsonian Institute, Showing the Operations, Expenditures, and Conditions of the Institute for the Year Ending June 30, 1902,* part 2. Washington, D.C.: U.S. Government Printing Office, 1904. Reprint ed. Glorieta, N.M.: Rio Grande Press, 1972.

————. *Basket-work of the North American Aborigines: Smithsonian Annual Report 1884.* Vol. 2. Washington, D.C.: U.S. National Museum, 1884. Facsimile reproduction. Shorey's Indian Series. Seattle, Wash.: Shorey Publications, 1983.

Maxwell, Philip Herbert, and Edouard Evartt Exline. *Valhalla in the Smokies.* Cleveland, Ohio: Privately published by George A. Exline, 1938.

Morton, Oren F. *A History of Pendleton County, West Virginia.* Franklin, W. Va.: 1910. Reprint ed. Baltimore, Md.: Regional Publishing Co., 1980.

Nylén, Anna-Maja. *Swedish Handcraft.* Translated by Anne-Charlotte Hanes Harvey. New York: Van Nostrand Reinhold, 1977.

Okey, Thomas. *The Art of Basketmaking.* London: Sir Issac Pitman & Sons, 1912. Reprint ed. Ware, England: Basketmakers' Association, 1986.

Panshin, A.J., and Carl de Zeeuw. *Textbook of Wood Technology.* 4th ed. New York: McGraw-Hill, 1980.

Peattie, Donald Culross. *A Natural History of Trees of Eastern and Central North America.* Boston: Houghton Mifflin, 1948.

Schweizerischen Vereins für Handarbeit und Schulreform. *Peddigrohrflechten — Vannerie.* 6th ed. [Liestal, Switzerland]: Schweizerischen Vereins für Handarbeit und Schulreform, 1979.

Seeler, Katherine, and Edgar Seeler. *Nantucket Lightship Baskets.* Nantucket, Mass.: Deermouse Press, 1972.

Scholtz, Sandra Clements. *Prehistoric Plies: A Structural and Comparative Analysis of Cordage, Netting, Basketry, and Fabric from Ozark Bluff Shelters.* Research Series no. 9. Fayetteville, Ark.: Arkansas Archeological Survey, 1975.

Schiffer, Nancy. *Baskets.* Exton, Pa.: Schiffer, 1984.

Shapiro, Henry D. *Appalachia on Our Mind: The Southern Mountains and Mountaineers in the American Consciousness, 1870–1920.* Chapel Hill: University of North Carolina Press, 1978.

Solomon, J.D.; F.I. McCracken; R.L. Anderson; R. Lewis, Jr.; F.L. Oliveria: T.H. Filer; and P.J. Barry. *Oak Pests: A Guide to Major Insects, Diseases, Air Pollution and Chemical Injury.* U.S. Department of Agriculture Forest Service. Washington, D.C.: U.S. Government Printing Office, 1980.

Steinmetz, Rollin, and Charles S. Rice. *Vanishing Crafts and Their Craftsmen.* New Brunswick, N.J.: Rutgers University Press, 1959.

Stephens, Cleo M. *Willow Spokes and Wickerwork.* Harrisburg, Pa.: Stackpole Books, 1975.

Stephenson, Sue H. *Basketry of the Appalachian Mountains.* New York: Van Nostrand Reinhold, 1977.

Swanton, John R. *The Indians of the Southeastern United States.* U.S. Smithsonian Institution, Bureau of American Ethnology, Bulletin 137. Washington, D.C.: U.S. Government Printing Office, 1946.

Teleki, Gloria Roth. *The Baskets of Rural America.* New York: E.P. Dutton, 1975.

————. *Collecting Traditional American Basketry.* New York: E.P. Dutton, 1979.

Thernstrom, Stephan, ed. *Harvard Encyclopedia of American Ethnic Groups.* Cambridge, Mass.: Belknap Press of Harvard University Press, 1980.

Thompson, Frances. *Antique Baskets and Basketry.* New York: A.S. Barnes, 1977.

Tod, Osma Gallinger. *Earth Basketry: A Popular Hand-book Containing Concise Basketry Directions With Clear Simple Diagrams – Designed for the Beginner as Well as the More Experienced Basket Weaver.* N.p.: Orange Judd Publishing Co., 1933.

Turnbaugh, Sarah Peabody, and William A. Turnbaugh. *Indian Baskets.* West Chester, Pa.: Schiffer, 1986.

Turner, Luther Weston. *The Basket Maker.* Worcester, Mass.: Davis Press, 1909.

United States Department of Interior. Indian Arts and Crafts Board. *Basketry by Emma Taylor: An Exhibition, May 11–June 30, 1975.* Exhibition brochure.

————. *Baskets of the Woods . . . A Collection by Carol S. Welch, August 1–October 1, 1977.* Exhibition brochure.

Wargo, Philip. *Defoliation by the Gypsy Moth: How it Hurts Your Tree.* U.S. Department of Agriculture, Home and Garden Bulletin No. 223. Washington, D.C.: U.S. Government Printing Office, 1978.

Wetherbee, Martha, and Nathan Taylor. *Legend of the Bushwhacker Basket.* Edited by Mary Lyn Ray. Sanbornton, N.H.: Martha Wetherbee Basket Shop, 1986.

————. *Shaker Baskets.* Edited by Mary Lyn Ray. Sanbornton, N.H.: Martha Wetherbee Basket Shop, 1988.

Whisnant, David E. *All That Is Native and Fine: The Politics of Culture in an American Region.* Chapel Hill: University of North Carolina Press, 1983.

White, Mary. *How to Make Baskets.* New York: Doubleday, Page & Co., 1901.

Will, Christoph. *International Basketry: For Weavers and Collectors.* Translated from the German by Edward Force. Exton, Pa.: Schiffer, 1985. Originally published as *Die Korbflechterei.* Munich: Callwey Verlag, 1978.

Wright, Dorothy. *The Complete Book of Baskets and Basketry.* 2d ed. North Pomfret, Vt.: David & Charles, 1983.

B. Articles and Other Published Materials

Includes: chapters from books; articles from journals, magazines, and newspapers; pamphlets; catalogs; brochures.

Alexander, Lawrence. "Basketmakers of Cannon County: An Overview." *Tennessee Folklore Society Bulletin* 52, no. 4 (1987):110–20.

Allanstand Cottage Industries, Inc. (ACI). *Price List*, ca. 1917. Archives of the Southern Highland Handicraft Guild, Asheville, N.C.

———. *Price List*, ca. 1920s. Archives of the Southern Highland Handicraft Guild, Asheville, N.C.

———. *Price List*, ca. 1930. Archives of the Southern Highland Handicraft Guild, Asheville, N.C.

Allen, A.B., ed. "Cultivation of the Osier." *American Agriculturalist* 7, no. 1 (1848):45–46, 86–87.

Bybee, Emma. "The Basket Makers of Wax." *Rural Kentuckian Magazine*, May 1963, pp. 2–7.

Cox, Jane. "Don't See How a Feller Can Keep House Without a Basket . . . Basket Maker of Lincoln County." [Richwood, W.Va.] *West Virginia Hillbilly*, 27 Jan. 1968.

Fackenthal, B.F., Jr. Comment on "Notes on Basketmaking." In *A Collection of Papers Read Before the Bucks County Historical Society*, edited by Henry Mercer et al., 5:196. Meadville, Pa.: Bucks County Historical Society, 1926.

Helm, Rudolf. "Hessische Vorratskörbe." *Fachzeitschrift für die Flechtwerk- und Kinderwagen-Wirtschaft*, Feb. 1961, pp. 46–50. Magazine published Neustadt b. Coburg, West Germany: Emil Patzschke.

Higginbotham, Wilma. "Linville Preserves True Native Craft." *Charleston W.Va. Daily Mail*, 8 June 1965.

Hill, Jennie Lester. "Fireside Industries in the Kentucky Mountains." *Southern Workman* 32 (Apr. 1903):208–13.

Horward, Frank. "Craftsman Begins Work on Basket: Basket Making Thrives Near Sewellsville." *Times-Leader*, Martins Ferry and Bellaire, Ohio, 4 Apr. 1951.

Lair, Eugene D. "Smooth Patch, A Bark Disease of Oak." *Journal of the Mitchell Society* 62 (Dec. 1946):212–20.

Lasansky, Jeannette. "Pennsylvania-German Round-Rod Oak Baskets." *The Magazine Antiques* 125 (Apr. 1984):886–95.

Lester, Joan. "'We Didn't Make Fancy Baskets Until We Were Discovered': Fancy-Basket Making in Maine." In *A Key into the Language of Woodsplint Baskets*, edited by Ann McMullen and Russell G. Handsman, 38–59. Washington, Conn.: American Indian Archaeological Institute, 1987.

Louis Stoughton Drake, Inc. *Everything for Basket Making*. Basket supply catalog. Boston: Louis Stoughton Drake, ca. 1918.

Marshall, Howard Wight. "Mr. Westfall's Baskets: Traditional Craftsmanship in Northcentral Missouri." *Mid-South Folklore* 2 (1974):43–60. Reprinted in *Readings in American Folklore*, edited by Jan H. Brunvand, 168–91. New York: Norton, 1979.

Martin-Perdue, Nancy J. "Case Study: On Eaton's Trail: A Genealogical Study of Virginia Basket Makers." In *Traditional Craftsmanship in America: A Diagnostic Report*, compiled and edited by Charles Camp, 79–101. Washington, D.C.: National Council for the Traditional Arts, 1983.

Mercer, Henry. "Splint Baskets Made by Peter Weirbach." In *A Collection of Papers Read Before the Bucks County Historical Society*, edited by Henry Mercer et al., 5:194–96. Meadville, Pa.: Bucks County Historical Society, 1926.

Milton Bradley Company. *Bradley's School-Materials and Books: Catalogue "A".* Philadelphia: Milton Bradley Co., 1923.

Romaine, Lawrence B. "Basketmaking." *Chronicle of the Early American Industries Association* 2, no. 8 (Mar. 1939):57–58.

Sattler, Richard. "Baskets of the Cherokees." In *Basketry of Southeastern Indians,* edited by Marshall Gettys, 25–34. Idabel, Okla.: Museum of the Red River, 1984.

Scheetz, Grier. "Basket Making." In *A Collection of Papers Read Before the Bucks County Historical Society,* edited by Henry Mercer et al., vol. 5:190–92. Meadville, Pa.: Bucks County Historical Society, 1926.

Smith, Tom. "It Takes Big Families to Weave Baskets." [Louisville, Ky.] *Courier Journal,* 24 Dec. 1940.

————. "It Takes Big Families to Weave Baskets." In *History of Hart County,* bk. 2, ch. 8, edited by Judge Roy Cann. Mimeographed. Munfordville, Ky.: Hart County Historical Society, n.d. Rewrite of article published in *Hart County (Ky.) News,* 1940.

Speck, Frank G. "Decorative Art and Basketry of the Cherokee." *Bulletin of the Public Museum of the City of Milwaukee* 2, no. 2 (July 1920):53–84.

Sutherland, David. "Traditional Basketmaking in Kentucky." *Kentucky Folklore Record* 18, no. 4 (1972):89–92.

II. Unpublished Sources

A. Manuscript Materials

Includes: mimeographed materials, unpublished theses, student papers, manuscripts, letters, lectures, photo albums, notes, and interviews.

Alvey, Leroy. Letter to Cynthia W. Taylor, 27 Jan. 1986. Collection of Cynthia W. Taylor.

Bavill, I. "Hart County Is Center of Kentucky Basket Industry." In *History of Hart County,* edited by Judge Roy Cann. Mimeographed. Munfordville, Ky.: Hart County Historical Society, n.d.

Benson, Chris. Notes from interview with Mildred Youngblood, Woodbury, Cannon County, Tenn., 1981. Private collection.

Brown, Jim, and Judith Schottenfeld. Tape-recorded interview with Rec Childress and Mrs. Childress, Cub Run, Hart County, Ky., 14 Sept. 1977. Folklore class project, Western Kentucky University, Bowling Green. Transcript in private collection.

Bucks County Historical Society. "Recent History, Natural History, and Science" (photo album). Bucks County Historical Society, Spruance Library, Doylestown, Pa.

————. "Archeology and Colonial History," photo album no. 1. Bucks County Historical Society, Spruance Library, Doylestown, Pa.

Bybee, Emma, Letter to Cynthia W. Taylor, 24 Oct. 1985. Collection of Cynthia W. Taylor.

Casteel, Catherine. "The Making of White Oak Baskets in Madison and Page Counties." Unpublished student paper, 1972. Folklore Archive, University of Virginia, Charlottesville, no. 1972–23.

Cogswell, Robert. "A Tradition of Inequity: Marketing Baskets in Kentucky and Tennessee." Paper presented at the annual meeting of the American Folklore Society, Baltimore, Md., 23 Oct. 1986.

Dalke, Peter. "Basketmaking: A Comparison Between Two Local Craftsmen." Unpublished student paper, 1979. Folklore Archive, University of Virginia, Charlottesville, no. 1979–9.

Davis, Gary, and Elizabeth Wilson. Tape-recorded interview with Gertie West, Cub Run, Hart County, Ky., 29 Sept. 1977. Folklore class project, Western Kentucky University, Bowling Green. Private collection.

Garvey, William. "Basket Builder." Unpublished student paper, 1975. Folklore Archive, University of Virginia, Charlottesville, no. 1975–38.

Hall, Deborah, and Roger Hall. Tape-recorded interview with Ralph Burbas and Mrs. Burbas, Edmonson County, Ky., 30 Sept. 1977. Folklore class project, Western Kentucky University, Bowling Green. Transcript in private collection.

Hall, Deborah, and Aza Moody. Tape-recorded interview with Ralph Burbas and Mrs. Burbas, Edmondson County, Ky., 19 Oct. 1977. Folklore class project, Western Kentucky University, Bowling Green. Transcript in private collection.

Harzoff, Elizabeth. "The Long Distance Basket Trade." Unpublished student paper, 1977. Folklore class project, Western Kentucky University, Bowling Green. Private collection.

———. Tape-recorded interviews with Stanley Cottrell, Hart County, Ky., 14 and 19 Sept. 1977. Folklore class project, Western Kentucky University, Bowling Green. Transcripts in private collection.

Helsley, Mildred. Letter to Cynthia W. Taylor, 31 March 1989. Collection of Cynthia W. Taylor.

Hopf, Carroll J. "Basketware of the Northeast: A Study of the Types of Basketware Used on the Farm from the Colonial Period to 1860." M.A. thesis, Cooperstown Graduate Program, State University of New York College at Oneonta, 1965.

Jaggers, Ben. "The Art of Basketmaking." Unpublished student paper, 1971. Folklife Archives, Western Kentucky University, Bowling Green, no. 1972–18.

Joyce, Rosemary O. Interview with Bertha Fridley, Lithopolis, Fairfield County, Ohio, 10 Mar. 1986. Private collection.

Joyce, Rosemary O. Letter to Cynthia W. Taylor, 6 May 1985. Collection of Cynthia W. Taylor.

Kiely, Denis O. "The Loving of the Game: A Study of Basketry in the Mammoth Cave Area." M.A. thesis, Western Kentucky University, Bowling Green, 1983.

———. Tape-recorded interview with Susan Barret, Cave City, Barren County, Ky., 30 Sept. 1977. Folklore class project, Western Kentucky University, Bowling Green. Transcript in private collection.

Korn, Michael and Denis Kiely. Tape-recorded interview with Thomas Fenwick, Wax, Grayson County, Ky., 16 Sept. 1977. Transcript in Folklife Archives, Western Kentucky University, Bowling Green, no. 1979–85.

Laird, Catherine Candace Irvine. "Basketry Notes" [concerning traditional basketry of W.Va.]. Mimeographed. 1967. Laird Collection, courtesy of Norman M. and Dorothy Irvine.

————. "How to Make Baskets from White Oak Splints, Related by Mr. Currence Dobbins" [of Glenville, Gilmer County, W.Va.]. Ca. 1960. Laird Collection, courtesy of Norman M. and Dorothy Irvine.

————. "The Manufacture of Split Oak Baskets: Basketmakers William Cody Cook and Lucy Cook and Directions from the Cooks" [of Luray, Page County, Va.]. Ca. 1960. Laird Collection, courtesy of Norman M. and Dorothy Irvine.

————. Notes from interviews with Claude Linville, Emmer Linville, and Ethel Bias, Griffithsville, Lincoln County, W.Va., ca. 1960. Laird Collection, courtesy of Norman M. and Dorothy Irvine.

————. Notes from interviews with Gertrude Lucky, Leroy, Wirt County, W.Va., ca. 1960. Laird Collection, courtesy of Norman M. and Dorothy Irvine.

————. Notes from interviews with Oscar Peters and Bess Peters, Lesage, Cabell County, W.Va., ca. 1960. Laird Collection, courtesy of Norman M. and Dorothy Irvine.

————. Notes from interviews with Elmer Propst, Franklin, Pendleton County, W.Va., 1969–1972. Laird Collection, courtesy of Norman M. and Dorothy Irvine.

Ludden, Keith. Tape-recorded interview with Audie Dennison, Cub Run, Hart County, Ky., 5 Sept. 1977. Tape in Folklife Archives, Western Kentucky University, Bowling Green, no. CT-452. Transcript in private collection.

Marshall, John, and Judith Schottenfeld. Tape-recorded interview with Anderson Childress, Munfordville, Hart County, Ky., 23 Sept. 1977. Folklore class project, Western Kentucky University, Bowling Green. Transcript in private collection.

Mercer, Henry. Accession ledger of Henry Mercer. Bucks County Historical Society and Mercer Museum, Doylestown, Pa.

Montell, Lynwood. Tape-recorded interview with Walter Dawson Logsdon and Bertha T. Skaggs, 1 Sept. 1977. Tape in Folklife Archives, Western Kentucky University, Bowling Green, no. CT-452.

Montell, Lynwood, and Molly Collins. Tape-recorded interview with Walker Thompson, Cub Run, Hart County, Ky., 1 Oct. 1977. Transcript in Folklife Archives, Western Kentucky University, Bowling Green, no. 1979-85.

Murphy, Valeria S., and Jorene McCubbins, Hart County Historical Society. Letter to Cynthia W. Taylor, 13 Jan. 1986. Collection of Cynthia W. Taylor.

Nason, Wayne C. "Rural Industries in Knott County, Kentucky: A Preliminary Report." U.S. Department of Agriculture, Bureau of Agricultural Economics, in coooperation with the Kentucky Agricultural Experiment Station. Mimeographed. Washington, D.C., 1932.

North, Keith, "Basket Weaving in Grayson Co." Unpublished student paper, 1975. Folklife Archives, Western Kentucky University, Bowling Green, no. 1976–5.

Ostrofsky, Martin B., and Jim Brown. Tape-recorded interview with Lloyd Meredith and Lilian Gunterman Meredith, Brownsville, Edmonson County, Ky., 28 Sept. 1977. Folklore class project, Western Kentucky University, Bowling Green. Transcript in private collection.

Payton, Lyndell. Tape-recorded interview with George Childress, Hart County, Ky., fall 1977. Tapes in Folklife Archives, Western Kentucky University, Bowling Green, nos. CT-873 and 874. Transcript in private collection.

Peters, Oscar. Letter to Catherine Candace Laird, ca. 1966. Laird Collection, courtesy of Norman M. and Dorothy Irvine.

Russell, Stanley. "The Southern Highland Handicraft Guild, 1928–1975." Ph.D. dissertation, Teachers College, Columbia University, New York, N.Y., 1976.

Sadewasser, Judi. "The Folkways of Walter D. Logsdon: Basketmaker." Unpublished student paper, 1974. Folklife Archives, Western Kentucky University, Bowling Green, no. 1974–94.

————. Tape-recorded interviews with Walter Dawson Logsdon, Brownsville, Edmonson County, Ky., 15 July 1974. Tape and transcript in Folklife Archives, Western Kentucky University, Bowling Green, no. 1974–94.

Sadewasser, Judi, and Steve Sadewasser. Tape-recorded interview with Walter Dawson Logsdon, Brownsville, Edmonson County, Ky., 27 June 1974. Tape and transcript in Folklife Archives, Western Kentucky University, Bowling Green, no. 1974–94.

Schottenfeld, Judith. "Construction of the White Oak Basket." Unpublished student paper, 1977. Folklife Archives, Western Kentucky University, Bowling Green, no. 1979–85.

Shobe, Annie Handley. Letter to David Nash, 29 July 1982. Collection of Rachel Nash Law.

————. Letter to Rachel Nash Law, 21 Jan. 1986. Collection of Rachel Nash Law.

Showen, Ellen Kay. "Three Types of Traditional Baskets." Unpublished student paper, 1978. Folklore Archive, University of Virginia, Charlottesville, no. 1978–28.

————. Interview with Lucy Cook, Luray, Page County, Va., 12 Mar. 1978. Transcript in Folklore Archive, University of Virginia, Charlottesville, no. 1978–28.

Sisto, Antonia L. "Basketmaking in Nelson County." Unpublished student paper, 1976. Folklore Archive, University of Virginia, Charlottesville, no. 1976–83.

————. Tape-recorded interview with Henry Beverley, Arrington, Nelson County, Va., 17 Apr. 1976. Tape and transcript in Folklore Archive, University of Virginia, Charlottesville, no. 1976–83.

Southern Highland Handicraft Guild. "Members Handbook." Mimeographed. Asheville, N.C., 1986.

Sutherland, David. "Traditional Basketmaking in Kentucky." Unpublished student paper, 1971. Folklife Archives, Western Kentucky University, Bowling Green, no. 1971–9.

Waldrop, Melanie. "Basketmaking for Walter Logsdon: A Way of Life." Unpublished student paper, 1975. Folklife Archives, Western Kentucky University, Bowling Green, no. 1976–13.

————. Tape-recorded interviews with Walter Dawson Logsdon, Brownsville, Edmonson County, 15 and 28 Nov. 1975. Transcripts in Folklife Archives, Western Kentucky University, Bowling Green, no. 1976–13.

Wilson, Elizabeth. "General Information of Basket Making and Weaving Interviews." [1977]. Folklore class project, Western Kentucky University, Bowling Green. Private collection.

B. Oral Sources: Interviews by the Authors

Alvey, Leroy. Cub Run, Hart County, Ky. Phone interview by Cynthia W. Taylor, 23 Jan. 1986.

Arthur, Ralph, and Sarah Arthur. Radford, Va. Informal interview by Rachel Nash Law and Cynthia W. Taylor, 11 Mar. 1985.

Bohn, Carol. Mifflinburg, Pa. Informal interview by Rachel Nash Law and Cynthia W. Taylor, 16 Oct. 1984.

Boggs, Elizabeth. Franklin, W.Va. Phone interview by Rachel Nash Law, 10 Feb. 1986.

Boyd, Clovis, and Roxie Boyd. Floyd, Floyd County, Va. Tape-recorded interview by Rachel Nash Law and Cynthia W. Taylor, 11 Mar. 1985.

Brunk, Robert S. Weaverville, N.C. Informal interview by Rachel Nash Law and Cynthia W. Taylor, 27 Nov. 1984.

Caldwell, Tishie. War Branch, Bell County, Ky. Pencil and pad interview by Rachel Nash Law and Cynthia W. Taylor, 25 May 1983.

Chesney, Ralph, and Trula Chesney. Luttrell, Union County, Tenn. Tape-recorded interview by Jesse Butcher, Rachel Nash Law, and Cynthia W. Taylor, 26 Nov. 1984. Pencil and pad interview by Law and Taylor, 4 Feb. 1985.

Childress, Lestel, and Ollie Childress. Park City, Edmonson County, Ky. Tape-recorded interview by Scott Gilbert, Beth Hester, Rachel Nash Law and Cynthia W. Taylor, 23 Mar. 1984. Tape-recorded interview by Law and Taylor, 20 Feb. 1985, also recorded with pencil and pad.

Cook, W. Bill. Mount Jackson, Shenandoah County, Va. Phone interview by Rachel Nash Law, 6 Dec. 1989.

Cook, William Cody, and Lucy Cook. Luray, Page County, Va. Tape-recorded interview by Rachel Nash Law and Cynthia W. Taylor, 14 Mar. 1985.

Curry, Betty. Salem, Dent County, Mo. Phone interview by Cynthia W. Taylor, 1 Dec. 1989.

Dalton, Kathleen. Coker Creek, Tenn. Interview by Rachel Nash Law and Cynthia W. Taylor, 1 Dec. 1984.

Davis, Ida Pearl; Thelma Davis Hibdon; and Billy Hibdon. Woodbury, Cannon County, Tenn. Pencil and pad interview by Rachel Nash Law and Cynthia W. Taylor, 7 May 1985.

Day, Oliver. Mount Jackson, Shenandoah County, Va. Phone interview by Cynthia W. Taylor, 13 Mar. 1985.

Devol, Jerry B. Marietta, Ohio. Phone interview by Cynthia W. Taylor, 20 Aug. 1989.

Doolin, Datha. Lancaster, Ky. Informal interview by Rachel Nash Law and Cynthia W. Taylor, 19 Feb. 1985.

Elder, J. Charlottesville, Va. Informal interview by Cynthia W. Taylor, 10 June 1983.

Elkins, Peggy. Location not listed. Informal interview by Rachel Nash Law and Cynthia W. Taylor, 9 May 1985.

Farmer, Ken, and Jane Farmer. Radford, Va. Informal interview by Rachel Nash Law and Cynthia W. Taylor, 11 Mar. 1985.

Faulkner, Teresa, and Charles Faulkner. Knoxville, Tenn. Informal interview by Rachel Nash Law and Cynthia W. Taylor, 28 Nov. 1984.

George, Jane, and Frank George. Spencer, W.Va. Tape-recorded interview by Rachel Nash Law and Cynthia W. Taylor, 9 Jan. 1985.

Gladden, Earl. Sewellsville, Ohio. Tape-recorded interview by Cynthia W. Taylor, 28 Sept. 1984, also recorded with pencil and pad.

Glass, Billie Jean. Lexington, Ky. Informal interview by Rachel Nash Law and Cynthia W. Taylor, 23 May 1983.

Hackley, Larry. North Middletown, Ky. Informal interview by Rachel Nash Law and Cynthia W. Taylor, 17 Feb. 1985.

Hamilton, Hazel. Lancaster, Ky. Informal interview by Rachel Nash Law and Cynthia W. Taylor, 18 Feb. 1985.

Haney, David. Marietta, Ohio. Informal interview by Cynthia W. Taylor, 14 Jan. 1986.

Helsley, Bruce, and Mildred Helsley. Woodstock, Va. Informal interview by Rachel Nash Law and Cynthia W. Taylor, 13 Mar. 1985; Tom's Brook, Va., 16 Mar. 1989.

Herr, Donald M., and Mrs. Donald M. Herr. Lancaster, Pa. Informal interview by Rachel Nash Law and Cynthia W. Taylor, 18 Oct. 1984.

Huddleston, C.B., and Donna Huddleston. Murfeesboro, Tenn. Informal interview by Rachel Nash Law and Cynthia W. Taylor, 29 Nov. 1984.

Jones, Martha, and Dan Jones. McMinnville, Warren County, Tenn. Pencil and pad interview by Rachel Nash Law and Cynthia W. Taylor, 7 May 1985.

Joyce, Rosemary O. Rockbridge, Ohio. Pencil and pad interview by Rachel Nash Law and Cynthia W. Taylor, 15 and 16 May 1984. Phone interviews by Cynthia W. Taylor, 8 Feb. 1985, 8 Apr. 1986, and 24 Aug. 1989.

Kemble, Marilyn. Norwich, Ohio. Informal interview by Rachel Nash Law and Cynthia W. Taylor, 23 Aug. 1985.

King, Marcus Farthing. Blountville, Tenn. Informal interview by Rachel Nash Law and Cynthia W. Taylor, 10 May 1985.

Knott, Edna. Glouster, Athens County, Ohio. Phone interview by Cynthia W. Taylor, 19 Aug. 1989.

Knott, Elmer E. Glouster, Athens County, Ohio. Phone interview by Cynthia W. Taylor, 19 Aug. 1989.

Knott, Elmer E., and Elmer L. Knott. Glouster, Athens County, Ohio. Tape-recorded interview by Cynthia W. Taylor, 20 Aug. 1989.

Kuster, Shirley. Selinsgrove, Pa. Informal interview by Rachel Nash Law and Cynthia W. Taylor, 16 Oct. 1984.

Kyle, Mrs. Clare. Torrisdale, Scotland. Informal conversation with Rachel Nash, 31 Aug. 1978.

Lasansky, Jeannette. Lewisburg, Pa. Interview by Rachel Nash Law and Cynthia W. Taylor, 15 Oct. 1984.

Long, Benny. New Market, Va. Informal interview by Rachel Nash Law and Cynthia W. Taylor, 14 Mar. 1985.

Lornell, Kip. Blue Ridge Institute, Ferrum, Va. Pencil and pad interview by Rachel Nash Law and Cynthia W. Taylor, 12 Mar. 1985.

Lott, Susan. Fleming, Ohio. Phone interview by Cynthia W. Taylor, 30 May 1985.

Luke, Bill. Marietta, Ohio. Pencil and pad interview by Cynthia W. Taylor, 22 Apr. 1985.

Malone, Therese. Marietta, Ohio. Informal interview by Cynthia W. Taylor, 22 Apr. 1985.

Martin-Perdue, Nancy J., and Charles L. Perdue, Jr. Charlottesville, Va. Informal interview by Rachel Nash Law and Cynthia W. Taylor, 13 Mar. 1985.

Mink, Dianne. Lancaster, Ky. Informal interview by Rachel Nash Law and Cynthia W. Taylor, 18 Feb. 1985.

Moore, J. Roderick. Blue Ridge Institute, Ferrum, Va. Tape-recorded interview by Rachel Nash Law and Cynthia W. Taylor, 20 June 1984; informal interviews, 12 Mar. 1985 and 16 Mar. 1989.

Myers, Edith Billetter. Barnesville, Ohio. Tape-recorded interview by Cynthia W. Taylor, 10 Oct. 1984.

Nash, David C., and Mary Nash. Berea, Ky. Informal conversation with Rachel Nash Law and Cynthia W. Taylor, 10 May 1988.

Nicholson, Irskel, and Charlotte Nicholson. Edinburg, Shenandoah County, Virginia. Phone interview by Cynthia W. Taylor, 13 Mar. 1985; tape-recorded interview by Taylor, 16 Mar. 1985.

Nicholson, Oral ("Nick"). Doddridge County, W.Va. Tape-recorded interview by Cynthia W. Taylor and Aaron Yakim, 3 Oct. 1984.

Noble, Ross. Highland Folk Museum, Kingussie, Scotland. Informal conversation with Rachel Nash, 22 Aug. 1978.

Pack, Ken. Moorefield, W.Va. Informal conversation with Rachel Nash, Apr. 1979.

Peters, John. Waverly, Wood County, W.Va. Phone interview by Cynthia W. Taylor, 1 Dec. 1989.

Price, Elmer D., Sr. New Market, Shenandoah County, Va. Tape-recorded interview by Rachel Nash Law and Cynthia W. Taylor, 14 Mar. 1985.

Ratsford, Jake. Moorefield, W.Va. Phone interview by Rachel Nash Law and Annie Handley Shobe, 15 Jan. 1986.

Rector Ed. Berea, Madison County, Ky. Phone interview by Rachel Nash Law, 5 Apr. 1986.

Rigsby, Bruce. Lancaster, Ky. Informal interview by Rachel Nash Law and Cynthia W. Taylor, 18 Feb. 1985.

Ross, Martha. Cherokee, Swain County, N.C. Pencil and pad interview by Rachel Nash Law and Cynthia W. Taylor, 8 May 1985.

Ross, Smith. Pine Knot, Ky. Phone interview by Rachel Nash Law, 19 Mar. 1985; pencil and pad interview by Law and C. David Nash, 5 Apr. 1986.

Rutter, Nora. Glouster, Athens County, Ohio. Phone interview by Cynthia W. Taylor, 19 Aug. 1989.

Shobe, Annie Handley. Moorefield, W.Va. Informal interview by Rachel Nash Law, 15 Jan. 1986.

Stump, Dwight, and Bob Mansberger. Rockbridge, Hocking County, Ohio. Tape-recorded interview by Rosemary Joyce, Rachel Nash Law, and Cynthia W. Taylor, 16 May 1984.

Stephenson, Sue H. Lynchburg, Va. Informal conversation with Rachel Nash Law and Cynthia W. Taylor, 15 Mar. 1985.

————. Informal conversation with Rachel Nash Law, 19–21 May 1986.

Summers, Homer, and Juanita Summers. Sissonville, Kanawha County, W.Va. Tape-recorded interviews by Rachel Nash Law and Cynthia W. Taylor, 24 Aug. 1984 and 13 Jan. 1985. Ripley, W.Va., pencil and pad interview by Taylor, 3 July 1985. Sissonville, informal interview by Taylor, 15 Sept. 1989.

Theophilus, Dan. Rhawndirmywn, Wales. Pencil and pad interview by Rachel Nash, 11 Aug. 1978.

Thierschmann, Michael. Beverly, W.Va. Informal interview by Rachel Nash Law, Sept. 1987.

Thomas, Earlean, and Lawson Thomas. Woodbury, Cannon County, Tenn. Tape-recorded interview by Rachel Nash Law and Cynthia W. Taylor, 30 Nov. 1984.

Tracey, Charlotte. Cherryville, Gaston County, N.C. Tape-recorded interview by Jim Gentry, Rachel Nash Law, and Cynthia W. Taylor, 27 Nov. 1984.

Turtschi, Werner. Beverly, W.Va. Informal interview by Rachel Nash Law, July 1986 and Sept. 1989.

Van Corbach, Dot. Elizabethtown, Ky. Informal interview by Rachel Nash Law and Cynthia W. Taylor, 20 Feb. 1985.

Ware, Pete. Bedford, Bedford County, Va. Tape-recorded interview by Rachel Nash Law and Cynthia W. Taylor, 15 Mar. 1985.

Watts, Elizabeth. Knoxville, Tenn. Pencil and pad interview by Rachel Nash Law and Cynthia W. Taylor, 26 Nov. 1984.

Young, Margaret. Beverly, Ky. Pencil and pad interview by Rachel Nash Law and Cynthia W. Taylor, 25 May 1983.

Youngblood, Estel. Woodbury, Cannon County, Tenn. Tape-recorded interview by Rachel Nash Law and Cynthia W. Taylor, 30 Nov. 1984.

Younger, Paul. Gladys, Campbell County, Va. Tape-recorded interview by Rachel Nash Law and Cynthia W. Taylor, 15 Mar. 1985.

Index

References to drawings and photographs or their captions are printed in boldface type. References to color plates are listed by plate number at the end of the listing. Foreign terms are in *italics*. Names of traditional basketmakers or family members participating in part of the basketmaking process are printed in CAPITALS. Traditional basketmakers are also cross-referenced by geographical location.

bases, split baskets. *See also* stakes (in splitwork)
— comparison of, 131
— hexagonally woven, 137–39, **138**
— rectangular bases, 143–50; closed-bottom, 143–46, **146, 147, 189** (*see also* fillers: in rectangular base constructions); with corner bye-stakes, 147, **148, 149**; cross-braced bottom, 147, **150**; doming of, **Cl. Pl. 16**; holding row for, 147, **149**; open plain woven, 134, **136**, 143, **144**; stake-and-filler, 146, **148, 198**; twill woven, 136, **137**, 143, **172**
— round bases, 151–63; doming, 153, **155, 156, Cl. Pl. 10**; stake layout, 151, **153**; stake tapering, 151, **156**; weaving, 140–42, **140, 141, 142, 161, 162**
— double-bottom round bases, 151–57, **155, 173, 177, 180, Cl. Pl. 14**; right-angle stake layout, 151, **153**; outside placement of second bottom, 151–53, **156**; spiral layouts, 151, **154, 178**; weaving, 154–56, **157**
— single-bottom round bases, 158–63; bye-staked, 158–63, **161, 162, 164**; medallion center, 158, **159**; split-stake, 158, **160, 161**; wickerwork construction, 163, **200**
— oval bases, 163–65; bye-staked, 141, **148**, 163, **166**; constructed with tapered stakes, 163, **165, 178, 200**
— plank bases, 166–67; baskets, **77, 167, Cl. Pl. 13**; sleigh, **168**
basket. *See also* basketmaker; basketmaking; rib baskets; rod baskets; rod/coil baskets; rod/rib baskets; rod/split baskets; split baskets
— bartering and peddling: barter for goods, 9–10, **13**, 116; peddling locally, 8–9, **11, 155, 209, 245**; long distance peddling from Kentucky, 12, 19–20, **21**, 68; long distance peddling from Tennessee, 20–22
— kinds of (names for): apple, **16, 215**; berry, 3; bird nest (bird house), **16**, 68, 121; "box," **76, Cl. Pl. 9**; burden, **128**; bushel, 12, 21, 67, **97, 160, 213**; bushel and related measure, 20, 73, 78, 209, **215, 245**; butter-fly, 75; buttocks, 74, **98**; cake, 75; cane-basket, 197, **198–99**; canoe, **16, 17**, 122, **122**; cheese making, 139; chip, 17; clam, 139; clothes, 3, **124**, 125, **215**; clover, 17; coal, 3, **117, 243**; cradle, 3, **7, 126–27**; *crealagh*, **120**; creel, 184, **184**; corn, 125, **213, 215**; "Dolly," 88, **Cl. Pl. 9**; Easter, 209,

215, **223**; eel trap, 3, **128**; egg, 3, 67, 74–75, 78, **99, 139, 152, 215**; Kentucky egg (old Kentucky or jug), 16, 17, 74, **74, Cl. Pl. 7**; fan, 88, **Cl. Pl. 8**; "fancy" baskets and novelties, 18, 68, **69, 200**; fanny, 74; farm, 10, 12, 67; feather, 3, 179, 197, **199**; feed, 125, **128**, 179, 182, **213**; field, 182, **184**, 251; fish, 179, **180, 184**; fish trap, 3, 125, **128**; flower, 68, **178, 257, Cl. Pl. 15**; flowervase, **97, 128, 131**; fruit, **16**, 68; garden, **16, 128**, 136, **198**; gizzard, 74; grain riddle, 3, 254, **256**; *gwyntell*, 70; hamper, **16**, 125, 128, **144–45, 215, 258**; hat, 200, **200**; hen, **120**, 121–22; hip, 4, 74; *Hutzelkörbe* (drying basket), **120**; key basket, 17, **76**; knitting, **16, 120**; laundry, 3, **218**; lunch, 128, **129**; magazine, 68, **97, 120–21**, 122; mail, 195; market (shopping), 67, 76, 99, 128, 176, **178, 182, 183, 193**; melon, 4, 6, **16, 17, 19, 57**, 67, 68, **82, 97, 98, 99, 119, Cl. Pl. 1**; melon favors, **16, 17**, 68, **99**; "Moses," 15; *mudag*, **120**; muzzle, 17; *Nußkörbe* (nut basket), **120, 121**; pack, 3, 166, **187, 189**; picking, **16, 17**; picnic, 68, **175**, 182, 197, **197–200, Cl. Pl. 11**; pie, 75, **118, 120–21**, 122, 257; potato, 66, 70; purse (handbag), 27, 128, 182, **183**, 197; rectangular rib (*see also* box basket), 76, **77, 95, Cl. Pl. 9**; scrap, 128, **136**; scuttle, 243, **243**; sewing, 3, **16**, 163, 197, 209, **212, 220, 230, 251–52, Cl. Pl. 18**; sieve, 3; sleigh, 167, **168**, 191; slop, 70; storage, **135**, 197, **198, 200**; swill, 70; table, 179; traveling, **204**; tray, **16**, 68, **74, 75, 75, 99, 114, 115–19, 215**; Tyrol, **16, 17**, 18; wall (side wall or wall pocket), **16, 17**, 68, **75–76, 76, 98–99, 119, 139**; waste-basket, 128, **135**, 163, **217**; watermelon, **16, 17**; White Rock, **16, 17**; winnowing, 3; wood, **16, 120–21**, 122, 128, **136**; wool, 3, 66, **115, 120, 121**, 197; work, 66, 67, **138**, 139
— materials. *See* ash, hickory, straw, willow, etc.
— white oak baskets: naming, xviii, 3, 67, 74–75, **125**; price of, **16, 23, 26**, 68, **97, 98**; regional styles and maker's signatures, xvii–xviii, 7–8, **9**, 63, 88, 143, **223**; structure of, 50; types of, three major: 4–5, **6**. *See also* rib baskets; rod baskets; rod/coil baskets; rod/rib baskets; rod/split baskets; split baskets
— use, 3, **66**, 67–68, 125, **126**. *See also* baskets, kinds of

basket stands, 1–2, 22, 23, 128–9, **152**

basketmaker, traditional: creativity of, **27**, **165, Cl. Pls. 8 and 9**; defined, xviii; demonstrating or marketing at fairs, festivals, museums, 24, 25, 26, **26, 27**, 157; knowledge possessed by, 31; using models, **15**, 17, 18. *See also names of traditional basketmakers*

basketmaking, white oak: division of labor, 63, 72, **73**, 172, 213, **Cl. Pl. 8**; future of, 5, 28, 209–10; influences on traditional basketmaking, 14–28, **15**, 62–63, **207**; occupations associated with, 8, 9, **155, 178**; storage of materials, 58–59; time required, 8, 63, **97**, 116; as traditional craft, 3, 7–8, **9**, 14, 25, 88–89, **144, 247**. *See also* basket, white oak baskets; basketmaker, traditional; rib baskets; rod baskets; rod/coil baskets; rod/rib baskets; rod/split baskets; split baskets

Bedford County, Virginia, 191, **191**. *See also* WARE, PETE

beech, 166

Belgium, 93

Bell County, Kentucky, **Cl. Pl. 1**. *See also* CALDWELL, TISHIE

Belmont County, Ohio, **9**, 124 153, **156**. *See also* BILLETER, CHARLES; BILLETER, SAMUEL E.; BILLETER, SARAH WAYT

Berea, Kentucky, **5, 245**

BERGSTRASSER, ABRAM, **119**

Berks County, Pennsylvania, **96**. *See also* STRAUSS (family)

BETHTRAIN, A., **207**

BEVERLEY, HENRY, **133**, 134, 191

Beverly, Kentucky, **5, 109, Cl. Pl. 1**

BIAS, ETHEL LINVILLE, **27**, 163, **200**

billet: defined, 45; dressing and shaping, 46–47, 48; for handle or hoop, **49**, 50, 78, 171, 175–76, 179; riving, **39**, 45–46, 50–54, **51**; for round materials, 50, 56. *See also* splitting

BILLETER, CHARLES A., **9**

BILLETER, SAMUEL E., **9, 124**

BILLETER, SARAH WAYT, 9, 153–54, **156**

binding. *See* lashing

birch, 125, 166

blackthorn, 70

Bland County, Virginia, **177**. *See also* LOVELL, NORMAN

BLAYLOCK, LAURA, **24**

bloodroot (puccoon), 60, 61, 62

Blue Ridge Mountains of Virginia: map, 5; basketmaking, 129, 158, 170, 172, **174, 175, Cl. Pl. 14**. *See also* COOK (family); CORBIN (family); NICHOLSON (family)

BOOP (family), 208

borders in rodwork, **211**, 232–43. *See also* stakes (in rodwork): foot-stakes

—combination top/foot, 235–41, **238**; baskets with, **219, 227, 239, 250, Cl. Pl. 18**

—Madeira-type, 240–41, **241**

—plain border, 232–35, **244**; three-rod plain (u1/o2/u1), **217, 234, 235, 239, 240**; three-rod plain (u2/o2/u1) foot border, **221, 235, 238, 242**; three-rod plain (u2/o2/u2) foot border, **217**; two-rod plain (u1/o1/u1/o1) top border, **221**, 234, **236, 237**

—scallop, 239–41, **240**; baskets with, **219, 239, 241, 242, Cl. Pls. 18 and 20**

—trac, **210, 232, 233, 246–47**

Botetourt County, Virginia, 141, **Cl. Pl. 10**

bottom-sticks. *See* bases, rod baskets: base slath

bow. *See* wrappings: bow; handles for split baskets: bow and tails

BOWMAN, GEORGE, **101**

BOYD, CLOVIS, 38, **39**, 54, 67–68, 79

Boyd, Roxie, 79

braid. *See* rib baskets: borders and braids

brake, 45

Britain, 125

British Isles, 67, 70, **103**, 121

broomsedge, 3

buckeye, 3

Bucks County, Pennsylvania, **66, 89, 98, 207**. *See also* BETHTRAIN, A.; FROHMAN, MICHAEL; WEIRBACH, PETER

Buncomb County, North Carolina, **184**

butternut, 60, 61

bye-stakes. *See* bases, split baskets: single-bottom round bases; bases, split baskets: oval bases; stakes (in splitwork): bye-stakes

Cabell County, West Virginia, 37, 158, **159**. *See also* PETERS, OSCAR

CALDWELL, TISHIE, **Cl. Pl. 1**

cambium, 40, **41**, 47

Campbell, Harry, 23

Campbell County, Virginia, 83. *See also* YOUNGER, PAUL

cane, 125. *See also* rivercane

Harlan County, Kentucky, 105, **109**. *See also* HOWARD, GOLDEN

Hart County, Kentucky: basket industry, 10–12; basket stands, **22**, 23; stories about, **21**, 36, 37–38. *See also* ALVEY, LEROY; CHILDRESS, ANDERSON; CHILDRESS, ELLA FRANCES THOMPSON; COTTRELL, STANLEY; GUESS, BILL; GUESS, MRS. BILL

Hawkins County, Tennessee, **107**

Haywood County, North Carolina, **128**

hazel, 67, 70, 94, 112, 125

heartwood (of white oak): as color accent in baskets, 60, 87–88, **95**, **135**, **226**; defined, 40, **41**; natural color of, 88; splitting, 45, 46, **47**; storage of, 38; use for baskets, 40, 72, 171

HENRY (family), 133, 182

HENRY, CALVIN, 133, **181**

HENRY, ROBERT, **181**

Heseltine, Alastair, xviii

Hessen district. *See* Germany

hexagonal weave. *See* weaves: hexagonal

HIBDON, BILLY, **73**

HIBDON, THELMA, **73**, **81**, 84

HICKEY (family), 209, **210**, 230, 232, 249

hickory, 3; frames and ribs in ribwork, 70, **Cl. Pl. 7**; handles in splitwork, 182, **183**, **Cl. Pl. 11**; rods, 203; splits, 70, 125

HIGDON (family), 10

HIGGINBOTHAM, OGEL, 232, 245, **247**

Hill, Jennie Lester, 67, 209, 258

Hindman, Kentucky, **5**, 66

Hindman Settlement School, 17–18, **19**, **20**, 74, **Cl. Pl. 7**

Hocking County, Ohio, 209, **214**, **215**, 229. *See also* MANSBERGER, BOB; STUMP, BOBBY; STUMP, DWIGHT

honeysuckle vine, **16**, **26**, 70, **Cl. Pl. 1**

hoops (in ribwork): defined (rim and handle), 68, **71**; dimensions, 72, 78; doubled rim hoops, **106**, **109**; hoop joins, **79**, **Cl. Pl. 3**; forming the frame, 79–80, **81**; shaping and bending, 78–79, **80**, **81**; shaping basket with hoop shape, 73–76, **Cl. Pl. 7**. *See also* billets: for handle or hoop; handles for rod baskets: overhead handles, D-ring; handles for split baskets: overhead, D-shaped handle hoops; rims: names for

HOWARD, GOLDEN, 105, **109**

HUNTER, MRS. WHYLE, 98

Illinois: map, **5**; as marketplace for Kentucky baskets, 12; willow cultivation, **207**

Indiana: map, **5**; as marketplace for Kentucky baskets, 12, **21**, 68; rodwork, 205

Indians (Native American): basketry, 4, 17, 125, 136; Delaware, 139; Mexican, 94. *See also* Cherokee

Iowa, 12

iron: "rapping," 230; Ware family stake piercing iron, 191, **191**. *See also* die

Iron Hill, Pennsylvania, **119**

Irwin, John Rice, xv–xvi, **82**

JAGGERS (family), 10

JAGGERS, 36

JAGGERS, NIMROD, 72

Jefferson County, Tennessee, 209, **210**. *See also* HICKEY (family)

JONES, DAN, **Cl. Pls. 8 and 9**

JONES, JESSIE, 78, 79, **82**

JONES, MARTHA, 25, 88, **Cl. Pls. 8 and 9**

Joyce, Rosemary O., 209, 213

Juniata County, Pennsylvania, 208, **244**. *See also* MOAD (family); MOAD, DAVID "PAPPY"; ZONG (family)

Kanawha County, West Virginia, **58**, 209, **246–47**. *See also* HIGGINBOTHAM, OGEL; PHILIPS, ROME; SUMMERS, HOMER

Kentucky: areas included in central Appalachian region, xvii; basket industry of southcentral Kentucky, 10–13, 19–20, **21**, **97**; basket stands, **1–2**, **22**, 23, 128–29, **152**; continuing basketmaking traditions, xvii, 67; Handicraft Revival, 17–18; industrialization of, 23; map, **5**; national park formation in, 22; ribwork styles and techniques associated with, 17, 70, **76**, 86, 90–92, 94, **97**, 107, **110**, 112, 113, **115**, **Cl. Pl. 1**; rodwork styles and techniques associated with, 216, 239–40, **239**, 244, **245**; rodwork traditions in, 205, 209; rod/ribwork, 258–61, **259**; splitwork styles and techniques associated with, **1**, **22**, 131, 151, **152**. *See also names of specific counties*

KESSINGER (family), 10
knife: for basketmaking, 63, **83**, **155**, **228**; to scrape splits, 54, **55**; as a splitting tool, 43, 50, 52, **52**, **53**; for whittling round rods or ribs, 56, **56**. *See also* split knife
Knock, A. G., xviii
KNOTT, ELMER E. (father), **144–45**, 192–93
KNOTT, ELMER L. (son), **144**
Knott County, Kentucky, **19**, **20**, 66, 74, **Cl. Pl. 7**. *See also* OWSLEY, BIRD; RITCHIE, AUNT CORD
Knox County, Tennessee, 209, **210**. *See also* HICKEY (family)

Lancaster County, Pennsylvania, 176, **178**, 208, 223, **Cl. Pl. 23**. *See also* LONGABAUGH, WALTER; MENTZER (family); MENTZER, JACOB
Landis, Henry, **7**
Landis Valley (Pennsylvania), 7, **7**
larch, 125
Lasansky, Jeannette, xv–xvi, 208
lashings or bindings, 131, **132**, 184–92; basic single, **172**, **177**, 185, **185**, **186**, **187**, 197; crossed, **132**, **173**, **176**, 192, **192**, **193**, 197, **228**, **Cl. Pl. 14**; crossed figure-eight, 192, **192**, **193**; double-wrapped, **161**, 185–87, **185**, **188**; figure-eight, **132**, **133**, **154**, **166**, **168**, **188**, 189–91, **190**, **191**, **194**, 197, **199**, **257**, **258**; laced, 187, **189**; laced two-rod, 254, **255**, **256**; single and crossed defined, 184–85; splices, 185, **185**; wrapped-rod, **190**, 254, **255**. *See also* stakes (in split-work): piercing or burning for lashing
latewood, 41–42, 54
Lebanon County, Pennsylvania, **226**. *See also* MASTLE, MARTIN
leg. *See* feet for split baskets
Lehigh County, Pennsylvania, **256**
lids: on rib baskets, 118, **119**, **Cl. Pl. 3**; on rod baskets, 204, 223, 231, 250, 253, **253**, **254**; on split baskets, 6, 135, 175, 179, 180, **181**, 184, 197–200, **198**, **199**, **200**, **Cl. Pls. 11 and 15**
Lincoln County, West Virginia, 27, 52, 86, 87, **94**, 163, **200**. *See also* BIAS, ETHEL LINVILLE; LINVILLE, CLAUDE; LINVILLE, EMMER
LINVILLE, CLAUDE: basketmaking tech-

niques used by, 86, 89, **90**; baskets, **27**, **94**; riving splits, **52**, **53**
LINVILLE, EMMER, **27**, 163
LINVILLE, MANDERVILLE, **27**
LOGSDON (family), 10
LOGSDON, WALTER, 3, 10–12, 23, 72
London, England, **Cl. Pl 15**
LONGABAUGH, WALTER, 143, 176, **178**
LOSSIAH, CHARLOTTE WELCH, 60, 61
Loudon County, Tennessee, **101**. *See also* BOWMAN, GEORGE
Louisville, Kentucky, **5**, 22
LOVELL, NORMAN, **177**
LUCKY, GERTRUDE, 80
LUKE, SHERMAN, 153, 154, **155**, 156

McCARTER, ARLINE, 69
McCARTER, MAC, 69, 77
machined strips for basketmaking. *See* splits: machined; veneer baskets
Madeira. *See* border, Madeira-type
Madeira Islands, 241
Madison County, Kentucky, 107, 244, **245**, 261. *See also* MOORE (family); RECTOR (family); RECTOR, ED; RECTOR, IKE
Madison County, North Carolina, 17, **98**. *See also* HUNTER, MRS. WHYLE
Madison County, Virginia, 157
Mammoth Cave National Park, 5, 22, 23
MANSBERGER, BOB: describing Stump's die, **214**
maple, 3; dye source, 62; for rib baskets, 49, 70; for rodwork, 203; for split baskets, 125, **183**
Marietta, Ohio, **5**, 130–31, 184
Martin-Perdue, Nancy J., 8
Maryland, **5**, 207
Massachusetts, 166
MASTLE, MARTIN, **226**
maul, 43, **44**, 45
MEADOWS, JIM, 209
MENTZER, JACOB, 223, **Cl. Pl. 23**
Mercer, Henry, **127**, **206**; Accession Ledger of, **256**
Mercer Museum. *See* Museums
MEREDITH, LILIAN, 37
Mifflin County, Pennsylvania, **244**. *See also* MOAD, DAVID "PAPPY"
MILES (family), 10
Missouri: as marketplace for Kentucky baskets, 12; split knife, 54

MOAD (family), 208
MOAD, DAVID "PAPPY," **244**
molds, 133–34, **133, 181, 190, Cl. Pl. 16**
Monroe County, West Virginia, **132, 150**
Montgomery County, Pennsylvania, 242
MOORE (family), 209, 261
Moore, Donna Billetter, **124**
MOYER (family), 208
Munfordville, Kentucky, **5, 22,** 152
Museums: Museum of the Cherokee Indian, 119; Mercer Museum, 119; Pennsylvania Farm Museum of Landis Valley, **7, Cl. Pl. 15**

Nashville, **5, 22**
national parks, 22–23. *See also* Cumberland Gap National Historic Park; Great Smoky Mountain National Park; Mammoth Cave National Park; Shenandoah National Park
NEFF, DAVID, 134
Nelson County, Virginia, 134, 191. *See also* BEVERLEY, HENRY
New England (northeastern United States), xviii, 134, 139, 182, 205
New Hope, Pennsylvania, **127**
New York, 182, **207**
NICHOLSON (family), 8, 129, **157,** 170, **174**
NICHOLSON, EDDIE, 29
NICHOLSON, IRSKEL: about basketmaking, 7–8, 129–30; basketmaking techniques, 155–56, 170–71, **173,** 175; on timber finding and splitting, 32, 36, 43
NICHOLSON, LANDON, **173**
NICHOLSON, ORAL ("NICK"), 55, **55, 157,** 175
NICHOLSON, THOMAS JACKSON, **173**
Nicholson, William, 9
Noble County, Ohio, **109,** 153, **155.** *See also* LUKE, SHERMAN
North Carolina: Handicraft Revival in, 14–17; map, **5;** marketplace for Tennessee baskets, 20–22; national park formation in, 22; ribwork occurrence, 67; ribwork styles and techniques associated with, **16, 17,** 70, 93, 94, 96, **98, 99, 101,** 102, **118,** 119; rod/ribwork, 258, **259;** rodwork occurrence, 205; rod/splitwork, 254, 257–58, **257, 258;** splitwork styles and techniques associated with, **16, 26, 128, 136, 139,** 158, **183, 191.** *See also* Cherokee; *names of specific counties;* Qualla Reservation

oak: ailments of white oak, 35; as a basket material in Europe, 70, 125; as a basket material in the United States, 3, 31, 70, 125, 203–5; as dye source, 62; *Quercus alba* (common white oak), 30, 31–32, 33; *Quercus michauxii* (swamp chestnut oak), **30,** 31, 33; red and white, 31; veneered splits of, 125–26. *See also* basket: white oak basket; earlywood; latewood; splitting; timber; wood
Ohio: as marketplace for Kentucky and Tennessee baskets, 12, 20–22; map, **5;** ribwork styles and techniques associated with, 103–4, **109,** rodwork traditions, 205–8, 209; rodwork styles and techniques associated with, **215, 216, Cl. Pl. 17;** splitwork styles and techniques associated with, 9, **136, 138, 139, 144–45,** 147, 149, 151, 153–54, **155, 156,** 187. *See also names of specific counties*
Okey, Thomas, xviii, **207**
Old Rag, Virginia, 9
OLMSTEAD (family), 208
Ornamentation. *See* color; decoration
OWSLEY, BIRD, **19, 74, Cl. Pl. 7**

Page County, Virginia, **157;** splitwork, 34, **55,** 156, 158, **160, 199;** rodwork, **237.** *See also* CAVE, TOM; COOK, LUCY; COOK, WILLIAM CODY
Paris, Kentucky, 112
Parton, Dolly, **Cl. Pl. 9**
Patrick County, Virginia, **118.** *See also* AYERS, KARRIE
peddling baskets. *See* basket: bartering and peddling
Pendleton County, West Virginia: peddling baskets in, 8, **11;** ribwork, 84, 102; rodwork, 249; splitwork, 134, **190.** *See also* EYE (family); EYE, LEVI; PROPST (family); PROPST, ABRAHAM; PROPST, ELMER
Pennsburg, Pennsylvania, **256**
Pennsylvania: Landis basket collection, 7; map, **5;** ribwork occurrence, 67; ribwork styles and techniques associated with, **66,** 82, 83, **89,** 93, **96, 98, 101, 103,** 112, 113, **119, 119,** 120; rodmaking tradition, 205–8, rodwork styles and techniques associated with, **204,** 216, **219, 222, 222, 223, 226, 227,** 239, **239, 243,** 244–45, **244,** 249–51,

splint, xviii

split baskets: decoration, 142–43, 163; definition and structure, xviii, 4–5, 130–31, **132**; identifying features (linked to maker or region), 143; material preparation and choice, 125, 131–33 (*see also* billet; splitting); on-going tradition of, 129–30; shaping the basket, 134, **135**, **136**, **162**, 170, **Cl. Pl. 16**; side weaving, **140**, **142**, **144–45**, **157**, 168–69; stake turndown and rims, 169–71; weaves for, 134–42. *See also* baskets: kinds of (names for); bases for split baskets; feet for split baskets; Handicraft Revival: influencing split baskets; handles for split baskets; lashings; lids for split baskets; molds; stakes; weaves; weaving techniques

split knife: for cutting splits, 54; for scraping splits, 55

splits (flat): machined splits vs. handsplit splits, 4, 125–26; shaved splits, 54; scraping, 54, 55, **55**, **155**; soaking, 59; splits vs. splints, xviii, storage of, 56, 58. *See also* color: natural coloring; color: dyes and stains; splitting: flat splits; weavers

splits (rounded). *See* rods

splitting white oak (riving): basic rules for splitting, 42, 50; frozen timber, 33; splitting on grain for flat splits, 50–56, **51**, **52**, **53**; growth ring size desired, 42; splitting for round materials (ribs or rods), 56; summarized, 4, 42; "run offs," 45, 50, 52; timber split radially (board splits), 42, 43–45, **44**, **47**; timber split tangentially (grain or bastard splits), 41, 45–47, **46**, **47**; tools, 43. *See also* axe; billet; drawknife; froe; shaving horse; split knife

spruce, 94, 112, 125, 187

stakes (in rodwork): baskets with foot-stakes, **221**, **244**, **245**, **251**, **Cl. Pl. 23**; foot-stakes, 232, 234–35, 243; side-stakes, 211–12, **211**, 228, 232; "pricking up" side-stakes, 228, **229**; replacing, 232. *See also* borders; floats; rod/split baskets

stakes (in splitwork): bye-stakes, 141, 147, **148**, **149**, **161**, **162**, 163, **164**; defined, 130–31, **132**; names for, 131; number needed, 131–33, 143, 151; piercing or burning for lashing, 185, 191, **191**, **194**, **256**; shaping the basket form with, 134, **136**, 151, 168–69; staves (in plank bottom

baskets), 167, **167**, **Cl. Pl. 13**; turn up for basket sides, **157**, **162**, 168; turndown of, 169, **170**, **Cl. Pl. 14**

STAMPER, LOTTIE, 26

staves. *See* stakes (in splitwork): staves

Steinmetz, Rollin, **178**

Stephenson, Sue H., xv–xvi, 93–94, 241, 261

Stone, May, 17, 18

Strange, Walton (basket peddler and basket merchant), 23, 40, 63

STRAUSS (family), **96**

straw, 3, **7**, 260, 261, **Cl. Pl. 15**

STUMP, BOBBY, 209

STUMP, DWIGHT: about Ohio rodmakers, 209, 213; die boards, and rod pulling, 58, **214**; basketmaking, **215**, **229**, 230

Sudetenland, 187

Sullivan County, Tennessee, **107**

sumac, 61

SUMMERS, HOMER, 58, 209, 232, **246–47**

Summers County, West Virginia, **196**

Swain County, North Carolina, **172**. *See also* ROSS, MARTHA

Swanton, John R., 125

Swiss basketry, 94

TAYLOR (family of Kentucky), 10

TAYLOR (family of Qualla Reservation), **120**

TAYLOR, EMMA, 63

Taylor, Nathan, 182

Tennessee: areas included in central Appalachian region, xvii; industrialization and work opportunities, 25; long-distance basket peddling from, 19, 20–22; map, **5**; national park formation, 22; ribwork occurrence, 67; ribwork styles and techniques associated with, **69**, **70**, **73**, **77**, **86**, **89**, 94, **95**, **101**, 103, **107**, 113, **116**, **Cls. Pl. 8** and 9; rodmaking tradition, 205, 209; rodwork styles and techniques associated with, **210**, **233**; rod/ribwork, 258; splitwork styles and techniques associated with, **137**, 146, 151, 158, **161**, **Cl. Pl. 12**. *See also names of specific counties*

terminology, xviii–xix; 7–8, 210–11

THOMAS, EARLEAN: on basket bartering and peddling, 9, 20–22; on basket materials and splitting, 42, 59, 70; rib basketmaking, 76–78, 87, 115, **116**

weaves (continued)

rod baskets with randed base and sides,
227, 228, 246–47; rod/split basket woven
with, **254, 255**; as a side weave, **210, 215,
216, 217, 231, Cl. Pl. 17**

—soumak, 143, **178**

—twill weave: defined and illustrated,
134–37, **137**; baskets with twill, **6, 137, 172,
Cl. Pl. 12**; weaving method associated
with, 140–41; use by traditional makers,
133, 136–37, 142

—three-rod wale: as base weave, **212, 221,
224, 237**; defined and illustrated, 218–19,
221; color and wale, **230, Cl. Pls. 22, 23,**
and **24**; floats and three-rod wale, 242, **Cl.
Pl. 20**; French randing and three-rod wale
as side weave, **210, 216, 218, 231, 244, 245**;
pairing and three-rod wale as side weave,
242; randing and three-rod wale as side
weave, **215, 217, 247, Cl. Pl. 17**; sides
uniformly waled, **212, 221, 226, 231, 237,
250, 251, Cl. Pl. 21**; three- and four-rod
wale as side weave, **253**

—four-rod wale: defined and illustrated,
222, **222**; as a side weave, **222, 242, 253**;
color blocks created with, **230, Cl. Pl. 19**

—five-rod wale: use of, 223; five-rod wale
(4/1) to make a foot, **230, 253, Cl. Pl. 22**;
five-rod wale (3/2) as a side weave, **242**

—six-rod wale, 223, 230; to make ledge for
lid, **253**

weaving methods. *See also* turnback; weaves

—chasing: defined and illustrated, 141, **142**;
in rodwork, 216, **226, 229, Cl. Pl. 17**; in
splitwork, **193, Cl. Pls. 10 and 15**

—coiling, 7, **260, 261**

—row-by-row, 139–40, **139**, 144–45, 172,
183, Cl. Pl. 11

—spiraling, 139, 140–42; by adding odd
number of bye-stakes, 141, **161, 162**;
skipped-stake spiral, 137, 141, **141**; split-
stake spiral, 140, **140, 176, 177, 180, 189,
198, Cl. Pl. 14**. (*See also* weaving methods:
chasing)

wedges, 43, **44**, 45

WEIRBACH, PETER, **89, 98**

WELCH, CAROL, 8

WEST, (family), 10

West Virginia: fair, **27**; as marketplace for
Tennessee baskets, 22; map, **5**; ribwork occurrence, 67, ribwork styles and techniques

associated with, **27**, 80, **84**, 86, **87, 90, 94**,
102; rodwork traditions, 205; rodwork
styles and techniques, 213, 222, 232, 242,
242, 245, **246–47**, 249, **Cl. Pl. 21**; peddling
baskets, 8, **11**; splitwork techniques
associated with, **27, 132, 147, 150, 158, 159,
168**, 185, **186, 190**, 191, **196, 200**. *See also*
Potomac River Valley; *names of specific
counties*

Wetherbee, Martha, 182

White, Mary, 241

white oak basketry. *See* basket: white oak
baskets; basketmaking, white oak; rib
baskets; rod baskets; rod/coil baskets;
rod/rib baskets; rod/split baskets; split
baskets; splitting white oak; timber

Whitley County, Kentucky, 239–40, **239**, 244.
See also SHELLY, EMBY

whittling, **56, 80**, 205

wickerwork, 203–5, **204**. *See also* willow:
techniques used in willow wickerwork

Will, Christoph, xvi, xviii

willow: availability and use by American
basketmakers, 3, 205, **206–7**, 244; baskets,
American-made, 7, 16, **208, Cl. Pls. 1** and
19; cultivation in the U.S., **206–7**; identifying characteristics of willow rods, 203,
206; importing of willow, 204, 205, **206–7**;
peeled vs. unpeeled, **206, Cl. Pl. 19**; split
willow ("skeins"), 125; ribwork in willow,
67, **120**, 261, **Cl. Pl. 1**; techniques used in
willow wickerwork, 215, 216, 230, 243,
252–53, **Cl. Pl. 20**; use in European
baskets, 67, 70, 125, 203

WILNOTY, ELENORA, **183**

WILNOTY, JOHN, **183**

Winchester, Virginia, 135

Wirt County, West Virginia, 80. *See also*
LUCKY, GERTRUDE

wood: anatomy of, 38–42, **41**; brash, 35, 37;
dimensions and planes, 42, **43**; "green," 37,
58, 170; growth rings, 41–42, **41**, 45, 203,
206; rays, 40–41, **41**, 45; seasoning,
shrinkage, and storage, 37–38, **39**, 58;
staining, 38, 59–60. *See also*: billet;
cambium; earlywood; heartwood;
latewood; pith; sapwood; splitting; timber

Wood County, West Virginia, 158. *See also*
PETERS, FRANK; PETERS, JOHN

Woodbury, Tennessee, **5**, 20, 86

wrappings (in ribwork), 88–101; bow, **15**, 89, **91**, **95**; cross, **76**, 89–90, **90**, **106**, **109**; figure-eight cross, 90, **91**, **96**; interwoven cross, 90, **96**, **Cl. Pl. 2**; Linville cross, 89, **90**, **94**; ear, **76**, 89, 90–92, **92**, 93–94, **97**, 102, **103**; fourfold-bond, 92–94, **92**, **98**, 102, **103**; woven fourfold-bond, **76**, 93, **93**, **98**, **99**, 118, **Cl. Pl. 4**; ring or "circle," 94–96, **Cl. Pl. 6**; ring or "circle" with cross, 96, **101**, **107**; ring and knot, 96, **100**, **101**; triangular, 93, **100**, **101**; V-shaped figure-eight cross, 90, **96**
WRATCHFORD, HUGH, **213**

Wright, Dorothy, xvi, xviii, 94
Wythe County, Virginia, 113, **114**, **118**

yellowroot, 60, 61
YOUNGBLOOD, ESTEL, 15, **95**
YOUNGBLOOD, GERTIE, **95**
YOUNGBLOOD, MILDRED, 54, 86
YOUNGER, PAUL, 83

ZONG (family) 208

Appalachian White Oak Basketmaking was designed by Dariel Mayer, composed by Lithocraft, Inc., and printed and bound by McNaughton & Gunn, Inc. The book is set in Caledonia and printed on Warren's 80–lb. Lustro Offset Enamel Dull white.